John Stuart Mill

AUTOBIOGRAPHY

EDITED WITH AN INTRODUCTION AND NOTES BY
JACK STILLINGER

OXFORD UNIVERSITY PRESS
LONDON   OXFORD
1971

Oxford University Press

LONDON OXFORD NEW YORK

GLASGOW TORONTO MELBOURNE WELLINGTON

CAPE TOWN SALISBURY IBADAN NAIROBI DAR ES SALAAM LUSAKA ADDIS ABABA

BOMBAY CALCUTTA MADRAS KARACHI LAHORE DACCA

KUALA LUMPUR SINGAPORE HONG KONG TOKYO

SBN 19 281097 9

This edition first published in the United States of
America by Houghton Mifflin Company, as a
Riverside Edition, 1969

First published as an Oxford University Press paperback
by Oxford University Press, London, 1971

*Printed lithographically in Great Britain
by Fletcher & Son Ltd, Norwich*

CONTENTS

INTRODUCTION

MILL'S *AUTOBIOGRAPHY:* IMAGINATION AND THE GROWTH OF A PHILOSOPHIC MIND

WHEN John Stuart Mill first drafted his *Autobiography,* in 1853–54, at the age of forty-seven, he had several specific aims in mind. He wanted, as he told his wife, "to stop the mouths of enemies hereafter"[1] who had thought and said scandalous things about their twenty-one-year relationship before their marriage. He wanted to record his intellectual obligations, of which the chief, in his view, was his debt to his wife. And, under the impression that both he and Harriet were deteriorating rapidly from consumption (she died in 1858, but he lived on until 1873), he wanted to set down before it was too late a great many ideas that he had not yet got into print — at this time his accomplishments lay mainly in logic and political economy, and he had yet to produce his major works on liberty, government, philosophy, and religion. "I feel bitterly," he confessed in his diary on 19 January 1854, "how I have procrastinated in the sacred duty of fixing in writing, so that it may not die with me, everything that I have in mind which is capable of assisting the destruction of error and prejudice and the growth of just feelings and true opinions." And he wrote to Harriet toward the end of February, after he had completed a substantial part of the draft that he had begun the year before: "we must do what we can while we are alive — the Life being the first thing — which independent of the personal matters which it will set right . . . is even now an unreserved proclamation of our opinions on religion, nature, & much else."[2]

"Much else" included education and an account of the development of a philosophic mind during a revolution in the ways of thinking, and when he added the opening paragraph he singled out these two related concerns as the primary justification of the work:

---

[1] F. A. Hayek, *John Stuart Mill and Harriet Taylor* (London, 1951), p. 190. For other references to the work in Mill's letters, see Hayek, pp. 190–200, and *The Early Draft of John Stuart Mill's "Autobiography,"* ed. Jack Stillinger (Urbana, 1961), pp. 5–11.

[2] Hayek, pp. 189–90, 200.

I have thought that in an age in which education, and its improvement, are the subject of more, if not of profounder study than
at any former period of English history, it may be useful that there
should be some record of an education which was unusual and
remarkable, and which . . . has proved how much more than is
commonly supposed may be taught, and well taught, in those early
years which, in the common modes of what is called instruction,
are little better than wasted. It has also seemed to me that in an
age of transition in opinions, there may be somewhat both of
interest and of benefit in noting the successive phases of any mind
which was always pressing forward, equally ready to learn and
to unlearn either from its own thoughts or from those of others.
(p. 3)[3]

For present purposes, nothing is more basic than Mill's steady consciousness that he lived in "an age of transition in opinions" —
narrowly, the nineteenth-century reaction against eighteenth-century rationalism, but in the larger view a transition from the past
into modern times — and that his own intellectual development was
representative of that transition.

The "age" was of course the same that the Romantics lived in,
and in our current zealousness to multiply distinctions, parceling
out our major writers into mutually exclusive categories — clean-
shaven poets in one course, bearded prose-writers in another — we
sometimes set up boundaries that work against the unity we are
trying to comprehend. Mill the Victorian was only eleven years
younger than Keats the Romantic, and was thus fourteen years
closer in age to Keats than the latter was to Wordsworth; he published his first writings in the same year in which Shelley died and
Byron produced *The Vision of Judgment;* he was well into his
forties before Wordsworth's long life came to an end. Mill was no
"romantic" — but then neither, in an important sense, were the
best of the Romantic poets just named. Though their methods were
as far apart as one could imagine, their largest aim was the same
— the improvement of society through what Mill calls the internal
culture of the individual. Mill's discovery of this shared preoccu-
pation is a main topic of the *Autobiography.*

[3] Parenthetical page numbers refer to the text (and in a few instances to
the notes) in the present edition. The penultimate sentence of this paragraph
in Mill's final version, "But a motive which weighs more with me . . . ," is
not in the early draft.

The nineteenth century, in both the Romantic and the Victorian periods, produced many accounts of painful and at the same time triumphant births into the modern world. Mill's specific connections with Wordsworth — he first read his poetry in 1828 in the course of recovering from the early mental crisis, defended him eloquently in a debating speech of 1829, met him in 1831, and wrote intelligently about him in a critical essay of 1833 — invite comparison of the *Autobiography* with that most substantial and impressive of earlier works treating education, intellectual obligations, and the growth of the mind. Although Wordsworth first completed *The Prelude* less than a year before Mill was born, Mill almost surely never read it (he was too busy for poetry of any sort when it was finally published in 1850). If he had, he would have seen some striking parallels with his own development, though he would not have been surprised since, even from reading the Intimations ode, he "found that [Wordsworth] too had had similar experience to mine" (p. 90). A brief account of some of those parallels may be helpful here as a means of centering immediately on the principal concern and structure of the *Autobiography*. Mill's work is of course many things besides: a reading list for any young genius who will take up the challenge, a series of character sketches of some of his most interesting contemporaries, a short history of a part of the political life of the nineteenth century, an account of the thought processes by which he developed his principal works, a concise statement of his considered opinions on the important subjects of his (and still, in many cases, also our own) time. But in the sense in which it has a continuous theme and a pattern transcending simple chronology, it is, considered over-all, an account of intellectual growth that follows a pattern similar to Wordsworth's of early development, crisis, and recovery.

Both the *Autobiography* and *The Prelude* give nearly half their pages to their subjects' early lives. Though nothing could be more unlike than their upbringings — Mill fits perfectly the description in Book V of *The Prelude* of the model child reared according to the latest educational theory, a "miracle of scientific lore" who is crammed with knowledge but who, because he has never developed imagination, cannot lose his self-consciousness, while Wordsworth is himself the Winander boy who hooted at owls (V, 293–425) — their respective educations and experiences lead them to the same general aspiration, the radical improvement of Man (at this point an abstraction, with nothing of the variety and complexity of actual

human beings taken into consideration), and they enter warmly
into the revolutionary enterprises of their time, Wordsworth with
the activists in France, Mill with the philosophic radicals in England. In their early twenties both suffer mental crises, and, while
here especially specific similarities cannot be pressed too hard, the
fundamental reason is the same, an awakening to defects in causes
that had hitherto seemed wholly good and in which they had invested all their hopes and energies. (Wordsworth retrospectively
associates his aspirations with "The attraction of a country in ro-
mance," in which Reason was "A prime enchantress" and those
were most ardent "who had fed their childhood upon dreams,"
IX, 437–65, XI, 109–44; Mill says that "the time came when I
awakened from this as from a dream," p. 80.) In reaction to the
Reign of Terror and to unexpected French aggression in Spain,
Italy, and elsewhere, Wordsworth abandons practical interest in
revolution and turns instead to "speculative schemes," to abstract
theorizing about man, anatomizing "the frame of social life . . . the
whole body of society," but without finding any answers to his
questions:

> till, demanding formal *proof*,
> And seeking it in every thing, I lost
> All feeling of conviction, and, in fine,
> Sick, wearied out with contrarieties,
> Yielded up moral questions in despair.
>
> This was the crisis of that strong disease,
> This the soul's last and lowest ebb . . . .   (XI, 301–307)

"Speculative schemes" of course played a large part in Mill's education, and Wordsworth's attitude toward them at this point in
The Prelude could be glossed by Mill's description in the early
draft of the *Autobiography* of the sectarian narrowness that he
overthrew: "we had at this time no idea of real culture. In our
schemes for improving human affairs we overlooked human beings" (p. 67 n.). A large trouble in each case was the gap between the rationalists' theoretical Man and the observed reality of
human feeling and behavior. By his own account, which relates his
personal situation to the philosophic currents of the time, Mill's
crisis was the product of a faulty view of human nature.

Recovery from crisis takes the same general course in both
works (it would be over-ingenious, and biographically quite wrong,

to see likenesses between Dorothy Wordsworth and Harriet, but both figure symbolically in leading their men to mental and moral, even poetical, health). It is marked by a discovery or rediscovery of feeling and imagination, and with these a more realistically based understanding of and sympathy with man. Wordsworth's most important gain from his experience, as he says toward the end of his poem, was

> A more judicious knowledge of the worth
> And dignity of individual man,
> No composition of the brain, but man
> Of whom we read, the man whom we behold
> With our own eyes.   (XIII, 80–84)

And Mill — having similarly thrown aside artificial compositions of the brain and examined not books but himself to learn about man's nature — now "for the first time, gave its proper place ; . . to the internal culture of the individual" (p. 86). For both of them, the idea of teaching the world what man *may* attain to becomes the governing motivation of a life's work.

It is lucky that Wordsworth recovered his creative powers, but not remarkable: he "had known / Too forcibly, too early in my life, / Visitings of imaginative power / For this [his impairment of imagination] to last" (XII, 201–204). Mill's case, to focus on it more directly now, was quite different in this respect, and his comment on his lack of religious belief — "I am thus one of the very few examples, in this country, of one who has, not thrown off religious belief, but never had it" (pp. 27–28) — would apply to a wider range of subjects and feelings, including imagination. Mill was brought up, in the words of James Mill to Jeremy Bentham, to be "a successor worthy of both of us."[4] The carefully worked out educational experiment, beginning with Greek at the age of three and including Latin at seven, logic at twelve, and a course of political economy at thirteen, was both a success and a failure: a success in that Mill could not possibly have achieved what he did without the wide reading, the foundation in logic, law, and psychology, and the general ideal of social reform that was early inculcated in him; and a failure in the personal and philosophic

[4] *The Works of Jeremy Bentham,* ed. John Bowring (Edinburgh, 1838–43), X, 473.

incompletenesses (he overcame only the latter) that were its result. Aiming entirely at the intellect, to the neglect of every other aspect of personality, it turned him out, as he described himself to Carlyle, "a school-boy fresh from the logic-school, [who] had never conversed with a reality; never seen one; knew not what manner of thing it was."[5] Characteristically he saw both the good and the bad aspects, implicitly affirming the former — he wrote the *Autobiography* in part to show how much more can be taught to children than was then attempted, and presents himself as one who "started . . . with an advantage of a quarter of a century over my cotemporaries" (p. 20) — and most movingly pointing up the latter — e.g., "My education, which was wholly his [James Mill's] work, had been conducted without any regard to the possibility of its ending in this result [the mental crisis]; and I saw no use in giving him the pain of thinking that his plans had failed, when the failure was probably irremediable" (p. 82).

Though not entirely the education of cram that his contemporaries thought it to be, Mill's upbringing does tend to illustrate Wordsworth's remark toward the end of *The Prelude,*

> How little those formalities, to which
> With overweening trust alone we give
> The name of Education, have to do
> With real feeling and just sense.   (XIII, 169–72)

"Real feeling" was not just neglected in the Mill household; it was positively banned. "For passionate emotions of all sorts, and for everything which has been said or written in exaltation of them," Mill's father "professed the greatest contempt. He regarded them as a form of madness. 'The intense' was with him a bye-word of scornful disapprobation. He regarded as an aberration of the moral standard of modern times, compared with that of the ancients, the great stress laid upon feeling" (p. 31). Mill's education had a number of drawbacks — his lifelong inability in things requiring manual dexterity, his habitual reserve which made him lonely even when surrounded by associates (Mill had almost no *friends*), his backwardness in assuming responsibility — but it is this starvation of the feelings that he makes most of in the *Autobiography*. In passages describing his life before the mental crisis, he speaks of it not just in connection with his father but in his contrast of the

5 *The Earlier Letters of John Stuart Mill,* ed. Francis E. Mineka, in *Collected Works of John Stuart Mill* (Toronto, 1963–   ), XII, 205.

French national character with the English (pp. 37–38)[6] and in his carefully considered account of the extent to which he fitted the common description of a Benthamite as "a mere reasoning machine" (pp. 66–68). In the latter, he explains that his zeal for speculative opinions "had not its root in genuine benevolence, or sympathy with mankind" and that "there was at that time an intermission of [these feelings'] natural aliment, poetical culture . . . . Add to this that, as already mentioned, my father's teachings tended to the undervaluing of feeling . . . . he thought that feeling could take care of itself."

In all of this Mill is of course setting a background to the famous "mental crisis," when at the age of twenty he paused to ask himself whether he would be happy if all his objects in life were immediately realized, and then had to answer, from an "irrepressible self-consciousness," that he would not. His first reading Bentham's *Traités de législation* five years earlier had been a turning point in his life — "It gave unity to my conceptions of things. I now had opinions; a creed, a doctrine, a philosophy; in one among the best senses of the word, a religion; the inculcation and diffusion of which could be made the principal outward purpose of a life" (p. 42). Now that purpose had suddenly become empty: "the whole foundation on which my life was constructed fell down. . . . I seemed to have nothing left to live for" (p. 81). What was at fault, as Mill laboriously explains it, was the artificiality of the associations created by his education. The ideas of good that had been impressed upon him by his father and up to this point always taken for granted were now put under analytic scrutiny (Mill does not say *why* he entered upon self-examination at this particular time, but it is pretty clearly nothing more startling than his beginning to think for himself); the unsettling result was a breakdown of associations and a sudden loss of the accustomed pleasure connected with those ideas. He had been taught but had never genuinely *felt* the kind of pleasure that should have been attached to a worthy object.

As a matter of biographical fact, Mill had several such attacks of morbid despondency ("to which," as he told Carlyle when he was

6 A specific detail in this passage, Jean Baptiste Say's life "made happy by warm affections, public and private," is obviously intended to contrast with the lack of feeling surrounding James Mill. In parts of the early draft Mill is much more explicit — e.g., "it must be mentioned as a most baneful [moral influence], that my father's children neither loved him, nor, with any warmth of affection, any one else" (see p. 33).

on the edge of one of them, "I have been indebted for all the most valuable of such insight as I have into the most important matters");[7] but only one of them is mentioned in the *Autobiography:* "A Crisis in My Mental History." An ordinary, perhaps even trivial experience in real life (it did not interfere with his regular work or his public speaking), this early event is placed almost exactly in the middle of the book, and is of large symbolic significance as marking the beginning of an "important transformation in my opinions and character," the "only actual revolution which has ever taken place in my modes of thinking," upon the completion of which he had "no further mental changes to tell of" (pp. 80, 114, 132). The event initiated Mill's growing up as a philosopher, his throwing off what he calls his "real inward sectarianism," and the beginning of his liberation from his father, Bentham, and the eighteenth-century rationalism they represented.

It is significant that his first relief from depression came from reading a tender passage in Marmontel's *Mémoires* and discovering that feeling was not dead within him — "I was no longer hopeless: I was not a stock or a stone" — and that he turned to poetry as "a medicine for my state of mind" (pp. 85, 89). Analyzing his reactions into "two very marked effects on my opinions and character," he speaks first of the importance of "anti-self-consciousness" and then of the "cultivation of the feelings," both of them directly necessary to any outgoing imaginative grasp of the feelings and needs of other human beings. At this point, he says, Wordsworth's poems

> seemed to be the very culture of the feelings, which I was in quest of. In them I seemed to draw from a source of inward joy, of sympathetic and imaginative pleasure, which could be shared in by all human beings; which had no connexion with struggle or imperfection, but would be made richer by every improvement in the physical or social condition of mankind. From them I seemed to learn what would be the perennial sources of happiness, when all the greater evils of life shall have been removed. And I felt myself at once better and happier as I came under their influence. (p. 89)

Poetry was *better* than push-pin, he might have added. From this time on, "The cultivation of the feelings became one of the cardinal points in my ethical and philosophical creed" (p. 86).

Mill first declared his new way of thinking in an 1829 debating speech in which he defended Wordsworth on the grounds that

[7] *Earlier Letters*, XII, 149.

poetry is an important branch of education both of the intellect and the feelings, and that, "far from [supposing] philosophy and poetry being unconnected, he ought to be called the greatest poet who is the greatest master of that branch of philosophy, which respects the education of the feelings, and has practised it most."

> I have learned from Wordsworth that it is possible by dwelling on certain ideas [and by] a proper regulation of the associations to keep up a constant freshness in the emotions which objects excite and which else they would cease to excite as we grow older — to connect cheerful and joyous states of mind with almost every object, to make everything speak to us of our own enjoyments or those of other sentient beings, and to multiply ourselves as it were in the enjoyments of other creatures: to make the good parts of human nature afford us more pleasure than the bad parts afford us pain — and to rid ourselves entirely of all feelings of hatred or scorn for our fellow creatures.

In sum, "Wordsworth illustrates all the most important features of the happiest and most virtuous character and unfolds [the] most recondite truths in morals and mental philosophy."[8]

Mill's new view (which led to the writing of the essays on poetry and the reviews of Tennyson, Browning, and Alfred de Vigny — all in the 1830's) runs through his letters of the time. "Poetry is higher than Logic, and . . . the union of the two is Philosophy," he wrote to Carlyle on 5 July 1833; and a letter to Edward Lytton Bulwer of 23 November 1836 explains that the utilitarianism of the *London and Westminster Review* was to comprehend "the whole of human nature . . . [holding] Feeling at least as valuable as Thought, & Poetry not only on a par with, but the necessary condition of, any true & comprehensive Philosophy."[9] His contemporaries reacted in different ways: the Coleridgians cheered, think-

[8] *John Stuart Mill: Literary Essays,* ed. Edward Alexander (Indianapolis, 1967), pp. 346, 353, 354. The quotations are from rough notes that Mill made in preparation for his speech.

[9] *Earlier Letters,* XII, 163, 312. See also pp. 80–82, 113, 173, 219. Like Wordsworth, Mill generally used "poetry" and "poetical culture" to refer not to written verse but to basic imaginative activity, "that which," as he defines Imagination in the 1838 essay on Bentham, "enables us, by a voluntary effort, to conceive the absent as if it were present, the imaginary as if it were real, and to clothe it in the feelings which, if it were indeed real, it would bring along with it. *This is the power by which one human being enters into the mind and circumstances of another*" (italics added). Poetry is not, then, opposed to philosophy (as in the remark quoted from Bowring just below), but to logic or science; and both kinds of intellectual activity are necessary to make a complete philosophy.

ing they had found an unexpected ally; his former associates were
appalled, one of them, John Bowring, saying that Mill "was most
emphatically a philosopher, but then he read Wordsworth and
that muddled him, and he has been in a strange confusion ever
since, endeavouring to unite poetry and philosophy."[10] "Strange
confusion" it has seemed to hostile critics from Mill's time to the
present day (who sometimes write as if the transformation actually
occurred in mid-career, as might appear from its place in the
Autobiography, rather than almost at the beginning). It is worth
keeping in mind that the change involved addition and enlargement,
not displacement and substitution. Mill's own precise account exactly states the case:

> I did not, for an instant, lose sight of, or undervalue, that part of
> the truth which I had seen before; I never turned recreant to
> intellectual culture, or ceased to consider the power and practice
> of analysis as an essential condition both of individual and of
> social improvement. But I thought that it had consequences
> which required to be corrected, by joining other kinds of culti-
> vation with it. The maintenance of a due balance among the
> faculties, now seemed to me of primary importance. (p. 86)

"I believe in spectacles," he told Carlyle, referring to the logic on
which he had been brought up, "but I think eyes necessary too."[11]

Renouncing half-truths, he took for his ideal Goethe's device of
many-sidedness, and, likening the contest between the eighteenth
and the nineteenth centuries to the battle between two knights over
the color of a shield, assumed the role of the third knight who clears
up the disagreement by showing both sides at once. An excellent
case in point is the extended comparison of Bentham and Coleridge
that he published in the *London and Westminster Review* in 1838
and 1840. "In every respect," he says near the beginning of the
essay on Coleridge, "the two men are each other's 'completing
counterpart': the strong points of each correspond to the weak
points of the other. Whoever could master the premises and combine the methods of both, would possess the entire English philosophy of their age." In pursuit of wholeness by means of "practical eclecticism,"[12] Mill incorporated the best of what he found in

10 Caroline Fox, *Memories of Old Friends,* ed. Horace N. Pym (London,
1882), p. 113 (journal entry for 7 August 1840).
11 *Earlier Letters,* XII, 347.
12 See *Earlier Letters,* XII, 42.

Coleridge and the Coleridgians, Goethe and other German writers, the Saint-Simonians, and Carlyle. The result, if not quite the complete synthesis that he ideally sought, was a far richer and more humane philosophy than the Benthamic utilitarianism with which he had begun. His major works for the improvement of human affairs do not, as his predecessors' in the same fields did, overlook the human beings.

However successful Mill was as a philosopher, in his personal relationships he remained as backward as ever. The particular combination of new strengths with old weaknesses may serve as partial explanation of the tremendous role that he gives to his wife in the *Autobiography* — she was "the source of a great part of all that I have attempted to do, or hope to effect hereafter, for human improvement," "the most admirable person I had ever known," and his published writings were "not the work of one mind, but of the fusion of two," "as much her work as mine" (pp. 111, 114, 145). She combined, he says, a character of feeling with a vigorous speculative intellect, a poetic and artistic nature, and an eminent practical capacity, "the qualities which in all other persons whom I had known I had been only too happy to find singly" (p. 112). More a poet than Carlyle, more a thinker than himself, at least as great a promoter of freedom as his father, she is pictured as both the ideal human being and the ideal poet-philosopher. "Only John Mill's reputation could have survived such an exhibition," George Grote is reported to have said.[13]

Few readers have suspended disbelief over Mill's encomiums, which are, it has to be admitted, a blemish on the work—not because we squirm at the notion that Mill owed so much to another, but simply because the claims do not carry conviction: we should object to such extravagances in fiction, and similarly must object to them in autobiography. It is reasonably clear in fact that Harriet was no originator of ideas, however much she may have aided Mill by ordinary wifely discussion and debate (Bain's view, probably the most reasonable among contemporaries, is that she helped set Mill's faculties in motion by "intelligently controverting" his ideas).[14] What must be grasped is the symbolic role she plays. Mill himself raises her to the symbolic level when he calls her

[13] Quoted in *The Early Draft*, p. 24.
[14] Alexander Bain, *John Stuart Mill* (London, 1882), p. 173.

influence "the presiding *principle* of my mental progress" (p. 114).
If, before his mental crisis, Benthamism was not only a philosophy
but "a religion," with James Mill as a type of priest-figure (the
ritualistic "put into my hands" occurs six times in the early pages
of the work), Mill's conversion[15] to a wider outlook also took on a
vaguely religious aspect. As an imagined embodiment of the union
of poetry and logic, Harriet becomes a saint to be worshipped, and
after her death he describes himself as working on "for her purposes with such diminished strength as can be derived from
thoughts of her, and communion with her memory"; "Her memory
is to me a religion" (pp. 143, 145).

The early draft of the *Autobiography,* supplemented by correspondence between Mill and Harriet in the Yale University Library, throws a good deal of light on their relationship and helps
to explain, if not excuse, the passages about her in his work.[16] What
appears most obvious is that the Harriet of the incomparable
intellect was (not only in the *Autobiography* but in his day-to-day
thinking as well) an idealization to answer Mill's peculiar personal
and philosophic needs. He tells at length in the draft how he suffered "great inaptness" in practical affairs; these Harriet had taken
complete charge of for him. Having grown up under a strong will,
he says that he lacked initiative and responsibility; she now supplied
the strong will, taking up, in his account, more or less where his
father had left off in directing his activities. There was his habitual
reserve, resulting in a loneliness that was unrelieved during his first
twenty-five years by any completely satisfactory personal relationship; again she answered the need: "from the time when I could
really call her my friend I wished for no other." And in his reaction
against the rationalism of his early education, she represented, as a
character of feeling, poetry, intuition, and humanity, just the qualities that he wished to unite with his own. It was but a short step,
by endowing her with his own logical and empirical traits, to make
her into a symbol of the perfect mind.

[15] Mill likens his mental condition at the beginning of his crisis to "the
state . . . in which converts to Methodism usually are, when smitten by
their first 'conviction of sin' " (p. 81); but in this sentence, a later addition
to the work, he is being humorous in an attempt to give some detachment
to his account.
[16] This and the next paragraph, along with a few sentences earlier, are
largely taken from my introduction in *The Early Draft.* The direct quotations are from pp. 178, 193, 198–99 of that book (see also pp. 23–24 n.,
33–34 n., in the present volume).

Two sentences from the original Part II of the draft are by their conjunction especially illuminating: "at a very early period of my knowledge of her she became to me a living type of the most admirable kind of human being. I had always wished for a friend whom I could admire wholly, without reservation & restriction, & I had now found one." On both the philosophic and personal levels, she represented a measure of success in the life he was retracing. In the original structure of the *Autobiography,* beginning with his education and proceeding through his mental crisis to a kind of salvation in his friendship and later marriage with her, the philosophic and personal concerns follow a parallel course throughout. In revising and adding the history of twenty more years of his life, Mill somewhat weakened and obscured this structure and Harriet's place in it, but it is still, in the final version, the basic scheme on which the account of his life is organized.

It is unfortunate that Mill did not simply thank his wife for encouragement, perhaps also for transcribing a manuscript or making an index, and let it go at that. But he was remarkably clear-sighted in most other things concerning his life and times, and his exaggeration in one part of the work ought not to stand in the way of understanding what he is trying to convey in the work at large. Though there will never be another movement as rigid and flinty-minded as the Benthamites, we are now much more than in Mill's day in an age of specialization, an age increasingly tending in social philosophy toward over-abstraction and in all fields toward the one-sidedness of half-truths. Mill may continue to remind us of the danger of narrowness, of the necessity for both a realistic grasp of things and an imaginative investment in them. The last point is of special importance. It may seem odd that this "Autobiography of a steam-engine"[17] should turn out to center on the fundamental role of imagination in the growth of the philosophic mind, but that is just what it does. As Lionel Trilling says, Mill "understood from his own experience that the imagination was properly the joint possession of the emotions and the intellect, that it was fed by the emotions, and that without it the intellect withers and dies, that without it the mind cannot work and cannot properly conceive itself."[18] We do not today, in our arguing over the two cultures,

[17] Carlyle's phrase, in a letter quoted by Emery Neff, *Carlyle and Mill,* 2nd ed. (New York, 1926), p. 52.
[18] Preface to *The Liberal Imagination* (New York, 1950), p. xiv.

in politics, in philosophy, even in the study of literature itself, have so large a play of imagination that we cannot learn something from Mill's account of his life.

A NOTE ON THE TEXT OF THE *AUTOBIOGRAPHY*

THE known facts of the history of the text and the relationship of the three extant manuscripts—the early draft in Mill's hand now in the University of Illinois Library, the final holograph version in the Columbia University Library, and the transcript from which the work was first published, written mainly in the months just after Mill's death by his stepdaughter Helen Taylor, his sister Mary Elizabeth Colman, and an unidentified French copyist, now in the John Rylands Library, Manchester — are given in the *Bulletin of the John Rylands Library,* XLIII (1960), 220–42, and in the introduction to *The Early Draft,* pp. 1–11. Mill began the work and wrote the equivalent of the first three-fourths of the final version (chapters I–VI plus the first dozen paragraphs of chapter VII) in 1853–54. His wife read this draft, marking passages with lines, X's, and question marks in the margin, deleting and sometimes rewriting Mill's text, occasionally making comments; and Mill followed many of her suggested alterations in the revisions made within the early MS. He further revised and recopied this version in 1861 in the first part of the MS now at Columbia, and then completed the work (or, rather, brought it up to date) in the continuation of this MS which he wrote in the winter of 1869–70. The rediscovery in 1959 of the third MS, which had been lost sight of for thirty-seven years, with the evidence it provides that Mill had no direct hand in the copy-text from which the posthumous first edition (1873) was printed, established the Columbia MS as the single authoritative source of text for the final version of the *Autobiography.* It is this MS (with thanks to the Columbia University Press for permission to use it) that is the basis of the present text.

Only one earlier edition has been made directly from the Columbia MS, that issued by the Columbia University Press, with a preface by John Jacob Coss, in 1924. The present text varies from it and improves on its accuracy in more than nine hundred particulars, including some seventy corrections of wording and several of paragraphing. I have silently emended the MS text in lowering superscript letters to the line; adding periods after abbreviations and (where they are missing) at the ends of sentences; adding commas and in a few instances other marks of punctuation where they were necessary or especially desirable (mainly to complete Mill's revisions but also in places where he used some other device — most often the end of the line in the MS — as a substitute for punctuation); expanding ampersand to "and" and spelling out most numbers and one abbreviation ("U. States" becomes "United States"). I have also corrected a title ("Système" to "Cours" on p. 147 n.), a date ("1861" to "1862" on p. 160), and the spelling of a few foreign words. In other respects I have followed the MS verbatim, retaining Mill's harmless oddities in spelling (e.g., "superintendance," "transcendant"), inconsistencies (e g., "stile" and "style," "developement" and "development"), and one archaism ("council" for "counsel" on p. 177) just as he wrote them. In the quotations from the early MS in the footnotes I have, while citing *The Early Draft,* slightly altered my text there to make the practices consistent with those used in the present text. The notes mainly translate foreign words and phrases, and identify quotations and allusions. Most persons and books mentioned in the text are briefly identified in the index.

CHRONOLOGY

1806   John Stuart Mill is born on May 20 in London, the eldest son of James and Harriet Mill. Eight sisters and brothers are added to the family between 1808 and 1825.

1809–20   Education at home, beginning with Greek at the age of three.

1820–21   A year's residence in France with the family of Sir Samuel Bentham.

1822   First publications — two letters in a newspaper.

1823   Forms Utilitarian Society (broken up in 1826). Begins career with East India Company as a clerk in the office of the Examiner of India Correspondence (subsequently promoted to assistant and, in 1856, to chief of the office).

1824   Founding of the *Westminster Review*.

1825   Edits Jeremy Bentham's *Rationale of Judicial Evidence* (published 1827). Helps found the London Debating Society.

1826–27   Mental crisis.

1830   Meets and soon falls in love with Harriet Taylor, wife of John Taylor. Visits Paris during the Revolution.

1831   Publishes a series of articles on "The Spirit of the Age" in the *Examiner*. Meets Carlyle.

1832   Death of Jeremy Bentham. Passing of the first Reform Bill.

1835–40   Founds and edits the *London Review* (title changed after the first year to *London and Westminster Review*).

1836   Death of James Mill. Several months of severe illness.

1843   Publication of *A System of Logic* (eight editions during his lifetime).

1844   Publication of *Essays on Some Unsettled Questions of Political Economy*.

1848   Publication of *Principles of Political Economy* (seven editions during his lifetime).

1851   Marries Harriet Taylor (her husband having died in 1849).

1858   Retires from the East India Company. Death of his wife in
            Avignon. Thereafter spends half of each year in Avignon.

1859   Publication of *On Liberty, Thoughts on Parliamentary Reform,*
            and *Dissertations and Discussions,* Volumes I and II.

1861   Publication of *Considerations on Representative Government.*

1863   Publication of *Utilitarianism* (reprinted from *Fraser's Maga-
            zine,* 1861).

1865   Publication of *An Examination of Sir William Hamilton's Phi-
            losophy* and *Auguste Comte and Positivism* (reprinted from the
            Westminster Review).

1865–68   M.P. for Westminster.

1867   Publication of *Inaugural Address Delivered to the University
            of St. Andrew's* and *Dissertations and Discussions,* Volume III.
            Passing of the second Reform Bill.

1868   Publication of *England and Ireland.*

1869   Publication of *The Subjection of Women* and a new edition of
            James Mill's *Analysis of the Phenomena of the Human Mind.*

1870   Publication of *Chapters and Speeches on the Irish Land Ques-
            tion* (reprinted from *Principles of Political Economy* and *Han-
            sard's Parliamentary Debates*).

1873   Dies on May 7 in Avignon. *Autobiography* published post-
            humously (also *Nature, the Utility of Religion, and Theism* in
            1874 and *Dissertations and Discussions,* Volume IV, in 1875).

SELECT BIBLIOGRAPHY

BIBLIOGRAPHICAL GUIDES

Bibliography of the Published Writings of John Stuart Mill, ed. Ney Mac-Minn, J. R. Hainds, and James McNab McCrimmon. Evanston, 1945. An annotated edition of a notebook copy of Mill's own MS bibliography.

Hascall, Dudley, and J. M. Robson. "Bibliography of the Writings on Mill," *Mill News Letter,* I (1965) — in progress. An annotated checklist, alphabetically by author.

See also the annual bibliographies of research in *PMLA* (1922–), *Modern Philology* (1933–57), *Victorian Studies* (1958–), and *Mill News Letter* (1965–).

MODERN EDITIONS

Collected Works of John Stuart Mill. F. E. L. Priestley, General Editor; J. M. Robson, Associate Editor. Toronto, 1963 — in progress. Six volumes to date, including *Principles of Political Economy, Essays on Economics and Society,* and *Earlier Letters* (see the next item).

The Earlier Letters of John Stuart Mill, 1812–1848, ed. Francis E. Mineka, in *Collected Works,* Vols. XII and XIII. Toronto, 1963.

The Early Draft of John Stuart Mill's "Autobiography," ed. Jack Stillinger. Urbana, 1961.

James & John Stuart Mill on Education, ed. F. A. Cavenagh. Cambridge, 1931.

John Mill's Boyhood Visit to France: Being a Journal and Notebook Written by John Stuart Mill in France, 1820–21, ed. Anna Jean Mill. Toronto, 1960.

John Stuart Mill: Literary Essays, ed. Edward Alexander. Indianapolis, 1967.

The Letters of John Stuart Mill, ed. Hugh S. R. Elliot. 2 vols. London, 1910. Still useful until the later letters are published in the collected edition.

The Spirit of the Age, ed. Frederick A. von Hayek. Chicago, 1942. A series of articles published in the *Examiner* in 1831.

BIOGRAPHY AND CRITICISM

Alexander, Edward. *Matthew Arnold and John Stuart Mill.* New York and London, 1965.

Alexander, Edward. "Mill's Theory of Culture: The Wedding of Literature and Democracy," *University of Toronto Quarterly,* XXXV (1965), 75–88.

Anschutz, R. P. *The Philosophy of J. S. Mill.* Oxford, 1953.

Bain, Alexander. *James Mill. A Biography.* London, 1882.
Bain, Alexander. *John Stuart Mill. A Criticism: with Personal Recollections.* London, 1882.
Britton, Karl. *John Stuart Mill.* London, 1953.
Cumming, Robert D. "Mill's History of His Ideas," *Journal of the History of Ideas,* XXV (1964), 235–56.
Durham, John. "The Influence of John Stuart Mill's Mental Crisis on His Thoughts," *American Imago,* XX (1963), 369–84.
Halévy, Elie. *The Growth of Philosophic Radicalism,* trans. Mary Morris. London, 1928.
Hamburger, Joseph. *Intellectuals in Politics: John Stuart Mill and the Philosophic Radicals.* New Haven, 1965.
Hamburger, Joseph. *James Mill and the Art of Revolution.* New Haven, 1963.
Hayek, F. A. *John Stuart Mill and Harriet Taylor.* London, 1951.
Levi, Albert William. "The 'Mental Crisis' of John Stuart Mill," *Psychoanalytic Review,* XXXII (1945), 86–101.
Levi, Albert William. "The Writing of Mill's *Autobiography,*" *Ethics,* LXI (1951), 284–96.
Mineka, Francis E. "The *Autobiography* and the Lady," *University of Toronto Quarterly,* XXXII (1963), 301–306.
Mueller, Iris Wessel. *John Stuart Mill and French Thought.* Urbana, 1956.
Neff, Emery. *Carlyle and Mill: Mystic and Utilitarian.* New York, 1924; 2nd ed., 1926.
Packe, Michael St. John. *The Life of John Stuart Mill.* London, 1954. The standard biography.
Pappe, H. O. *John Stuart Mill and the Harriet Taylor Myth.* Melbourne, 1960.
Rinehart, Keith. "John Stuart Mill's *Autobiography:* Its Art and Appeal," *University of Kansas City Review,* XIX (1953), 265–73.
Robson, John M. "Harriet Taylor and John Stuart Mill: Artist and Scientist," *Queen's Quarterly,* LXXIII (1966), 167–86.
Robson, John M. *The Improvement of Mankind: The Social and Political Thought of John Stuart Mill.* Toronto, 1968.
Robson, John M. "John Stuart Mill and Jeremy Bentham, with Some Observations on James Mill," *Essays in English Literature . . . Presented to A. S. P. Woodhouse,* ed. Millar MacLure and F. W. Watt (Toronto, 1964), pp. 245–68.
Robson, John M. "Mill and Arnold: Liberty and Culture — Friends or Enemies?" *Humanities Association Bulletin,* XII (1961), 20–32.
Robson, John M. "Mill's 'Autobiography' — the Public and the Private Voice," *College Composition and Communication,* XVI (1965), 97–101.
Stephen, Leslie. *The English Utilitarians.* 3 vols. New York and London, 1900.
Stillinger, Jack. "The Text of John Stuart Mill's *Autobiography,*" *Bulletin of the John Rylands Library,* XLIII (1960), 220–42.

AUTOBIOGRAPHY

AUTOBIOGRAPHY

CHAPTER I

CHILDHOOD, AND EARLY EDUCATION

IT seems proper that I should prefix to the following biographical sketch, some mention of the reasons which have made me think it desirable that I should leave behind me such a memorial of so uneventful a life as mine. I do not for a moment imagine that any part of what I have to relate, can be interesting to the public as a narrative, or as being connected with myself. But I have thought that in an age in which education, and its improvement, are the subject of more, if not of profounder study than at any former period of English history, it may be useful that there should be some record of an education which was unusual and remarkable, and which, whatever else it may have done, has proved how much more than is commonly supposed may be taught, and well taught, in those early years which, in the common modes of what is called instruction, are little better than wasted. It has also seemed to me that in an age of transition in opinions, there may be somewhat both of interest and of benefit in noting the successive phases of any mind which was always pressing forward, equally ready to learn and to unlearn either from its own thoughts or from those of others. But a motive which weighs more with me than either of these, is a desire to make acknowledgment of the debts which my intellectual and moral development owes to other persons; some of them of recognized eminence, others less known than they deserve to be, and the one to whom most of all is due,[1] one whom the world had no opportunity of knowing. The reader whom these things do not interest, has only himself to blame if he reads farther, and I do not desire any other indulgence from him than that of bearing in mind, that for him these pages were not written.

[1] His wife.

I was born in London, on the 20th of May 1806, and was the eldest son of James Mill, the author of the History of British India. My father, the son of a petty tradesman and (I believe) small farmer, at Northwater Bridge, in the county of Angus, was, when a boy, recommended by his abilities to the notice of Sir John Stuart, of Fettercairn, one of the Barons of the Exchequer in Scotland, and was, in consequence, sent to the University of Edinburgh at the expense of a fund established by Lady Jane Stuart (the wife of Sir John Stuart) and some other ladies for educating young men for the Scottish Church. He there went through the usual course of study, and was licensed as a Preacher, but never followed the profession; having satisfied himself that he could not believe the doctrines of that or any other Church. For a few years he was a private tutor in various families in Scotland, among others that of the Marquis of Tweeddale; but ended by taking up his residence in London, and devoting himself to authorship. Nor had he any other means of support until 1819, when he obtained an appointment in the India House.

In this period of my father's life there are two things which it is impossible not to be struck with: one of them unfortunately a very common circumstance, the other a most uncommon one. The first is, that in his position, with no resource but the precarious one of writing in periodicals, he married and had a large family; conduct than which nothing could be more opposed, both as a matter of good sense and of duty, to the opinions which, at least at a later period of life, he strenuously upheld.[2] The other circumstance, is the extraordinary energy which was required to lead the life he led, with the disadvantages under which he laboured from the first, and with those which he brought upon himself by his marriage. It would have been no small thing, had he done no more than to support himself and his family during so many years by writing, without ever being in debt, or in any pecuniary difficulty; holding, as he did, opinions, both in politics and in religion, which were more odious to all persons of influence, and to the common run of prosperous Englishmen, in that generation than either before or since; and being not only a man whom nothing would have induced to

[2] The original MS continues the sentence with an indirect reference to Mill's mother: "and to which he had not, and never could have supposed that he had, the inducements of kindred intellect, tastes, or pursuits" (*The Early Draft*, p. 36).

write against his convictions, but one who invariably threw into everything he wrote, as much of his convictions as he thought the circumstances would in any way permit: being, it must also be said, one who never did anything negligently; never undertook any task, literary or other, on which he did not conscientiously bestow all the labour necessary for performing it adequately. But he, with these burthens on him, planned, commenced, and completed, the History of India; and this in the course of about ten years, a shorter time than has been occupied (even by writers who had no other employment) in the production of almost any other historical work of equal bulk, and of anything approaching to the same amount of reading and research. And to this is to be added, that during the whole period, a considerable part of almost every day was employed in the instruction of his children: in the case of one of whom, myself, he exerted an amount of labour, care, and perseverance rarely, if ever, employed for a similar purpose, in endeavouring to give, according to his own conception, the highest order of intellectual education.

A man who, in his own practice, so vigorously acted up to the principle of losing no time, was likely to adhere to the same rule in the instruction of his pupil. I have no remembrance of the time when I began to learn Greek. I have been told that it was when I was three years old. My earliest recollection on the subject, is that of committing to memory what my father termed Vocables, being lists of common Greek words, with their signification in English, which he wrote out for me on cards. Of grammar, until some years later, I learnt no more than the inflexions of the nouns and verbs, but, after a course of vocables, proceeded at once to translation; and I faintly remember going through Æsop's Fables, the first Greek book which I read. The Anabasis,[3] which I remember better, was the second. I learnt no Latin until my eighth year. At that time I had read, under my father's tuition, a number of Greek prose authors, among whom I remember the whole of Herodotus, and of Xenophon's Cyropædia and Memorials of Socrates; some of the lives of the philosophers by Diogenes Laertius; part of Lucian, and Isocrates ad Demonicum and ad Nicoclem. I also read, in 1813, the first six dialogues (in the common arrangement) of Plato, from the Euthyphron to the Theætetus inclusive: which last dialogue, I

---

[3] Of Xenophon.

venture to think, would have been better omitted, as it was totally
impossible I should understand it.[4] But my father, in all his teaching, demanded of me not only the utmost that I could do, but much
that I could by no possibility have done. What he was himself willing to undergo for the sake of my instruction, may be judged from
the fact, that I went through the whole process of preparing my
Greek lessons in the same room and at the same table at which he
was writing: and as in those days Greek and English Lexicons were
not, and I could make no more use of a Greek and Latin Lexicon
than could be made without having yet begun to learn Latin, I was
forced to have recourse to him for the meaning of every word which
I did not know. This incessant interruption he, one of the most
impatient of men, submitted to, and wrote under that interruption
several volumes of his History and all else that he had to write
during those years.

The only thing besides Greek, that I learnt as a lesson in this part
of my childhood, was arithmetic: this also my father taught me: it
was the task of the evenings, and I well remember its disagreeable-
ness. But the lessons were only a part of the daily instruction I
received. Much of it consisted in the books I read by myself, and
my father's discourses to me, chiefly during our walks. From 1810
to the end of 1813 we were living in Newington Green, then an
almost rustic neighbourhood. My father's health required considerable and constant exercise, and he walked habitually before
breakfast, generally in the green lanes towards Hornsey. In these
walks I always accompanied him, and with my earliest recollections
of green fields and wild flowers, is mingled that of the account I
gave him daily of what I had read the day before. To the best of
my remembrance, this was a voluntary rather than a prescribed
exercise. I made notes on slips of paper while reading, and from
these, in the morning walks, I told the story to him; for the books
were chiefly histories, of which I read in this manner a great number: Robertson's histories, Hume, Gibbon; but my greatest delight,
then and for long afterwards, was Watson's Philip the Second and
Third. The heroic defence of the Knights of Malta against the
Turks, and of the revolted provinces of the Netherlands against
Spain, excited in me an intense and lasting interest. Next to Wat-

---

[4] The "common arrangement" varied from edition to edition, but the first
four dialogues were usually the *Euthyphro, Apology, Crito*, and *Phaedo*.
The *Theaetetus* treats the meaning of knowledge.

son, my favorite historical reading was Hooke's History of Rome. Of Greece I had seen at that time no regular history, except school abridgments and the last two or three volumes of a translation of Rollin's Ancient History, beginning with Philip of Macedon. But I read with great delight Langhorne's translation of Plutarch. In English history, beyond the time at which Hume leaves off, I remember reading Burnet's History of his Own Time, though I cared little for anything in it except the wars and battles; and the historical part of the Annual Register, from the beginning to about 1788, where the volumes my father borrowed for me from Mr. Bentham left off. I felt a lively interest in Frederic of Prussia during his difficulties, and in Paoli, the Corsican patriot; but when I came to the American War, I took my part, like a child as I was (until set right by my father) on the wrong side, because it was called the English side. In these frequent talks about the books I read, he used, as opportunity offered, to give me explanations and ideas respecting civilization, government, morality, mental cultivation, which he required me afterwards to restate to him in my own words. He also made me read, and give him a verbal account of, many books which would not have interested me sufficiently to induce me to read them of myself: among others, Millar's Historical View of the English Government, a book of great merit for its time, and which he highly valued; Mosheim's Ecclesiastical History, McCrie's Life of John Knox, and even Sewell's and Rutty's Histories of the Quakers. He was fond of putting into my hands books which exhibited men of energy and resource in unusual circumstances, struggling against difficulties and overcoming them: of such works I remember Beaver's African Memoranda, and Collins's account of the first settlement of New South Wales. Two books which I never wearied of reading were Anson's Voyage, so delightful to most young persons, and a Collection (Hawkesworth's, I believe) of Voyages round the World, in four volumes, beginning with Drake and ending with Cook and Bougainville. Of children's books, any more than of playthings, I had scarcely any, except an occasional gift from a relation or acquaintance: among those I had, Robinson Crusoe was preeminent, and continued to delight me through all my boyhood. It was no part however of my father's system to exclude books of amusement, though he allowed them very sparingly. Of such books he possessed at that time next to none, but he borrowed several for me; those which I remember are, the Arabian Nights, Cazotte's

Arabian Tales, Don Quixote, Miss Edgeworth's "Popular Tales," and a book of some reputation in its day, Brooke's Fool of Quality.

In my eighth year I commenced learning Latin, in conjunction with a younger sister, to whom I taught it as I went on, and who afterwards repeated the lessons to my father: and from this time, other sisters and brothers being successively added as pupils, a considerable part of my day's work consisted of this preparatory teaching. It was a part which I greatly disliked; the more so, as I was held responsible for the lessons of my pupils, in almost as full a sense as for my own: I however derived from this discipline the great advantage, of learning more thoroughly and retaining more lastingly the things which I was set to teach: perhaps, too, the practice it afforded in explaining difficulties to others, may even at that age have been useful. In other respects, the experience of my boyhood is not favorable to the plan of teaching children by means of one another. The teaching, I am sure, is very inefficient as teaching, and I well know that the relation between teacher and taught is not a good moral discipline to either. I went in this manner through the Latin grammar, and a considerable part of Cornelius Nepos and Cæsar's Commentaries, but afterwards added to the superintendance of these lessons, much longer ones of my own.

In the same year in which I began Latin, I made my first commencement in the Greek poets with the Iliad. After I had made some progress in this, my father put Pope's translation into my hands. It was the first English verse I had cared to read, and it became one of the books in which for many years I most delighted: I think I must have read it from twenty to thirty times through. I should not have thought it worth while to mention a taste apparently so natural to boyhood, if I had not, as I think, observed that the keen enjoyment of this brilliant specimen of narrative and versification is not so universal with boys, as I should have expected both *a priori* and from my individual experience. Soon after this time I commenced Euclid, and somewhat later, algebra, still under my father's tuition.

From my eighth to my twelfth year the Latin books which I remember reading were, the Bucolics of Virgil, and the first six books of the Æneid; all Horace except the Epodes; the fables of Phædrus; the first five books of Livy (to which from my love of the subject I voluntarily added, in my hours of leisure, the remainder of the first decad); all Sallust; a considerable part of Ovid's Metamorphoses;

some plays of Terence; two or three books of Lucretius; several of the Orations of Cicero, and of his writings on oratory; also his letters to Atticus, my father taking the trouble to translate to me from the French the historical explanations in Mongault's notes. In Greek I read the Iliad and Odyssey through; one or two plays of Sophocles, Euripides, and Aristophanes, though by these I profited little; all Thucydides; the Hellenics of Xenophon; a great part of Demosthenes, Æschines, and Lysias; Theocritus; Anacreon; part of the Anthology; a little of Dionysius; several books of Polybius; and lastly, Aristotle's Rhetoric, which, as the first expressly scientific treatise on any moral or psychological subject which I had read, and containing many of the best observations of the ancients on human nature and life, my father made me study with peculiar care, and throw the matter of it into synoptic tables. During the same years I learnt elementary geometry and algebra thoroughly, the differential calculus and other portions of the higher mathematics far from thoroughly: for my father, not having kept up this part of his early acquired knowledge, could not spare time to qualify himself for removing my difficulties, and left me to deal with them, with little other aid than that of books: while I was continually incurring his displeasure by my inability to solve difficult problems for which he did not see that I had not the necessary previous knowledge.

As to my private reading, I can only speak of what I remember. History continued to be my strongest predilection, and most of all ancient history. Mitford's Greece I read continually. My father had put me on my guard against the Tory prejudices of this writer, and his perversions of facts for the whitewashing of despots, and blackening of popular institutions. These points he discoursed on, exemplifying them from the Greek orators and historians, with such effect that in reading Mitford, my sympathies were always on the contrary side to those of the author, and I could, to some extent, have argued the point against him: yet this did not diminish the ever new pleasure with which I read the book. Roman history, both in my old favorite, Hooke, and in Ferguson, continued to delight me. A book which, in spite of what is called the dryness of its stile, I took great pleasure in, was the Ancient Universal History: through the incessant reading of which, I had my head full of historical details concerning the obscurest ancient people, while about modern history, except detached passages such as the Dutch war of independence, I knew and cared comparatively little. A voluntary exercise to which throughout my boyhood I was much addicted, was what I called writing histories. I successively composed a Roman history, picked out of Hooke; an abridgment of the Ancient Universal History; a History of Holland, from my favorite Watson and from an anonymous compilation; and in my eleventh and twelfth year I occupied myself with writing what I flattered myself was something serious. This was no less than a history of the Roman Government, compiled (with the assistance of Hooke) from Livy and Dionysius: of which I wrote as much as would have made an octavo volume, extending to the epoch of the Licinian Laws. It was, in fact, an account of the struggles between the patricians and plebeians, which now engrossed all the interest in my mind which I had previously felt in the mere wars and conquests of the Romans. I discussed all the constitutional points as they arose: though quite ignorant of Niebuhr's researches, I, by such lights as my father had given me, vindicated the Agrarian Laws on the evidence of Livy, and upheld to the best of my ability the Roman democratic party. A few years later, in my contempt of my childish efforts, I destroyed all these papers, not then anticipating that I could ever feel any curiosity about my first attempts at writing and reasoning. My father encouraged me in this useful amusement, though, as I think judiciously, he never asked to see what I wrote; so that I did not feel that in writing it I was accountable to any one, nor had the chilling sensation of being under a critical eye.

But though these exercises in history were never a compulsory lesson, there was another kind of composition which was so, namely writing verses, and it was one of the most disagreeable of my tasks. Greek or Latin verses I did not write, nor learnt the prosody of those languages. My father, thinking this not worth the time it required, contented himself with making me read aloud to him, and correcting false quantities. I never composed at all in Greek, even in prose, and but little in Latin: not that my father could be indifferent to the value of this practice, in giving a thorough knowledge of those languages, but because there really was not time for it. The verses I was required to write were English. When I first read Pope's Homer, I ambitiously attempted to compose something of the same kind, and achieved as much as one book of a continuation of the Iliad. There, probably, the spontaneous promptings of my poetical ambition would have stopped; but the exercise, begun from choice, was continued by command. Conformably to my father's usual practice of explaining to me, as far as possible, the reasons for what he required me to do, he gave me, for this, as I well remember, two reasons highly characteristic of him. One was, that some things could be expressed better and more forcibly in verse than in prose: this, he said, was a real advantage. The other was, that people in general attached more value to verse than it deserved, and the power of writing it was, on this account, worth acquiring. He generally left me to choose my own subjects, which, as far as I remember, were mostly addresses to some mythological personage or allegorical abstraction; but he made me translate into English verse many of Horace's shorter poems: I also remember his giving me Thomson's "Winter" to read, and afterwards making me attempt (without book) to write something myself on the same subject. The verses I wrote were of course the merest rubbish, nor did I ever attain any facility of versification, but the practice may have been useful in making it easier for me, at a later period, to acquire readiness of expression.[5] I had read, up to this time, very little English poetry. Shakespeare my father had put into my hands, chiefly for the sake of the historical plays, from which however I went on to the others. My father never was a great admirer of Shakespeare, the English idolatry of whom he used to attack with some severity. He cared little for any English poetry except Milton (for whom he had the highest admiration), Goldsmith, Burns, and Gray's Bard, which he preferred to his Elegy: perhaps I may add Cowper and Beattie. He had some value for Spenser, and I remember his reading to me (unlike his usual practice of making me read to him) the first book of the Fairie Queene; but I took little pleasure in it. The poetry of the present century he saw scarcely any merit in, and I hardly became acquainted with any of it till I was grown up to manhood, except the metrical romances of Walter Scott, which I read at his recommendation and was intensely delighted with; as I always was with animated narrative. Dryden's Poems were among my father's books, and many of these

[5] In a subsequent stage of boyhood, when these exercises had ceased to be compulsory, like most youthful writers I wrote tragedies; under the inspiration not so much of Shakespeare as of Joanna Baillie, whose "Constantine Paleologus" in particular appeared to me one of the most glorious of human compositions. I still think it one of the best dramas of the last two centuries (Mill's note).

he made me read, but I never cared for any of them except Alexander's Feast, which, as well as many of the songs in Walter Scott, I used to sing internally, to a music of my own: to some of the latter indeed I went so far as to compose airs, which I still remember. Cowper's short poems I read with some pleasure, but never got far into the longer ones; and nothing in the two volumes interested me like the prose account of his three hares. In my thirteenth year I met with Campbell's Poems, among which Lochiel, Hohenlinden, the Exile of Erin, and some others, gave me sensations I had never before experienced from poetry. Here, too, I made nothing of the longer poems, except the striking opening of Gertrude of Wyoming, which long kept its place in my feelings as the perfection of pathos.

During this part of my childhood, one of my greatest amusements was experimental science; in the theoretical, however, not the practical sense of the word; not trying experiments, a kind of discipline which I have often regretted not having had — nor even seeing, but merely reading about them. I never remember being so wrapt up in any book, as I was in Joyce's Scientific Dialogues; and I was rather recalcitrant to my father's criticisms of the bad reasoning respecting the first principles of physics which abounds in the early part of that work. I devoured treatises on Chemistry, especially that of my father's early friend and schoolfellow Dr. Thomson, for years before I attended a lecture or saw an experiment.

From about the age of twelve, I entered into another and more advanced stage in my course of instruction; in which the main object was no longer the aids and appliances of thought, but the thoughts themselves. This commenced with Logic, in which I began at once with the Organon, and read it to the Analytics inclusive, but profited little by the Posterior Analytics,[6] which belong to a branch of speculation I was not yet ripe for. Contemporaneously with the Organon, my father made me read the whole or parts of several of the Latin treatises on the scholastic logic; giving each day to him, in our walks, a minute account of what I had read, and answering his numerous and searching questions. After this, I went, in a similar manner, through the "Computatio sive Logica" of Hobbes, a work of a much higher order of thought than the books of the school logicians, and which he estimated very highly;

[6] The "Prior Analytics" and "Posterior Analytics" are parts of Aristotle's *Organon*.

in my own opinion beyond its merits, great as these are. It was his invariable practice, whatever studies he exacted from me, to make me as far as possible understand and feel the utility of them: and this he deemed peculiarly fitting in the case of the syllogistic logic, the usefulness of which had been impugned by so many writers of authority. I well remember how, and in what particular walk, in the neighbourhood of Bagshot Heath (where we were on a visit to his old friend Mr. Wallace, then one of the Mathematical Professors at Sandhurst) he first attempted by questions to make me think on the subject, and frame some conception of what constituted the utility of the syllogistic logic, and when I had failed in this, to make me understand it by explanations. The explanations did not make the matter at all clear to me at the time; but they were not therefore useless; they remained as a nucleus for my observations and reflections to crystallize upon; the import of his general remarks being interpreted to me, by the particular instances which came under my notice afterwards. My own consciousness and experience ultimately led me to appreciate quite as highly as he did, the value of an early practical familiarity with the school logic. I know of nothing, in my education, to which I think myself more indebted for whatever capacity of thinking I have attained. The first intellectual operation in which I arrived at any proficiency, was dissecting a bad argument, and finding in what part the fallacy lay: and though whatever capacity of this sort I attained, was due to the fact that it was an intellectual exercise in which I was most perseveringly drilled by my father, yet it is also true that the school logic, and the mental habits acquired in studying it, were among the principal instruments of this drilling. I am persuaded that nothing, in modern education, tends so much, when properly used, to form exact thinkers, who attach a precise meaning to words and propositions, and are not imposed on by vague, loose, or ambiguous terms. The boasted influence of mathematical studies is nothing to it; for in mathematical processes, none of the real difficulties of correct ratiocination occur. It is also a study peculiarly adapted to an early stage in the education of philosophical students, since it does not presuppose the slow process of acquiring, by experience and reflection, valuable thoughts of their own. They may become capable of disentangling the intricacies of confused and self-contradictory thought, before their own thinking faculties are much advanced; a power which, for want of some such discipline, many otherwise able men altogether lack; and when they have to answer opponents, only endeavour, by such arguments as they can command, to support the opposite conclusion, scarcely even attempting to confute the reasonings of their antagonists; and therefore, at the utmost, leaving the question, as far as it depends on argument, a balanced one.

During this time, the Latin and Greek books which I continued to read with my father were chiefly such as were worth studying not for the language merely, but also for the thoughts. This included much of the orators, and especially Demosthenes, some of whose principal orations I read several times over, and wrote out, by way of exercise, a full analysis of them. My father's comments on these orations when I read them to him were very instructive to me. He not only drew my attention to the insight they afforded into Athenian institutions, and the principles of legislation and government which they often illustrated, but pointed out the skill and art of the orator — how everything important to his purpose was said at the exact moment when he had brought the minds of his audience into the state most fitted to receive it; how he made steal into their minds, gradually and by insinuation, thoughts which if expressed in a more direct manner would have roused their opposition. Most of these reflections were beyond my capacity of full comprehension at the time; but they left seed behind, which germinated in due season. At this time I also read the whole of Tacitus, Juvenal, and Quintilian. The latter, owing to his obscure stile and to the scholastic details of which many parts of his treatise are made up, is little read and seldom sufficiently appreciated. His book is a kind of encyclopædia of the thoughts of the ancients on the whole field of education and culture; and I have retained through life many valuable ideas which I can distinctly trace to my reading of him, even at that early age. It was at this period that I read, for the first time, some of the most important dialogues of Plato, in particular the Gorgias, the Protagoras, and the Republic. There is no author to whom my father thought himself more indebted for his own mental culture, than Plato, or whom he more frequently recommended to young students. I can bear similar testimony in regard to myself. The Socratic method, of which the Platonic dialogues are the chief example, is unsurpassed as a discipline for correcting the errors, and clearing up the confusions incident to the *intellectus sibi permissus*,[7] the understanding which has made up all its bundles of associations under the guidance of popular phraseology. The close, searching *elenchus* by which the man of vague generalities is constrained either to express his meaning to himself in definite terms, or to confess that he does not know what he is talking about; the perpetual testing of all general statements by particular instances; the siege in form which is laid to the meaning of large abstract terms, by fixing upon some still larger class-name which includes that and more, and dividing down to the thing sought—marking out its limits and definition by a series of accurately drawn distinctions between it and each of the cognate objects which are successively parted off from it — all this, as an education for precise thinking, is inestimable, and all this, even at that age, took such hold of me that it became part of my own mind. I have felt ever since that the title of Platonist belongs by far better right to those who have been nourished in, and have endeavoured to practise Plato's mode of investigation, than to those who are distinguished only by the adoption of certain dogmatical conclusions, drawn mostly from the least intelligible of his works, and which the character of his mind and writings makes it uncertain whether he himself regarded as anything more than poetic fancies, or philosophic conjectures.[8]

In going through Plato and Demosthenes, since I could now read these authors, as far as the language was concerned, with perfect ease, I was not required to construe them sentence by sentence, but to read them aloud to my father, answering questions when asked: but the particular attention which he paid to elocution (in which his own excellence was remarkable) made this reading aloud to him a most painful task. Of all things which he required me to do, there was none which I did so constantly ill, or in which he so perpetually lost his temper with me. He had thought much on the principles of the art of reading, especially the most neglected part of it, the inflexions of the voice, or *modulation* as writers on elocution call it (in contrast with *articulation* on the one side, and *ex-*

[7] The mind left to itself (Bacon's phrase in *Novum Organum*, I, ii, xx, xxi).

[8] In place of this last sentence of the paragraph the original MS reads: "and I have ever felt myself, beyond any modern that I know of except my father and perhaps beyond even him, a pupil of Plato, and cast in the mould of his dialectics" (*The Early Draft*, p. 48).

pression on the other), and had reduced it to rules, grounded on
the logical analysis of a sentence. These rules he strongly impressed upon me, and took me severely to task for every violation
of them: but I even then remarked (though I did not venture to
make the remark to him) that though he reproached me when I
read a sentence ill, and *told* me how I ought to have read it, he
never, by reading it himself, *shewed* me how it ought to be read.
A defect running through his otherwise admirable modes of instruction, as it did through all his modes of thought, was that of trusting
too much to the intelligibleness of the abstract, when not embodied
in the concrete. It was at a much later period of my youth, when
practising elocution by myself, or with companions of my own age,
that I for the first time understood the object of his rules, and saw
the psychological grounds of them. At that time I and others followed out the subject into its ramifications, and could have composed a very useful treatise, grounded on my father's principles.
He himself left those principles and rules unwritten. I regret that
when my mind was full of the subject, from systematic practice, I
did not put them, and our improvements of them, into a formal
shape.

A book which contributed largely to my education, in the best
sense of the term, was my father's History of India. It was published in the beginning of 1818. During the year previous, while
it was passing through the press, I used to read the proofsheets to
him; or rather, I read the manuscript to him while he corrected the
proofs. The number of new ideas which I received from this remarkable book, and the impulse and stimulus as well as guidance
given to my thoughts by its criticisms and disquisitions on society
and civilization in the Hindoo part, on institutions and the acts of
governments in the English part, made my early familiarity with it
eminently useful to my subsequent progress. And though I can
perceive deficiencies in it now as compared with a perfect standard,
I still think it, if not the most, one of the most instructive histories
ever written, and one of the books from which most benefit may be
derived by a mind in the course of making up its opinions.

The Preface, among the most characteristic of my father's writings, as well as the richest in materials of thought, gives a picture
which may be entirely depended on, of the sentiments and expectations with which he wrote the History. Saturated as the book is
with the opinions and modes of judgment of a democratic radi-

calism then regarded as extreme; and treating with a severity at that time most unusual the English Constitution, the English law, and all parties and classes who possessed any considerable influence in the country; he may have expected reputation, but certainly not advancement in life, from its publication; nor could he have supposed that it would raise up anything but enemies for him in powerful quarters: least of all could he have expected favour from the East India Company, to whose commercial privileges he was unqualifiedly hostile, and on the acts of whose government he had made so many severe comments: though, in various parts of his book, he bore a testimony in their favour, which he felt to be their just due, namely, that no government had on the whole given so much proof, to the extent of its lights, of good intention towards its subjects; and that if the acts of any other government had the light of publicity as completely let in upon them, they would, in all probability, still less bear scrutiny.

On learning, however, in the spring of 1819, about a year after the publication of the History, that the East India Directors desired to strengthen the part of their home establishment which was employed in carrying on the correspondence with India, my father declared himself a candidate for that employment, and, to the credit of the Directors, successfully. He was appointed one of the Assistants of the Examiner of India Correspondence; officers whose duty it was to prepare drafts of despatches to India, for consideration by the Directors, in the principal departments of administration. In this office, and in that of Examiner, which he subsequently attained, the influence which his talents, his reputation, and his decision of character gave him, with superiors who really desired the good government of India, enabled him to a great extent to throw into his drafts of despatches, and to carry through the ordeal of the Court of Directors and Board of Control, without having their force much weakened, his real opinions on Indian subjects. In his History he had set forth, for the first time, many of the true principles of Indian administration: and his despatches, following his History, did more than had ever been done before to promote the improvement of India, and teach Indian officials to understand their business. If a selection of them were published, they would, I am convinced, place his character as a practical statesman fully on a level with his eminence as a speculative writer.

This new employment of his time caused no relaxation in his

attention to my education. It was in this same year, 1819, that
he took me through a complete course of political economy. His
loved and intimate friend, Ricardo, had shortly before published the
book which formed so great an epoch in political economy;[9] a book
which never would have been published or written, but for the
entreaty and strong encouragement of my father; for Ricardo, the
most modest of men, though firmly convinced of the truth of his
doctrines, deemed himself so little capable of doing them justice
in exposition and expression, that he shrank from the idea of publicity. The same friendly encouragement induced Ricardo, a year
or two later, to become a member of the House of Commons;
where during the few remaining years of his life, unhappily cut
short in the full vigour of his intellect, he rendered so much service
to his and my father's opinions both in political economy and on
other subjects.

Though Ricardo's great work was already in print, no didactic
treatise embodying its doctrines, in a manner fit for learners, had
yet appeared. My father, therefore, commenced instructing me in
the science by a sort of lectures, which he delivered to me in our
walks. He expounded each day a portion of the subject, and I gave
him next day a written account of it, which he made me rewrite
over and over again until it was clear, precise, and tolerably complete. In this manner I went through the whole extent of the science; and the written outline of it which resulted from my daily
compte rendu,[10] served him afterwards as notes from which to write
his Elements of Political Economy. After this I read Ricardo, giving an account daily of what I read, and discussing, in the best manner I could, the collateral points which offered themselves in our
progress. On Money, as the most intricate part of the subject, he
made me read in the same manner Ricardo's admirable pamphlets,
written during what was called the Bullion controversy. To these
succeeded Adam Smith; and in this reading it was one of my
father's main objects to make me apply to Smith's more superficial
view of political economy, the superior lights of Ricardo, and detect
what was fallacious in Smith's arguments, or erroneous in any of
his conclusions. Such a mode of instruction was excellently calculated to form a thinker; but it required to be worked by a thinker,
as close and vigorous as my father. The path was a thorny one even

[9] *On the Principles of Political Economy and Taxation* (1817).
[10] Report.

to him, and I am sure it was so to me, notwithstanding the strong interest I took in the subject. He was often, and much beyond reason, provoked by my failures in cases where success could not have been expected; but in the main his method was right, and it succeeded. I do not believe that any scientific teaching ever was more thorough, or better fitted for training the faculties, than the mode in which logic and political economy were taught to me by my father. Striving, even in an exaggerated degree, to call forth the activity of my faculties, by making me find out everything for myself, he gave his explanations not before, but after, I had felt the full force of the difficulties; and not only gave me an accurate knowledge of these two great subjects, as far as they were then understood, but made me a thinker on both. I thought for myself almost from the first, and occasionally thought differently from him, though for a long time only on minor points, and making his opinion the ultimate standard. At a later period I even occasionally convinced him, and altered his opinion on some points of detail: which I state to his honour, not my own. It at once exemplifies his perfect candour, and the real worth of his method of teaching.

At this point concluded what can properly be called my lessons. When I was about fourteen I left England for more than a year; and after my return, though my studies went on under my father's general direction, he was no longer my schoolmaster. I shall therefore pause here, and turn back to matters of a more general nature connected with the part of my life and education included in the preceding reminiscences.

In the course of instruction which I have partially retraced, the point most superficially apparent is the great effort to give, during the years of childhood, an amount of knowledge in what are considered the higher branches of education, which is seldom acquired (if acquired at all) until the age of manhood. The result of the experiment shews the ease with which this may be done, and places in a strong light the wretched waste of so many precious years as are spent in acquiring the modicum of Latin and Greek commonly taught to schoolboys; a waste, which has led so many educational reformers to entertain the ill-judged proposal of discarding these languages altogether from general education. If I had been by nature extremely quick of apprehension, or had possessed a very accurate and retentive memory, or were of a remarkably active and energetic character, the trial would not be conclusive; but in all these natural gifts I am rather below than above par. What I could do, could assuredly be done by any boy or girl of average capacity and healthy physical constitution: and if I have accomplished anything, I owe it, among other fortunate circumstances, to the fact that through the early training bestowed on me by my father, I started, I may fairly say, with an advantage of a quarter of a century over my cotemporaries.

There was one cardinal point in this training, of which I have already given some indication, and which, more than anything else, was the cause of whatever good it effected. Most boys or youths who have had much knowledge drilled into them, have their mental capacities not strengthened, but overlaid by it. They are crammed with mere facts, and with the opinions or phrases of other people, and these are accepted as a substitute for the power to form opinions of their own. And thus, the sons of eminent fathers, who have spared no pains in their education, so often grow up mere parroters of what they have learnt, incapable of using their minds except in the furrows traced for them. Mine, however, was not an education of cram. My father never permitted anything which I learnt, to degenerate into a mere exercise of memory. He strove to make the understanding not only go along with every step of the teaching, but if possible, precede it. Anything which could be found out by thinking, I never was told, until I had exhausted my efforts to find it out for myself. As far as I can trust my remembrance, I acquitted myself very lamely in this department; my recollection of such matters is almost wholly of failures, hardly ever of success. It is true, the failures were often in things in which success in so early a stage of my progress, was almost impossible. I remember at some time in my thirteenth year, on my happening to use the word idea, he asked me what an idea was; and expressed some displeasure at my ineffectual efforts to define the word: I recollect also his indignation at my using the common expression that something was true in theory but required correction in practice; and how, after making me vainly strive to define the word theory, he explained its meaning, and shewed the fallacy of the vulgar form of speech which I had used; leaving me fully persuaded that in being unable to give a correct definition of Theory, and in speaking of it as something which might be at variance with practice, I had shewn unparalleled ignorance. In this he seems, and perhaps was, very unreasonable; but I think, only in being angry at my failure. A pupil from whom nothing is ever demanded which he cannot do, never does all he can.

One of the evils most liable to attend on any sort of early proficiency, and which often fatally blights its promise, my father most anxiously guarded against. This was self conceit. He kept me, with extreme vigilance, out of the way of hearing myself praised, or of being led to make self-flattering comparisons between myself and others. From his own intercourse with me I could derive none but a very humble opinion of myself; and the standard of comparison he always held up to me, was not what other people did, but what a man could and ought to do. He completely succeeded in preserving me from the sort of influences he so much dreaded. I was not at all aware that my attainments were anything unusual at my age. If I accidentally had my attention drawn to the fact that some other boy knew less than myself — which happened less often than might be imagined — I concluded, not that I knew much, but that he, for some reason or other, knew little, or that his knowledge was of a different kind from mine. My state of mind was not humility, but neither was it arrogance. I never thought of saying to myself, I am, or I can do, so and so. I neither estimated myself highly nor lowly: I did not estimate myself at all. If I thought anything about myself, it was that I was rather backward in my studies, since I always found myself so, in comparison with what my father expected from me. I assert this with confidence, though it was not the impression of various persons who saw me in my childhood. They, as I have since found, thought me greatly and disagreeably self-conceited; probably because I was disputatious, and did not scruple to give direct contradictions to things which I heard said. I suppose I acquired this bad habit from having been encouraged in an unusual degree to talk on matters beyond my age, and with grown persons, while I never had inculcated on me the usual respect for them. My father did not correct this ill breeding and impertinence, probably from not being aware of it, for I was always too much in awe of him to be otherwise than extremely subdued and quiet in his presence.[11] Yet with all this I had no notion of any superiority in myself; and well was it for me that I had not. I remember the very place in Hyde Park where, in my fourteenth year, on the eve

---

[11] In the original MS Mill wrote and then (following his wife's markings) deleted at this point: "My mother did tax me with it, but for her remonstrances I never had the slightest regard" (*The Early Draft*, p. 56 n.).

of leaving my father's house for a long absence, he told me that
I should find, as I got acquainted with new people, that I had been
taught many things which youths of my age did not commonly
know; and that many persons would be disposed to talk to me of
this, and to compliment me upon it. What other things he said on
this topic I remember very imperfectly; but he wound up by saying,
that whatever I knew more than others, could not be ascribed to
any merit in me, but to the very unusual advantage which had
fallen to my lot, of having a father who was able to teach me, and
willing to give the necessary trouble and time; that it was no matter
of praise to me, if I knew more than those who had not had a similar advantage, but the deepest disgrace to me if I did not. I have a
distinct remembrance, that the suggestion thus for the first time
made to me, that I knew more than other youths who were considered well educated, was to me a piece of information, to which,
as to all other things which my father told me, I gave implicit
credence, but which did not at all impress me as a personal matter.
I felt no disposition to glorify myself upon the circumstance that
there were other persons who did not know what I knew; nor had
I ever flattered myself that my acquirements, whatever they might
be, were any merit of mine: but, now when my attention was called
to the subject, I felt that what my father had said respecting my
peculiar advantages was exactly the truth and common sense of
the matter, and it fixed my opinion and feeling from that time
forward.

It is evident that this, among many other of the purposes of my
father's scheme of education, could not have been accomplished if
he had not carefully kept me from having any great amount of
intercourse with other boys. He was earnestly bent upon my escap-
ing not only the ordinary corrupting influence which boys exercise
over boys, but the contagion of vulgar modes of thought and feeling; and for this he was willing that I should pay the price of
inferiority in the accomplishments which schoolboys in all countries
chiefly cultivate. The deficiencies in my education were principally
in the things which boys learn from being turned out to shift for
themselves, and from being brought together in large numbers.
From temperance and much walking, I grew up healthy and hardy,
though not muscular; but I could do no feats of skill or physical
strength, and knew none of the ordinary bodily exercises. It was
not that play, or time for it, was refused me. Though no holidays

were allowed, lest the habit of work should be broken, and a taste for idleness acquired, I had ample leisure in every day to amuse myself; but as I had no boy companions, and the animal need of physical activity was satisfied by walking, my amusements, which were mostly solitary, were in general of a quiet, if not a bookish turn, and gave little stimulus to any other kind even of mental activity than that which was already called forth by my studies. I consequently remained long, and in a less degree have always remained, inexpert in anything requiring manual dexterity; my mind, as well as my hands, did its work very lamely when it was applied, or ought to have been applied, to the practical details which, as they are the chief interest of life to the majority of men, are also the things in which whatever mental capacity they have, chiefly shews itself. I was constantly meriting reproof by inattention, inobservance, and general slackness of mind in matters of daily life. My father was the extreme opposite in these particulars: his senses and mental faculties were always on the alert; he carried decision and energy of character in his whole manner, and into every action of life: and this, as much as his talents, contributed to the strong impression which he always made upon those with whom he came into personal contact. But the children of energetic parents, frequently grow up unenergetic, because they lean on their parents, and the parents are energetic for them. The education which my father gave me, was in itself much more fitted for training me to *know* than to *do*. Not that he was unaware of my deficiencies; both as a boy and as a youth I was incessantly smarting under his severe admonitions on the subject. There was anything but insensibility or tolerance on his part towards such shortcomings: but, while he saved me from the demoralizing effects of school life, he made no effort to provide me with any sufficient substitute for its practicalizing influences. Whatever qualities he himself, probably, had acquired without difficulty or special training, he seems to have supposed that I ought to acquire as easily. He had not, I think, bestowed the same amount of thought and attention on this, as on most other branches of education; and here, as well as in some other points of my tuition, he seems to have expected effects without causes.[12]

[12] In canceled passages of the original MS Mill speaks more specifically of "the very considerable drawbacks" that attended his education, drawbacks "which have pursued me through life." "I grew up," he says, "with great

inaptness in the common affairs of every day life. I was far longer than children generally are before I could put on my clothes. I know not how many years passed before I could tie a knot. My articulation was long imperfect; one letter, *r,* I could not pronounce until I was nearly sixteen. I never could, nor can I now, do anything requiring the smallest manual dexterity, but I never put even a common share of the exercise of understanding into practical things. I was continually acquiring odd or disagreeable tricks which I very slowly and imperfectly got rid of. I was, besides, utterly inobservant: I was, as my father continually told me, like a person who had not the organs of sense: my eyes and ears seemed of no use to me, so little did I see or hear what was before me, and so little, even of what I did see or hear, did I observe and remember. . . . [My father] could not endure stupidity, nor feeble and lax habits, in whatever manner displayed, and I was perpetually exciting his anger by manifestations of them. From the earliest time I can remember he used to reproach me, and most truly, with a general habit of inattention; owing to which, he said, I was constantly acquiring bad habits, and never breaking myself of them; was constantly forgetting what I ought to remember, and judging and acting like a person devoid of common sense; and which would make me, he said, grow up a mere oddity, looked down upon by everybody, and unfit for all the common purposes of life. . . . I had also the great misfortune of having, in domestic matters, everything done for me. Circumstanced as I was, nothing but being thrown as much as possible, in daily matters, upon my own powers of contriving and of executing could have given me the proper use of my faculties for the occasions of life. This discipline, I presume my father did not see the necessity of; and it would never have occurred to my mother, who without misgivings of any sort worked from morning till night for her children." Mill wrote three successive accounts of these deficiencies. At his wife's insistence the subject was finally dropped altogether from the draft (to be reintroduced in this final paragraph of the chapter in the Columbia MS). His repeated attempts to include some mention of it, and the bitterness of some of his language (references to ungainliness, awkwardness, and "a thoroughly ineffective and bungling manner" occur in one deleted sentence), bear witness to a strong feeling in the matter. See *The Early Draft,* pp. 18, 178–82.

CHAPTER II

MORAL INFLUENCES IN EARLY YOUTH. MY
FATHER'S CHARACTER AND OPINIONS

IN my education, as in that of every one, the moral influences, which are so much more important than all others, are also the most complicated, and the most difficult to specify with any approach to completeness. Without attempting the hopeless task of detailing the circumstances by which, in this respect, my early character may have been shaped, I shall confine myself to a few leading points, which form an indispensable part of any true account of my education.

I was brought up from the first without any religious belief, in the ordinary acceptation of the term. My father, educated in the creed of Scotch presbyterianism, had by his own studies and reflexions been early led to reject not only the belief in revelation, but the foundations of what is commonly called Natural Religion. I have heard him say, that the turning point of his mind on the subject was reading Butler's Analogy. That work, of which he always continued to speak with respect, kept him, as he said, for some considerable time, a believer in the divine authority of Christianity; by proving to him, that whatever are the difficulties in believing that the Old and New Testaments proceed from, or record the acts of, a perfectly wise and good being, the same and still greater difficulties stand in the way of the belief, that a being of such a character can have been the Maker of the universe. He considered Butler's argument as conclusive against the only opponents for whom it was intended. Those who admit an omnipotent as well as perfectly just and benevolent maker and ruler of such a world as this, can say little against Christianity but what can, with at least equal force, be retorted against themselves. Finding, therefore, no halting place in Deism, he remained in a state of perplexity, until, doubtless after many struggles, he yielded to the conviction, that concerning the origin of things nothing whatever can be known. This is the only correct statement of his opinion; for dogmatic atheism he looked upon as absurd; as most of those, whom the world has considered atheists, have always done. These particulars are important, because they shew that my father's rejection of all that is called religious belief, was not, as many might suppose, primarily a matter of logic and evidence: the grounds of it were moral, still more than intellectual. He found it impossible to believe that a world so full of evil was the work of an Author combining infinite power with perfect goodness and righteousness. His intellect spurned the subtleties by which men attempt to blind themselves to this open contradiction. The Sabæan, or Manichæan theory of a Good and an Evil Principle, struggling against each other for the government of the universe, he would not have equally condemned; and I have heard him express surprise, that no one revived it in our time. He would have regarded it as a mere hypothesis; but he would have ascribed to it no depraving influence. As it was, his aversion to religion, in the sense usually attached to the term, was of the same kind with that of Lucretius: he regarded it with the feelings due not to a mere mental delusion, but to a great moral evil. He looked upon it as the greatest enemy of morality: first, by setting up factitious excellencies, — belief in creeds, devotional feelings, and ceremonies, not connected with the good of human kind, — and causing these to be accepted as substitutes for genuine virtues: but above all, by radically vitiating the standard of morals; making it consist in doing the will of a being, on whom it lavishes indeed all the phrases of adulation, but whom in sober truth it depicts as eminently hateful. I have a hundred times heard him say, that all ages and nations have represented their gods as wicked, in a constantly increasing progression; that mankind have gone on adding trait after trait till they reached the most perfect conception of wickedness which the human mind could devise, and have called this God, and prostrated themselves before it. This *ne plus ultra* of wickedness he considered to be embodied in what is commonly presented to mankind as the creed of Christianity. Think (he used to say) of a being who would make a Hell — who would create the human race with the infallible foreknowledge, and therefore with the intention, that the great majority of them were to be consigned to horrible and everlasting torment. The time, I believe, is drawing near when this dreadful conception of an object of worship will be no longer identified with Christianity; and when all persons, with any sense of moral good and evil, will look upon it with the same indignation with which my father regarded it. My father was as well aware as any one that Christians do not, in general, undergo the demoralizing consequences which seem inherent in such a creed, in the manner or to the extent which might have been expected from it. The same slovenliness of thought, and subjection of the reason to fears, wishes, and affections, which enable them to accept a theory involving a contradiction in terms, prevents them from perceiving the logical consequences of the theory. Such is the facility with which mankind believe at one and the same time things inconsistent with one another, and so few are those who draw from what they receive as truths, any consequences but those recommended to them by their feelings, that multitudes have held the undoubting belief in an Omnipotent Author of Hell, and have nevertheless identified that being with the best conception they were able to form of perfect goodness. Their worship was not paid to the demon which such a Being as they imagined would really be, but to their own ideal of excellence. The evil is, that such a belief keeps the ideal wretchedly low; and opposes the most obstinate resistance to all thought which has a tendency to raise it higher. Believers shrink from every train of ideas which would lead the mind to a clear conception and an elevated standard of excellence, because they feel (even when they do not distinctly see) that such a standard would conflict with many of the dispensations of nature, and with much of what they are accustomed to consider as the Christian creed. And thus morality continues a matter of blind tradition, with no consistent principle, nor even any consistent feeling, to guide it.

It would have been wholly inconsistent with my father's ideas of duty, to allow me to acquire impressions contrary to his convictions and feelings respecting religion: and he impressed upon me from the first, that the manner in which the world came into existence was a subject on which nothing was known: that the question "Who made me?" cannot be answered, because we have no experience or authentic information from which to answer it; and that any answer only throws the difficulty a step further back, since the question immediately presents itself, Who made God? He, at the same time, took care that I should be acquainted with what had been thought by mankind on these impenetrable problems. I have mentioned at how early an age he made me a reader of ecclesiastical history; and he taught me to take the strongest interest in the Reformation, as the great and decisive contest against priestly tyranny for liberty of thought.

I am thus one of the very few examples, in this country, of one who has, not thrown off religious belief, but never had it: I grew up in a negative state with regard to it. I looked upon the modern exactly as I did upon the ancient religion, as something which in no way concerned me. It did not seem to me more strange that English people should believe what I did not, than that the men whom I read of in Herodotus should have done so. History had made the variety of opinions among mankind a fact familiar to me, and this was but a prolongation of that fact. This point in my early education had however incidentally one bad consequence deserving notice. In giving me an opinion contrary to that of the world, my father thought it necessary to give it as one which could not prudently be avowed to the world. This lesson of keeping my thoughts to myself, at that early age, was attended with some moral disadvantages; though my limited intercourse with strangers, especially such as were likely to speak to me on religion, prevented me from being placed in the alternative of avowal or hypocrisy. I remember two occasions in my boyhood, on which I felt myself in this alternative, and in both cases I avowed my disbelief and defended it. My opponents were boys, considerably older than myself: one of them I certainly staggered at the time, but the subject was never renewed between us: the other, who was surprised and somewhat shocked, did his best to convince me for some time, without effect.

The great advance in liberty of discussion, which is one of the most important differences between the present time and that of my childhood, has greatly altered the moralities of this question; and I think that few men of my father's intellect and public spirit, holding with such intensity of moral conviction as he did, unpopular opinions on religion, or on any other of the great subjects of thought, would now either practise or inculcate the withholding of them from the world, unless in the cases, becoming fewer every day, in which frankness on these subjects would either risk the loss of means of subsistence, or would amount to exclusion from some sphere of usefulness peculiarly suitable to the capacities of the individual. On religion in particular the time appears to me to have come, when it is the duty of all who being qualified in point of knowledge, have on mature consideration satisfied themselves that the current opinions are not only false but hurtful, to make their dissent known; at least, if they are among those whose station, or reputation, gives their opinion a chance of being attended to. Such an avowal would put an end, at once and for ever, to the vulgar prejudice, that what is called, very improperly, unbelief, is connected with any bad qualities either of mind or heart. The world would be astonished if it knew how great a proportion of its brightest ornaments — of those most distinguished even in popular estimation for wisdom and virtue — are complete sceptics in religion; many of them refraining from avowal, less from personal considerations, than from a conscientious, though now in my opinion a most mistaken apprehension lest by speaking out what would tend to weaken existing beliefs, and by consequence (as they suppose) existing restraints, they should do harm instead of good.

Of unbelievers (so called) as well as of believers, there are many species, including almost every variety of moral type. But the best among them, as no one who has had opportunities of really knowing them will hesitate to affirm (believers rarely have that opportunity), are more genuinely religious, in the best sense of the word religion, than those who exclusively arrogate to themselves the title. The liberality of the age, or in other words the weakening of the obstinate prejudice, which makes men unable to see what is before their eyes because it is contrary to their expectations, has caused it to be very commonly admitted that a Deist may be truly religious: but if religion stands for any graces of character and not for mere dogma, the assertion may equally be made of many whose belief is far short of Deism. Though they may think the proof incomplete that the universe is a work of design, and though they assuredly disbelieve that it can have an Author and Governor who is absolute in power as well as perfect in goodness, they have that which constitutes the principal worth of all religions whatever, an ideal conception of a Perfect Being, to which they habitually refer as the guide of their conscience; and this ideal of Good is usually far nearer to perfection than the objective Deity of those, who think themselves obliged to find absolute goodness in the author of a world so crowded with suffering and so deformed by injustice as ours.

My father's moral convictions, wholly dissevered from religion, were very much of the character of those of the Greek philosophers; and were delivered with the force and decision which characterized all that came from him. Even at the very early age at which I read with him the Memorabilia of Xenophon, I imbibed from that work and from his comments a deep respect for the character of Socrates; who stood in my mind as a model of ideal excellence: and I well remember how my father at that time impressed upon me the lesson of the "Choice of Hercules."[1] At a somewhat later period the lofty moral standard exhibited in the writings of Plato operated upon me with great force. My father's moral inculcations were at all times mainly those of the "Socratici viri";[2] justice, temperance (to which he gave a very extended application), veracity, perseverance, readiness to encounter pain and especially labour; regard for the public good; estimation of persons according to their merits, and of things according to their intrinsic usefulness; a life of exertion, in contradiction to one of self-indulgent sloth. These and other moralities he conveyed in brief sentences, uttered as occasion arose, of grave exhortation, or stern reprobation and contempt.

But though direct moral teaching does much, indirect does more; and the effect my father produced on my character, did not depend solely on what he said or did with that direct object, but also, and still more, on what manner of man he was.

In his views of life he partook of the character of the Stoic, the Epicurean, and the Cynic, not in the modern but the ancient sense of the word. In his personal qualities the Stoic predominated. His standard of morals was Epicurean, inasmuch as it was utilitarian, taking as the exclusive test of right and wrong, the tendency of actions to produce pleasure or pain. But he had (and this was the Cynic element) scarcely any belief in pleasure; at least in his later years, of which alone, on this point, I can speak confidently. He was not insensible to pleasures; but he deemed very few of them worth the price which, at least in the present state of society, must be paid for them. The greatest number of miscarriages in life, he considered to be attributable to the overvaluing of pleasures. Accordingly, temperance, in the large sense intended by the Greek philosophers — stopping short at the point of moderation in all indulgences — was with him, as with them, almost the central point of educational precept. His inculcations of this virtue fill a large place in my childish remembrances. He thought human life a poor thing at best, after the freshness of youth and of unsatisfied curiosity had gone by. This was a topic on which he did not often speak, especially, it may be supposed, in the presence of young persons: but when he did, it was with an air of settled and profound con-

[1] The choice between Virtue and Vice, in Xenophon's *Memorabilia*, II, i, 21–34.
[2] Disciples of Socrates.

viction. He would sometimes say, that if life were made what it might be, by good government and good education, it would be worth having: but he never spoke with anything like enthusiasm even of that possibility. He never varied in rating intellectual enjoyments above all others, even in value as pleasures, independently of their ulterior benefits. The pleasures of the benevolent affections he placed high in the scale; and used to say, that he had never known a happy old man, except those who were able to live over again in the pleasures of the young. For passionate emotions of all sorts, and for everything which has been said or written in exaltation of them, he professed the greatest contempt. He regarded them as a form of madness. "The intense" was with him a bye-word of scornful disapprobation. He regarded as an aberration of the moral standard of modern times, compared with that of the ancients, the great stress laid upon feeling. Feelings, as such, he considered to be no proper subjects of praise or blame. Right and wrong, good and bad, he regarded as qualities solely of conduct — of acts and omissions; there being no feeling which may not lead, and does not frequently lead, either to good or to bad actions: conscience itself, the very desire to act right, often leading people to act wrong. Consistently carrying out the doctrine, that the object of praise and blame should be the discouragement of wrong conduct and the encouragement of right, he refused to let his praise or blame be influenced by the motive of the agent. He blamed as severely what he thought a bad action, when the motive was a feeling of duty, as if the agents had been consciously evil doers. He would not have accepted as a plea in mitigation for inquisitors, that they sincerely believed burning heretics to be an obligation of conscience. But though he did not allow honesty of purpose to soften his disapprobation of actions, it had its full effect on his estimation of characters. No one prized conscientiousness and rectitude of intention more highly, or was more incapable of valuing any person in whom he did not feel assurance of it. But he disliked people quite as much for any other deficiency, provided he thought it equally likely to make them act ill. He disliked, for instance, a fanatic in any bad cause, as much or more than one who adopted the same cause from self-interest, because he thought him even more likely to be practically mischievous. And thus, his aversion to many intellectual errors, or what he regarded as such, partook, in a certain sense, of the character of a moral feeling. All this is merely saying that he, in a degree once common, but now very unusual, threw his feelings into his opinions; which truly it is difficult to understand how any one, who possesses much of both, can fail to do. None but those who do not care about opinions, will confound it with intolerance. Those who, having opinions which they hold to be immensely important, and their contraries to be prodigiously hurtful, have any deep regard for the general good, will necessarily dislike, as a class and in the abstract, those who think wrong what they think right, and right what they think wrong: though they need not therefore be, nor was my father, insensible to good qualities in an opponent, nor governed in their estimation of individuals by one general presumption, instead of by the whole of their character. I grant that an earnest person, being no more infallible than other men, is liable to dislike people on account of opinions which do not merit dislike; but if he neither himself does them any ill office, nor connives at its being done by others, he is not intolerant: and the forbearance, which flows from a conscientious sense of the importance to mankind of the equal freedom of all opinions, is the only tolerance which is commendable, or, to the highest moral order of minds, possible.

It will be admitted, that a man of the opinions, and the character, above described, was likely to leave a strong moral impression on any mind principally formed by him, and that his moral teaching was not likely to err on the side of laxity or indulgence. The element which was chiefly deficient in his moral relation to his children, was that of tenderness. I do not believe that this deficiency lay in his own nature. I believe him to have had much more feeling than he habitually shewed, and much greater capacities of feeling than were ever developed. He resembled most Englishmen in being ashamed of the signs of feeling, and, by the absence of demonstration, starving the feelings themselves. If we consider further that he was in the trying position of sole teacher, and add to this that his temper was constitutionally irritable, it is impossible not to feel true pity for a father who did, and strove to do, so much for his children, who would have so valued their affection, yet who must have been constantly feeling that fear of him was drying it up at its source. This was no longer the case, later in life and with his younger children. They loved him tenderly: and if I cannot say so much of myself, I was always loyally devoted to him. As regards my own education, I hesitate to pronounce whether I was more a loser or gainer by his severity.[3] It was not such as to prevent me

³ In place of this and the preceding three sentences the original MS reads: "In an atmosphere of tenderness and affection he would have been tender and affectionate; but his ill assorted marriage and his asperities of temper disabled him from making such an atmosphere. It was one of the most unfavourable of the moral agencies which acted on me in my boyhood, that mine was not an education of love but of fear" (*The Early Draft,* p. 66). Canceled passages in the MS enlarge on this and some other drawbacks: "I once heard him say, that there was always the greatest sympathy between him and his children until the time of lessons began but that the lessons always destroyed it. . . . This is true only of the elder children: with the younger he followed an entirely different system, to the great comfort of the later years of his life. But in respect to what I am here concerned with, the moral agencies which acted on myself, it must be mentioned as a most baneful one, that my father's children neither loved him, nor, with any warmth of affection, any one else. I do not mean that things were worse in this respect than they are in most English families; in which genuine affection is altogether exceptional; what is usually found being more or less of an attachment of mere habit, like that to inanimate objects, and a few conventional proprieties of phrase and demonstration. I believe there is less personal affection in England than in any other country of which I know anything, and I give my father's family not as peculiar in this respect but only as a too faithful exemplification of the ordinary fact. That rarity in England, a really warm hearted mother, would in the first place have made my father a totally different being, and in the second would have made the children grow up loving and being loved. But my mother with the very best intentions, only knew how to pass her life in drudging for them. Whatever she could do for them she did, and they liked her, because she was kind to them, but to make herself loved, looked up to, or even obeyed, required qualities which she unfortunately did not possess.

"I thus grew up in the absence of love and in the presence of fear: and many and indelible are the effects of this bringing-up, in the stunting of my moral growth. One of these, which it would have required a quick sensibility and impulsiveness of natural temperament to counteract, was habitual reserve. Without knowing or believing that I was reserved, I grew up with an instinct of closeness. I had no one to whom I desired to express everything which I felt; and the only person I was in communication with, to whom I looked up, I had too much fear of, to make the communication to him of any act or feeling ever a matter of frank impulse or spontaneous inclination. Instead of a character whose instinct and habit are openness, but who can command reserve when duty or prudence require it, my circumstances tended to form a character, close and reserved from habit and want of impulse, not from will, and therefore, while destitute of the frank communicativeness which wins and deserves sympathy, yet continually failing in retinence where it is suitable and desirable.

"Another evil I shared with many of the sons of energetic fathers. To have been, through childhood, under the constant rule of a strong will, certainly is not favourable to strength of will. I was so much accustomed to expect to be told what to do, either in the form of direct command or of rebuke for not doing it, that I acquired a habit of leaving my responsibility as a moral agent to rest on my father, my conscience never speaking to me except by his voice. The things I ought *not* to do were mostly provided for by his precepts, rigorously enforced whenever violated, but the things which I *ought* to do I hardly ever did of my own mere motion, but waited till he told me to do them; and if he forbore or forgot to tell me, they were gen-

from having a happy childhood. And I do not believe, that boys can be induced to apply themselves with vigour, and what is so much more difficult, perseverance, to dry and irksome studies, by the sole force of persuasion and soft words. Much must be done, and much must be learnt, by children, for which rigid discipline, and known liability to punishment, are indispensable as means. It is, no doubt, a very laudable effort, in modern teaching, to render as much as possible of what the young are required to learn, easy and interesting to them. But when this principle is pushed to the length of not requiring them to learn anything *but* what has been made easy and interesting, one of the chief objects of education is sacrificed. I rejoice in the decline of the old brutal and tyrannical system of teaching, which however did succeed in enforcing habits of application; but the new, as it seems to me, is training up a race of men who will be incapable of doing anything which is disagreeable to them. I do not, then, believe that fear, as an element in education, can be dispensed with; but I am sure that it ought not to be the main element; and when it predominates so much as to preclude love and confidence on the part of the child to those who should be the unreservedly trusted advisers of after years, and perhaps to seal up the fountains of frank and spontaneous communicativeness in the child's nature, it is an evil for which a large abatement must be made from the benefits, moral and intellectual, which may flow from any other part of the education.

During this first period of my life, the habitual frequenters of my father's house were limited to a very few persons, most of them little known to the world, but whom personal worth, and more or less of congeniality with at least his political opinions (not so frequently to be met with then as since) inclined him to cultivate; and his conversations with them I listened to with interest and instruction. My being an habitual inmate of my father's study made me acquainted with the dearest of his friends, David Ricardo, who by his benevolent countenance, and kindliness of manner, was very attractive to young persons, and who after I became a student of

---

erally left undone. I thus acquired a habit of backwardness, of waiting to follow the lead of others, an absence of moral spontaneity, an inactivity of the moral sense and even to a large extent, of the intellect, unless roused by the appeal of some one else, — for which a large abatement must be made from the benefits, either moral or intellectual, which flowed from any other part of my education" (*The Early Draft*, pp. 183–85). Much of this text was first marked for deletion by Mill's wife.

political economy, invited me to his house and to walk with him in order to converse on the subject. I was a more frequent visitor (from about 1817 or 1818) to Mr. Hume, who, born in the same part of Scotland as my father, and having been, I rather think, a younger schoolfellow or college companion of his, had on returning from India renewed their youthful acquaintance, and who coming like many others greatly under the influence of my father's intellect and energy of character, was induced partly by that influence to go into Parliament, and there adopt the line of conduct which has given him an honorable place in the history of his country. Of Mr. Bentham I saw much more, owing to the close intimacy which existed between him and my father. I do not know how soon after my father's first arrival in England they became acquainted. But my father was the earliest Englishman of any great mark, who thoroughly understood, and in the main adopted, Bentham's general views of ethics, government, and law: and this was a natural foundation for sympathy between them, and made them familiar companions in a period of Bentham's life during which he admitted much fewer visitors than was the case subsequently. At this time Mr. Bentham passed some part of every year at Barrow Green House, in a beautiful part of the Surrey hills, a few miles from Godstone, and there I each summer accompanied my father in a long visit. In 1813 Mr. Bentham, my father, and I made an excursion, which included Oxford, Bath and Bristol, Exeter, Plymouth, and Portsmouth. In this journey I saw many things which were instructive to me, and acquired my first taste for natural scenery, in the elementary form of fondness for a "view." In the succeeding winter we moved into a house very near Mr. Bentham's, which my father rented from him, in Queen Square, Westminster. From 1814 to 1817 Mr. Bentham lived during half of each year at Ford Abbey, in Somersetshire (or rather in a part of Devonshire surrounded by Somersetshire), which intervals I had the advantage of passing at that place. This sojourn was, I think, an important circumstance in my education. Nothing contributes more to nourish elevation of sentiments in a people, than the large and free character of their habitations. The middle-age architecture, the baronial hall, and the spacious and lofty rooms, of this fine old place, so unlike the mean and cramped externals of English middle class life, gave the sentiment of a larger and freer existence, and were to me a sort of poetic cultivation, aided also by the character of the grounds in which the Abbey stood; which were riant and secluded, umbrageous, and full of the sound of falling waters.[4]

I owed another of the fortunate circumstances in my education, a year's residence in France, to Mr. Bentham's brother, General Sir Samuel Bentham. I had seen Sir Samuel Bentham and his family at their house near Gosport in the course of the tour already mentioned (he being then Superintendant of the Dockyard at Portsmouth) and during a stay of a few days which they made at Ford Abbey shortly after the peace,[5] before going to live on the Continent. In 1820 they invited me for a six months visit to them in the South of France, which their kindness ultimately prolonged to nearly a twelvemonth. Sir Samuel Bentham, though of a character of mind different from that of his illustrious brother, was a man of very considerable attainments and general powers, with a decided genius for mechanical art. His wife, a daughter of the celebrated chemist Dr. Fordyce, was a woman of strong will and decided character, much general knowledge, and great practical good sense of the Edgeworth kind:[6] she was the ruling spirit of the household, as she deserved, and was well qualified, to be. Their family consisted of one son (the eminent botanist) and three

[4] The original MS contains a note at this point which Mill, following his wife's instructions, deleted: "The mode of life at Ford Abbey was the following. Mr. Bentham and my father studied and wrote in the same large room (a different room however in summer and in winter). My father commenced at about seven, summer and winter: and as Mr. Bentham did not make his appearance till some time after nine, I and the other children worked at our lessons in the same room during those two hours. The general hour of breakfast was nine, but Mr. Bentham always breakfasted at one o'clock among his books and papers, his breakfast being laid early in the morning on his study table. The party at the general breakfast consisted of my father and mother, Mr. Bentham's amanuensis for the time being, and the visitors, if, as not unfrequently happened, any were staying in the house. Before his one o'clock breakfast Mr. Bentham regularly went out for the same invariable walk, a circuit of about half an hour, in which my father almost always joined him. The interval between breakfast and this walk my father employed in hearing lessons, which when weather permitted, was always done in walking about the grounds. The hours from one to six my father passed in study and this was the time regularly allotted to us children for learning lessons. Six was the dinner hour, and the remainder of the evening Mr. Bentham passed in social enjoyment, of which he had a keen relish. I was never present on these evenings except a few times when Mr. Bentham good-naturedly sent for me to teach me to play at chess" (*The Early Draft,* pp. 68–69 n.).

[5] At the end of 1815.

[6] A reference to Maria Edgeworth's *Moral Tales for Young People* (1801).

daughters, the youngest about two years my senior. I am indebted to them for much and various instruction, and for an almost parental interest in my welfare. When I first joined them, in May 1820, they occupied the Château of Pompignan (still belonging to a descendant of Voltaire's enemy) on the heights overlooking the plain of the Garonne between Montauban and Toulouse. I accompanied them in an excursion to the Pyrenees, including a stay of some duration at Bagnères de Bigorre, a journey to Pau, Bayonne, and Bagnères de Luchon, and an ascent of the Pic du Midi de Bigorre. This first introduction to the highest order of mountain scenery made the deepest impression on me, and gave a colour to my tastes through life. In October we proceeded by the beautiful mountain route of Castres and St. Pons, from Toulouse to Montpellier, in which last neighbourhood Sir Samuel had just bought the estate of Restinclière, near the foot of the singular mountain of St. Loup. During this residence in France I acquired a familiar knowledge of the French language, and acquaintance with the ordinary French literature; I took lessons in various bodily exercises, in none of which however I made any proficiency; and at Montpellier I attended the excellent winter courses of lectures at the Faculté des Sciences, those of M. Anglada on chemistry, of M. Provençal on zoology, and of a very accomplished representative of the eighteenth century metaphysics, M. Gergonne, on logic, under the name of Philosophy of the Sciences. I also went through a course of the higher mathematics under the private tuition of M. Lenthéric, a professor at the Lycée of Montpellier. But the greatest, perhaps, of the many advantages which I owed to this episode in my education, was that of having breathed for a whole year the free and genial atmosphere of Continental life. This advantage was not the less real though I could not then estimate, nor even consciously feel it. Having so little experience of English life, and the few people I knew being mostly such as had public objects, of a large and personally disinterested kind, at heart, I was ignorant of the low moral tone of what, in England, is called society; the habit of, not indeed professing, but taking for granted in every mode of implication, that conduct is of course always directed towards low and petty objects; the absence of high feelings which manifests itself by sneering depreciation of all demonstrations of them, and by general abstinence (except among a few of the stricter religionists) from professing any high principles of action at all, except in those

preordained cases in which such profession is put on as part of
the costume and formalities of the occasion. I could not then
know or estimate the difference between this manner of existence,
and that of a people like the French, whose faults, if equally real,
are at all events different; among whom sentiments, which by comparison at least may be called elevated, are the current coin of
human intercourse, both in books and in private life; and though
often evaporating in profession, are yet kept alive in the nation at
large by constant exercise, and stimulated by sympathy, so as to
form a living and active part of the existence of great numbers of
persons, and to be recognized and understood by all. Neither could
I then appreciate the general culture of the understanding, which
results from the habitual exercise of the feelings, and is thus carried
down into the most uneducated classes of several countries on the
Continent, in a degree not equalled in England among the so called
educated, except where an unusual tenderness of conscience leads
to a habitual exercise of the intellect on questions of right and
wrong. I did not know the way in which, among the ordinary
English, the absence of interest in things of an unselfish kind, except occasionally in a special thing here and there, and the habit of
not speaking to others, nor much even to themselves, about the
things in which they do feel interest, causes both their feelings and
their intellectual faculties to remain undeveloped, or develope
themselves only in some single and very limited direction; reducing
them, considered as spiritual beings, to a kind of negative existence.
All these things I did not perceive till long afterwards; but I even
then felt, though without stating it clearly to myself, the contrast
between the frank sociability and amiability of French personal
intercourse, and the English mode of existence in which everybody
acts as if everybody else (with few, or no, exceptions) was either
an enemy or a bore. In France, it is true, the bad as well as the
good points both of individual and of national character come more
to the surface, and break out more fearlessly in ordinary intercourse, than in England: but the general habit of the people is to
shew, as well as to expect, friendly feeling in every one towards
every other, wherever there is not some positive cause for the
opposite. In England it is only of the best bred people, in the
upper or upper middle ranks, that anything like this can be said.

In my way through Paris, both going and returning, I passed
some time in the house of M. Say, the eminent political economist,

who was a friend and correspondent of my father, having become acquainted with him on a visit to England a year or two after the peace. He was a man of the later period of the French Revolution, a fine specimen of the best kind of French republican, one of those who had never bent the knee to Bonaparte though courted by him to do so; a truly upright, brave, and enlightened man. He lived a quiet and studious life, made happy by warm affections, public and private. He was acquainted with many of the chiefs of the Liberal party, and I saw various noteworthy persons while staying at his house; among whom I have pleasure in the recollection of having once seen Saint-Simon, not yet the founder either of a philosophy or a religion, and considered only as a clever *original*. The chief fruit which I carried away from the society I saw, was a strong and permanent interest in Continental Liberalism, of which I ever afterwards kept myself *au courant,* as much as of English politics: a thing not at all usual in those days with Englishmen, and which had a very salutary influence on my development, keeping me free from the error always prevalent in England, and from which even my father with all his superiority to prejudice was not exempt, of judging universal questions by a merely English standard. After passing a few weeks at Caen with an old friend of my father's, I returned to England in July 1821; and my education resumed its ordinary course.

CHAPTER III

LAST STAGE OF EDUCATION, AND FIRST
OF SELF-EDUCATION

FOR the first year or two after my visit to France, I continued my old studies, with the addition of some new ones. When I returned, my father was just finishing for the press his "Elements of Political Economy," and he made me perform an exercise on the manuscript, which Mr. Bentham practised on all his own writings — making what he called "marginal contents"; a short abstract of every paragraph, to enable the writer more easily to judge of, and improve, the order of the ideas, and the general character of the exposition. Soon after, my father put into my hands Condillac's Traité des Sensations, and the logical and metaphysical volumes of his Cours d'Etudes; the first (notwithstanding the superficial resemblance between Condillac's psychological system and my father's) quite as much for a warning as for an example. I am not sure whether it was in this winter or the next that I first read a history of the French Revolution. I learnt with astonishment, that the principles of democracy, then apparently in so insignificant and hopeless a minority everywhere in Europe, had borne all before them in France thirty years earlier, and had been the creed of the nation. As may be supposed from this, I had previously a very vague idea of that great commotion. I knew only that the French had thrown off the absolute monarchy of Louis XIV and XV, had put the king and queen to death, guillotined many persons, one of whom was Lavoisier, and had ultimately fallen under the despotism of Bonaparte. From this time, as was natural, the subject took an immense hold of my feelings. It allied itself with all my juvenile aspirations to the character of a democratic champion. What had happened so lately, seemed as if it might easily happen again; and the most transcendant glory I was capable of conceiving, was that of figuring, successful or unsuccessful, as a Girondist in an English Convention.

During the winter of 1821/2, Mr. John Austin, with whom at the time of my visit to France my father had but lately become acquainted, kindly allowed me to read Roman law with him. My father, notwithstanding his abhorrence of the chaos of barbarism

40

called English Law, had turned his thoughts towards the bar as on the whole less ineligible for me than any other profession: and these readings with Mr. Austin, who had made Bentham's best ideas his own, and added much to them from other sources and from his own mind, were not only a valuable introduction to legal studies, but an important portion of general education. With Mr. Austin I read Heineccius on the Institutes, his Roman Antiquities, and part of his exposition of the Pandects; to which was added a considerable portion of Blackstone. It was at the commencement of these studies that my father, as a needful accompaniment to them, put into my hands Bentham's principal speculations, as interpreted to the Continent, and indeed to all the world, by Dumont, in the Traité de Législation. The reading of this book was an epoch in my life; one of the turning points in my mental history.

My previous education had been, in a certain sense, already a course of Benthamism. The Benthamic standard of "the greatest happiness" was that which I had always been taught to apply; I was even familiar with an abstract discussion of it, forming an episode in an unpublished dialogue on Government, written by my father on the Platonic model. Yet in the first pages of Bentham it burst upon me with all the force of novelty. What thus impressed me was the chapter[1] in which Bentham passed judgment on the common modes of reasoning in morals and legislation, deduced from phrases like "law of nature," "right reason," "the moral sense," "natural rectitude," and the like, and characterized them as dogmatism in disguise imposing its sentiments upon others under cover of sounding expressions which convey no reason for the sentiment, but set up the sentiment as its own reason. It had not struck me before, that Bentham's principle put an end to all this. The feeling rushed upon me, that all previous moralists were superseded, and that here indeed was the commencement of a new era in thought. This impression was strengthened by the manner in which Bentham put into scientific form the application of the happiness principle to the morality of actions, by analyzing the various classes and orders of their consequences. But what struck me at that time most of all, was the Classification of Offences; which is much more clear,

[1] Chapter III of the work edited and translated into French by Dumont (1802). For the English version, see *An Introduction to the Principles of Morals and Legislation*, ch. II, the long footnote to sec. XIV (in Bentham's *Works*, ed. John Bowring [1838–43], I, 8–9).

compact, and imposing, in Dumont's *rédaction,* than in the original
work of Bentham from which it was taken. Logic, and the dialectics of Plato, which had formed so large a part of my previous
training, had given me a strong relish for accurate classification.
This taste had been strengthened and enlightened by the study of
botany, on the principles of what is called the Natural Method,
which I had taken up with great zeal, though only as an amusement,
during my stay in France; and when I found scientific classification
applied to the great and complex subject of Punishable Acts, under
the guidance of the ethical principle of Pleasurable and Painful
Consequences, followed out in the method of detail introduced into
these subjects by Bentham, I felt taken up to an eminence from
which I could survey a vast mental domain, and see stretching out
into the distance intellectual results beyond all computation. As I
proceeded farther, there seemed to be added to this intellectual
clearness, the most inspiring prospects of practical improvement in
human affairs. To Bentham's general views of the construction of
a body of law I was not altogether a stranger, having read with
attention that admirable compendium, my father's article "Jurisprudence":[2] but I had read it with little profit, and scarcely any
interest, no doubt from its extremely general and abstract character,
and also because it concerned the form more than the substance of
the *corpus juris,* the logic rather than the ethics of law. But Bentham's subject was Legislation, of which Jurisprudence is only the
formal part: and at every page he seemed to open a clearer and
broader conception of what human opinions and institutions ought
to be, how they might be made what they ought to be, and how far
removed from it they now are. When I laid down the last volume
of the Traité I had become a different being. The "principle of
utility" understood as Bentham understood it, and applied in the
manner in which he applied it through these three volumes, fell
exactly into its place as the keystone which held together the detached and fragmentary component parts of my knowledge and
beliefs. It gave unity to my conceptions of things. I now had
opinions; a creed, a doctrine, a philosophy; in one among the best
senses of the word, a religion; the inculcation and diffusion of
which could be made the principal outward purpose of a life. And
I had a grand conception laid before me of changes to be effected

[2] In the supplement to the *Encyclopaedia Britannica,* 1820.

in the condition of mankind through that doctrine. The Traité de Législation wound up with what was to me a most impressive picture of human life as it would be made by such opinions and such laws as were recommended in the treatise. The anticipations of practicable improvement were studiously moderate, deprecating and discountenancing as reveries of vague enthusiasm many things which will one day seem so natural to human beings, that injustice will probably be done to those who once thought them chimerical. But, in my state of mind, this appearance of superiority to illusion added to the effect which Bentham's doctrines produced on me, by heightening the impression of mental power. And the vista of improvement which he did open was sufficiently large and brilliant to light up my life, as well as to give a definite shape to my aspirations.

After this I read, from time to time, the most important of the other works of Bentham which had then seen the light, either as written by himself or as edited by Dumont. This was my private reading: while, under my father's direction, my studies were carried into the higher branches of analytic psychology. I now read Locke's Essay, and wrote out an account of it, consisting of a complete abstract of every chapter, with such remarks as occurred to me: which was read by, or (I think) to, my father, and discussed throughout. I performed the same process with Helvetius de l'Esprit, which I read of my own choice. This preparation of abstracts, subject to my father's censorship, was of great service to me, by compelling precision in conceiving and expressing psychological doctrines, whether accepted as truths or only regarded as the opinions of others. After Helvetius, my father made me study what he deemed the really master-production in the philosophy of mind, Hartley's Observations on Man. This book, though it did not, like the Traité de Législation, give a new colour to my existence, made a very similar impression on me in regard to its immediate subject. Hartley's explanation, incomplete as in many points it is, of the more complex mental phenomena by the law of association, commended itself to me at once as a real analysis, and made me feel by contrast the insufficiency of the merely verbal generalizations of Condillac, and even of the instructive gropings and feelings about for psychological explanations, of Locke. It was at this very time that my father commenced writing his Analysis of the Mind, which carried Hartley's mode of explaining the mental phenomena to so much greater length and depth. He could only command the con-

centration of thought necessary for this work, during the complete
leisure of his holiday of a month or six weeks annually; and he commenced it in the summer of 1822, in the first holiday he passed
at Dorking; in which neighbourhood, from that time to the end of
his life, with the exception of two years, he lived, as far as his
official duties permitted, for six months of every year. He worked
at the Analysis during several successive vacations, up to the year
1829 when it was published, and allowed me to read the manuscript, portion by portion, as it advanced. The other principal
English writers on mental philosophy I read as I felt inclined, particularly Berkeley, Hume's Essays, Reid, Dugald Stewart, and
Brown on Cause and Effect. Brown's Lectures I did not read until
two or three years later, nor at that time had my father himself
read them.

Among the works read in the course of this year, which contributed materially to my development, I ought to mention a book
(written on the foundation of some of Bentham's manuscripts and
published under the pseudonyme of Philip Beauchamp)[3] entitled
"Analysis of the Influence of Natural Religion on the Temporal
Happiness of Mankind." This was an examination not of the truth,
but of the usefulness of religious belief, in the most general sense,
apart from the peculiarities of any special Revelation; which, of all
the parts of the discussion concerning religion, is the most important in this age, in which real belief in any religious doctrine is
feeble and precarious, but the opinion of its necessity for moral
and social purposes almost universal; and when those who reject
revelation, very generally take refuge in an optimistic Deism, a worship of the order of Nature and the supposed course of Providence,
at least as full of contradictions, and perverting to the moral sentiments, as any of the forms of Christianity, if only it is as completely
realized. Yet, very little, with any claim to a philosophical character, has been written by sceptics against the usefulness of this form
of belief. The volume bearing the name of Philip Beauchamp had
this for its special object. Having been shewn to my father in
manuscript, it was put into my hands by him, and I made a marginal analysis of it as I had done of the Elements of Political Economy. Next to the Traité de Législation, it was one of the books
which by the searching character of its analysis produced the great-

[3] The author was George Grote (on whom see the second paragraph
below).

est effect upon me. On reading it lately after an interval of many years, I find it to have some of the defects as well as the merits of the Benthamic modes of thought, and to contain, as I now think, many weak arguments, but with a great overbalance of sound ones, and much good material for a more completely philosophic and conclusive treatment of the subject.

I have now, I believe, mentioned all the books which had any considerable effect on my early mental developement. From this point I began to carry on my intellectual cultivation by writing still more than by reading. In the summer of 1822 I wrote my first argumentative essay. I remember very little about it, except that it was an attack on what I regarded as the aristocratic prejudice, that the rich were, or were likely to be, superior in moral qualities to the poor. My performance was entirely argumentative, without any of the declamation which the subject would admit ot, and might be expected to suggest to a young writer. In that department however I was, and remained, very inapt. Dry argument was the only thing I could manage, or willingly attempted; though passively I was very susceptible to the effect of all composition, whether in the form of poetry or oratory, which appealed to the feelings on any basis of reason. My father, who knew nothing of this essay until it was finished, was well satisfied, and as I learnt from others, even pleased with it; but, perhaps from a desire to promote the exercise of other mental faculties than the purely logical, he advised me to make my next exercise in composition one of the oratorical kind: on which suggestion, availing myself of my familiarity with Greek history and ideas and with the Athenian orators, I wrote two speeches, one an accusation, the other a defence of Pericles on a supposed impeachment for not marching out to fight the Lacedæmonians on their invasion of Attica. After this I continued to write papers on subjects often very much beyond my capacity, but with great benefit both from the exercise itself, and from the discussions which it led to with my father.

I had now also begun to converse, on general subjects, with the instructed men with whom I came in contact: and the opportunities of such contact naturally became more numerous. The two friends of my father from whom I derived most, and with whom I most associated, were Mr. Grote and Mr. John Austin. The acquaintance of both with my father was recent, but had ripened rapidly into intimacy. Mr. Grote was introduced to my father by Mr. Ricardo,

I think in 1819 (being then about twenty-five years old), and
sought assiduously his society and conversation. Already a highly
instructed man, he was yet, by the side of my father, a tyro on the
great subjects of human opinion; but he rapidly seized on my
father's best ideas; and in the department of political opinion he
made himself known as early as 1820, by a pamphlet in defence of
Radical Reform, in reply to a celebrated article by Sir James
Mackintosh, then lately published in the Edinburgh Review. Mr.
Grote's father, the banker, was, I believe, a thorough Tory, and his
mother intensely Evangelical; so that for his liberal opinions he was
in no way indebted to home influences. But, unlike most persons
who have the prospect of being rich by inheritance, he had, though
actively engaged in the business of banking, devoted a great portion
of time to philosophic studies; and his intimacy with my father
did much to decide the character of the next stage in his mental
progress. Him I often visited, and my conversations with him on
political, moral, and philosophical subjects gave me, in addition to
much valuable instruction, all the pleasure and benefit of sympathetic communion with a man of the high intellectual and moral
eminence which his life and writings have since manifested to the
world.

Mr. Austin, who was four or five years older than Mr. Grote,
was the eldest son of a retired miller in Suffolk, who had made
money by contracts during the war, and who must have been a man
of remarkable qualities, as I infer from the fact that all his sons
were of more than common ability and all eminently gentlemen.
The one with whom we are now concerned, and whose writings on
jurisprudence have made him celebrated, was for some time in the
army, and served in Sicily under Lord William Bentinck. After
the peace he sold his commission and studied for the bar, to which
he had been called for some time before my father knew him. He
was not, like Mr. Grote, to any extent a pupil of my father, but he
had attained, by reading and thought, a considerable number of
the same opinions, modified by his own very decided individuality
of character. He was a man of great intellectual powers which in
conversation appeared at their very best; from the vigour and rich-
ness of expression with which, under the excitement of discussion,
he was accustomed to maintain some view or other of most general
subjects; and from an appearance of not only strong, but deliberate
and collected will; mixed with a certain bitterness, partly derived
from temperament, and partly from the general cast of his feelings

and reflexions. The dissatisfaction with life and the world, felt more or less in the present state of society and intellect by every discerning and highly conscientious mind, gave in his case a rather melancholy tinge to the character, very natural to those whose passive moral susceptibilities are more than proportioned to their active energies. For it must be said, that the strength of will, of which his manner seemed to give such strong assurance, expended itself principally in manner. With great zeal for human improvement, a strong sense of duty, and capacities and acquirements the extent of which is proved by the writings he has left, he hardly ever completed any intellectual task of magnitude. He had so high a standard of what ought to be done, so exaggerated a sense of deficiencies in his own performances, and was so unable to content himself with the amount of elaboration sufficient for the occasion and the purpose, that he not only spoiled much of his work for ordinary use by overlabouring it, but spent so much time and exertion in superfluous study and thought, that when his task ought to have been completed, he had generally worked himself into an illness, without having half finished what he undertook. From this mental infirmity (of which he is not the sole example among the accomplished and able men whom I have known), combined with liability to frequent attacks of disabling though not dangerous ill health, he accomplished, through life, little in comparison with what he seemed capable of; but what he did produce is held in the very highest estimation by the most competent judges; and, like Coleridge, he might plead as a set-off that he had been to many persons, through his conversation, a source not only of much instruction but of great elevation of character. On me his influence was most salutary. It was moral in the best sense. He took a sincere and kind interest in me, far beyond what could have been expected towards a mere youth from a man of his age, standing, and what seemed austerity of character. There was in his conversation and demeanour a tone of highmindedness which did not shew itself so much, if the quality existed as much, in any of the other persons with whom at that time I associated. My intercourse with him was the more beneficial, owing to his being of a different mental type from all other intellectual men whom I frequented, and he from the first set himself decidedly against the prejudices and narrownesses which are almost sure to be found in a young man formed by a particular mode of thought or a particular social circle.

His younger brother, Charles Austin, of whom at this time and for the next year or two I saw much, had also a great effect on me, though of a very different description. He was but a few years older than myself, and had then just left the University, where he had shone with great éclat as a man of intellect and a brilliant orator and converser. The effect he produced on his Cambridge cotemporaries deserves to be accounted an historical event; for to it may in part be traced the tendency towards Liberalism in general, and the Benthamic and politico-economic form of it in particular, which shewed itself in a portion of the more active-minded young men of the higher classes from this time to 1830. The Union Debating Society, at that time at the height of its reputation, was an arena where what were then thought extreme opinions, in politics and philosophy, were weekly asserted, face to face with their opposites, before audiences consisting of the élite of the Cambridge youth: and though many persons afterwards of more or less note (of whom Lord Macaulay is the most celebrated) gained their first oratorical laurels in those debates, the really influential mind among these intellectual gladiators was Charles Austin. He continued, after leaving the University, to be, by his conversation and personal ascendancy, a leader among the same class of young men who had been his associates there; and he attached me among others to his car. Through him I became acquainted with Macaulay, Hyde and Charles Villiers, Strutt (now Lord Belper), Romilly (now Lord Romilly and Master of the Rolls), and various others who subsequently figured in literature or politics, and among whom I heard discussions on many topics, as yet to a certain degree new to me. The influence of Charles Austin over me differed from that of the persons I have hitherto mentioned, in being not the influence of a man over a boy, but that of an elder cotemporary. It was through him that I first felt myself, not a pupil under teachers, but a man among men. He was the first person of intellect whom I met on a ground of equality, though as yet much his inferior on that common ground. He was a man who never failed to impress greatly those with whom he came in contact, even when their opinions were the very reverse of his. The impression he gave was that of boundless strength, together with talents which, combined with such apparent force of will and character, seemed capable of dominating the world. Those who knew him, whether friendly to him or not, always anticipated that he would play a conspicuous part in public life. It is seldom that men produce so great an immediate effect by speech, unless they, in some degree, lay themselves out for it; and he did this in no ordinary degree. He loved to strike, and even to startle. He knew that decision is the greatest element of effect, and he uttered his opinions with all the decision he could throw into them, never so well pleased as when he astonished any one by their audacity. Very unlike his brother, who made war against the narrower interpretations and applications of the principles they both professed, he on the contrary presented the Benthamic doctrines in the most startling form of which they were susceptible, exaggerating every thing in them which tended to consequences offensive to any one's preconceived feelings. All which, he defended with such verve and vivacity, and carried off by a manner so agreeable as well as forcible, that he always either came off victor, or divided the honours of the field. It is my belief that much of the notion popularly entertained of the tenets and sentiments of what are called Benthamites or Utilitarians, had its origin in paradoxes thrown out by Charles Austin. It must be said, however, that his example was followed, *haud passibus æquis,*[4] by younger proselytes, and that to *outrer*[5] whatever was by anybody considered offensive in the doctrines and maxims of Benthamism, became at one time the badge of a small coterie of youths. All of these who had anything in them, myself among others, quickly outgrew this boyish vanity; and those who had not, became tired of differing from other people, and gave up both the good and the bad part of the heterodox opinions they had for some time professed.

It was in the winter of 1822/23 that I formed the plan of a little society, to be composed of young men agreeing in fundamental principles — acknowledging Utility as their standard in ethics and politics, and a certain number of the principal corollaries drawn from it in the philosophy I had accepted — and meeting once a fortnight to read essays and discuss questions conformably to the premises thus agreed on. The fact would hardly be worth mentioning, but for the circumstance, that the name I gave to the society I had planned was the Utilitarian Society. It was the first time that any one had taken the title of Utilitarian; and the term made its way into the language from this humble source. I did not invent the word, but found it in one of Galt's novels, the "Annals of the Parish," in which the Scotch clergyman, of whom the book is a

---

[4] With steps that by no means matched his (*Aeneid,* II, 724).
[5] Exaggerate.

supposed autobiography, is represented as warning his parishioners not to leave the Gospel and become utilitarians. With a boy's fondness for a name and a banner I seized on the word, and for some years called myself and others by it as a sectarian appellation; and it came to be occasionally used by some others holding the opinions which it was intended to designate. As those opinions attracted more notice, the term was repeated by strangers and opponents, and got into rather common use just about the time when those who had originally assumed it, laid down that along with other sectarian characteristics. The Society so called consisted at first of no more than three members, one of whom, being Mr. Bentham's amanuensis, obtained for us permission to hold our meetings in his house. The number never, I think, reached ten, and the society was broken up in 1826. It had thus an existence of about three years and a half. The chief effect of it as regards myself, over and above the benefit of practice in oral discussion, was that of bringing me in contact with several young men at that time less advanced than myself, among whom, as they professed the same opinions, I was for some time a sort of leader, and had considerable influence on their mental progress. Any young man of education who fell in my way, and whose opinions were not incompatible with those of the Society, I endeavoured to press into its service; and some others I probably should never have known, had they not joined it. Those of the members who became my intimate companions — no one of whom was in any sense of the word a disciple, but all of them independent thinkers on their own basis — were William Eyton Tooke, son of the eminent political economist, a young man of singular worth both moral and intellectual, lost to the world by an early death; his friend William Ellis, an original thinker in the field of political economy, now honorably known by his apostolic exertions for the improvement of education; George Graham, afterwards an official assignee of the Bankruptcy Court, a thinker of originality and power on almost all abstract subjects; and (from the time when he came first to England to study for the bar in 1824 or 1825) a man who has made considerably more noise in the world than any of these, John Arthur Roebuck.

In May 1823, my professional occupation and status for the next thirty-five years of my life, were decided by my father's obtaining for me an appointment from the East India Company, in the office of the Examiner of India Correspondence, immediately under himself. I was appointed in the usual manner, at the bottom of the list of clerks, to rise, at least in the first instance, by seniority; but with the understanding, that I should be employed from the beginning in preparing drafts of despatches, and be thus trained up as a successor to those who then filled the higher departments of the office. My drafts of course required, for some time, much revision from my immediate superiors, but I soon became well acquainted with the business, and by my father's instructions and the general growth of my own powers, I was in a few years qualified to be, and practically was, the chief conductor of the correspondence with India in one of the leading departments, that of the Native States. This continued to be my official duty until I was appointed Examiner, only two years before the time when the abolition of the East India Company as a political body determined my retirement. I do not know any one of the occupations by which a subsistence can now be gained, more suitable than such as this to any one who, not being in independent circumstances, desires to devote a part of the twenty-four hours to private intellectual pursuits. Writing for the press, cannot be recommended as a permanent resource to any one qualified to accomplish anything in the higher departments of literature or thought: not only on account of the uncertainty of this means of livelihood, especially if the writer has a conscience, and will not consent to serve any opinions except his own; but also because the writings by which one can live, are not the writings which themselves live, and are never those in which the writer does his best. Books destined to form future thinkers take too much time to write, and when written come in general too slowly into notice and repute, to be relied on for subsistence. Those who have to support themselves by their pen must depend on literary drudgery, or at best on writings addressed to the multitude; and can employ in the pursuits of their own choice only such time as they can spare from those of necessity; which is generally less than the leisure allowed by office occupations, while the effect on the mind is far more enervating and fatiguing. For my own part, I have, through life, found office duties an actual rest from the other mental occupations which I have carried on simultaneously with them. They were sufficiently intellectual not to be a distasteful drudgery, without being such as to cause any strain upon the mental powers of a person used to abstract thought, or to the labour of careful literary composition. The drawbacks, for every

mode of life has its drawbacks, were not, however, unfelt by me.
I cared little for the loss of the chances of riches and honours held
out by some of the professions, particularly the bar, which had
been, as I have already said, the profession thought of for me. But
I was not indifferent to exclusion from Parliament, and public life:
and I felt very sensibly the more immediate unpleasantness of con-
finement to London; the holiday allowed by India-house practice
not exceeding a month in the year, while my taste was strong for a
country life, and my sojourn in France had left behind it an ardent
desire of travelling. But though these tastes could not be freely indulged, they were at no time entirely sacrificed. I passed most Sun-
days, throughout the year, in the country, taking long rural walks
on that day even when residing in London. The month's holiday
was, for a few years, passed at my father's house in the country:
afterwards a part or the whole was spent in tours, chiefly pedes-
trian, with some one or more of the young men who were my
chosen companions; and at a later period, in longer journeys or
excursions, alone or with other friends. France, Belgium, and
Rhenish Germany were within easy reach of the annual holiday:
and two longer absences, one of three, the other of six months,
under medical advice, added Switzerland, the Tyrol, and Italy to
my list. Fortunately, also, both these journeys occurred rather
early, so as to give the benefit and charm of the remembrance to a
large portion of life.

I am disposed to agree with what has been surmised by others,
that the opportunity which my official position gave me of learning
by personal observation the necessary conditions of the practical
conduct of public affairs, has been of considerable value to me as a
theoretical reformer of the opinions and institutions of my time.
Not, indeed, that public business transacted on paper, to take effect
on the other side of the globe, was of itself calculated to give much
practical knowledge of life. But the occupation accustomed me to
see and hear the difficulties of every course, and the means of ob-
viating them, stated and discussed deliberately, with a view to
execution; it gave me opportunities of perceiving when public
measures, and other political facts, did not produce the effects
which had been expected of them, and from what causes; above all
it was valuable to me by making me, in this portion of my activity,
merely one wheel in a machine, the whole of which had to work
together. As a speculative writer, I should have had no one to con-

sult but myself, and should have encountered in my speculations none of the obstacles which would have started up whenever they came to be applied to practice. But as a Secretary conducting political correspondence, I could not issue an order or express an opinion, without satisfying various persons very unlike myself, that the thing was fit to be done. I was thus in a good position for finding out by practice the mode of putting a thought which gives it easiest admittance into minds not prepared for it by habit; while I became practically conversant with the difficulties of moving bodies of men, the necessities of compromise, the art of sacrificing the non-essential to preserve the essential. I learnt how to obtain the best I could, when I could not obtain everything; instead of being indignant or dispirited because I could not have entirely my own way, to be pleased and encouraged when I could have the smallest part of it; and when even that could not be, to bear with complete equanimity the being overruled altogether. I have found, through life, these acquisitions to be of the greatest possible importance for personal happiness, and they are also a very necessary condition for enabling any one, either as theorist or as practical man, to effect the greatest amount of good compatible with his opportunities.

CHAPTER IV

YOUTHFUL PROPAGANDISM. THE
WESTMINSTER REVIEW

THE occupation of so much of my time by office work did not relax my attention to my own pursuits, which were never carried on more vigorously. It was about this time that I began to write in newspapers. The first writings of mine which got into print were two letters published towards the end of 1822, in the Traveller evening newspaper. The Traveller (which afterwards grew into the "Globe and Traveller" by the purchase and incorporation of the Globe) was then the property of the well known political economist Colonel Torrens. Under the editorship of an able man, Mr. Walter Coulson (who after being an amanuensis of Mr. Bentham, became a reporter, then an editor, next a barrister and conveyancer, and died Counsel to the Home Office), it had become one of the most important newspaper organs of liberal politics. Col. Torrens himself wrote much of the political economy of his paper; and had at this time made an attack upon some opinion of Ricardo and my father, to which at my father's instigation I attempted an answer, and Coulson out of consideration for my father and good will to me, inserted it. There was a reply by Torrens, to which I again rejoined. I soon after attempted something considerably more ambitious. The prosecutions of Richard Carlile and his wife and sister for publications hostile to Christianity, were then exciting much attention, and nowhere more than among the people I frequented. Freedom of discussion even in politics, much more in religion, was at that time far from being, even in theory, the conceded point which it at least seems to be now; and the holders of obnoxious opinions had to be always ready to argue and reargue for the liberty of expressing them. I wrote a series of five letters, under the signature of Wickliffe,[1] going over the whole length and breadth of the question of free publication of all opinions on religion, and offered them to the Morning Chronicle. Three of them were published in January and February 1823; the other two, containing things too outspoken for that journal, never appeared at all. But a paper which

---

[1] After the great fourteenth-century religious reformer, John Wycliffe.

I wrote soon after on the same subject, *à propos* of a debate in the House of Commons, was inserted as a leading article; and during the whole of this year, 1823, a considerable number of my contributions were printed in the Chronicle and Traveller: sometimes notices of books, but oftener letters, commenting on some nonsense talked in Parliament, or some defect of the law, or misdoings of the magistracy or the courts of justice. In this last department the Chronicle was now rendering signal service. After the death of Mr. Perry, the editorship and management of the paper had devolved on Mr. John Black, long a reporter on its establishment; a man of most extensive reading and information, great honesty and simplicity of mind; a particular friend of my father, imbued with many of his and Bentham's ideas, which he reproduced in his articles, among other valuable thoughts, with great facility and skill. From this time the Chronicle ceased to be the merely Whig organ it was before, and during the next ten years became to a considerable extent a vehicle of the opinions of the Utilitarian radicals. This was mainly by what Black himself wrote, with some assistance from Fonblanque, who first shewed his eminent qualities as a writer by articles and *jeux d'esprit* in the Chronicle. The defects of the law, and of the administration of justice, were the subject on which that paper rendered most service to improvement. Up to that time hardly a word had been said, except by Bentham and my father, against that most peccant part of English institutions and of their administration. It was the almost universal creed of Englishmen, that the law of England, the judicature of England, the unpaid magistracy of England, were models of excellence. I do not go beyond the mark in saying, that after Bentham, who supplied the principal materials, the greatest share of the merit of breaking down this wretched superstition belongs to Black, as editor of the Morning Chronicle. He kept up an incessant fire against it, exposing the absurdities and vices of the law and the courts of justice, paid and unpaid, until he forced some sense of them into people's minds. On many other questions he became the organ of opinions much in advance of any which had ever before found regular advocacy in the newspaper press. Black was a frequent visitor of my father, and Mr. Grote used to say that he always knew by the Monday morning's article, whether Black had been with my father on the Sunday. Black was one of the most influential of the many channels through which my father's conversation and personal influence made his opinions tell on the world; cooperating with the effect of his writings in making him a power in the country, such as it has rarely been the lot of an individual in a private station to be, through the mere force of intellect and character: and a power which was often acting the most efficiently where it was least seen and suspected. I have already noticed how much of what was done by Ricardo, Hume, and Grote, was the result, in part, of his prompting and persuasion. He was the good genius by the side of Brougham in most of what he did for the public, either on education, law reform, or any other subject. And his influence flowed in minor streams too numerous to be specified. This influence was now about to receive a great extension, by the foundation of the Westminster Review.

Contrary to what may have been supposed, my father was in no degree a party to setting up the Westminster Review. The need of a Radical organ to make head against the Edinburgh and Quarterly (then in the period of their greatest reputation and influence) had been a topic of conversation between him and Mr. Bentham many years earlier, and it had been a part of their *château en Espagne*[2] that my father should be the editor, but the idea had never assumed any practical shape. In 1823, however, Mr. Bentham determined to establish the review at his own cost, and offered the editorship to my father, who declined it as incompatible with his India House appointment. It was then entrusted to Mr. (now Sir John) Bowring, at that time a merchant in the City. Mr. Bowring had been for two or three years previous an assiduous frequenter of Mr. Bentham, to whom he was recommended by many personal good qualities, by an ardent admiration for Bentham, a zealous adoption of many though not all of his opinions, and, not least, by an extensive acquaintanceship and correspondence with Liberals of all countries, which seemed to qualify him for being a powerful agent in spreading Bentham's fame and doctrines through all quarters of the world. My father had seen little of Bowring, but knew enough of him to have formed a strong opinion, that he was a man of an entirely different type from what my father considered suitable for conducting a political and philosophical review: and he augured so ill of the enterprise that he regretted it altogether, feeling persuaded not only that Mr. Bentham would lose his money, but

---

[2] I.e., castle in the air.

that discredit would probably be brought upon radical principles. He could not however desert Mr. Bentham, and he consented to write an article for the first number. As it had been a favorite portion of the scheme formerly talked of, that part of the work should be devoted to reviewing the other Reviews, this article of my father's was to be a general criticism of the Edinburgh Review from its commencement. Before writing it he made me read through all the volumes of the Review, or as much of each as seemed of any importance (which was not so arduous a task in 1823 as it would be now), and make notes for him of the articles which I thought he would wish to examine, either on account of their good or their bad qualities. This paper of my father's was the chief cause of the sensation which the Westminster Review produced at its first appearance, and is, both in conception and in execution, one of the most striking of all his writings. He began by an analysis of the tendencies of periodical literature in general; pointing out, that it cannot, like books, wait for success, but must succeed immediately, or not at all, and is hence almost certain to profess and inculcate the opinions already held by the public to which it addresses itself, instead of attempting to rectify or improve those opinions. He next, to characterize the position of the Edinburgh Review as a political organ, entered into a complete analysis, from the Radical point of view, of the British Constitution. He held up to notice its thoroughly aristocratic character: the nomination of a majority of the House of Commons by a few hundred families; the entire identification of the more independent portion, the county members, with the great landholders; the different classes whom this narrow oligarchy was induced, for convenience, to admit to a share of power; and finally, what he called its two props, the Church, and the legal profession. He pointed out the natural tendency of an aristocratic body of this composition, to group itself into two parties, one of them in possession of the executive, the other endeavouring to supplant the former and become the predominant section by the aid of public opinion, without any essential sacrifice of the aristocratical predominance. He described the course likely to be pursued, and the political ground occupied, by an aristocratic party in opposition, coquetting with popular principles for the sake of popular support. He shewed how this idea was realized in the conduct of the Whig party, and of the Edinburgh Review as its chief literary organ. He described, as their main characteristic, what he termed "seesaw"; writing alternately on both sides of every question which touched the power or interest of the governing classes; sometimes in different articles, sometimes in different parts of the same article: and illustrated his position by copious specimens. So formidable an attack on the Whig party and policy had never before been made; nor had so great a blow been ever struck, in this country, for radicalism: nor was there, I believe, any living person capable of writing that article, except my father.[3]

In the meantime the nascent review had formed a junction with another project, of a purely literary periodical, to be edited by Mr. Henry Southern, afterwards a diplomatist, then a literary man by profession. The two editors agreed to unite their corps, and divide the editorship, Bowring taking the political, Southern the literary department. Southern's review was to have been published by Longman, and that firm, though part proprietors of the Edinburgh, were willing to be the publishers of the new journal. But when all the arrangements had been made, and the prospectuses sent out, the Longmans saw my father's attack on the Edinburgh, and drew back. My father was now appealed to for his interest with his own publisher, Baldwin, which was exerted with a successful result. And so, in April 1824, amidst anything but hope on my father's part, and that of most of those who afterwards aided in carrying on the review, the first number made its appearance.

That number was an agreeable surprise to most of us. The average of the articles was of much better quality than had been expected. The literary and artistic department had rested chiefly on Mr. Bingham, a barrister (subsequently a Police Magistrate) who had been for some years a frequenter of Bentham, was a friend of both the Austins, and had adopted with great ardour Mr. Bentham's philosophical opinions. Partly from accident, there were in the first number as many as five articles by Bingham; and we were extremely pleased with them. I well remember the mixed feeling I myself had about the Review; the joy at finding, what we did not at all expect, that it was sufficiently good to be capable of being made a creditable organ of those who held the opinions it professed; and extreme vexation, since it was so good on the whole, at what

---

[3] The continuation of this article in the second number of the review was written by me under my father's eye, and (except as practice in composition, in which respect it was, to me, more useful than anything else I ever wrote) was of little or no value (Mill's note).

we thought the blemishes of it. When, however, in addition to our generally favourable opinion of it, we learned that it had an extraordinarily large sale for a first number, and found that the appearance of a Radical review, with pretensions equal to those of the established organs of parties, had excited much attention, there could be no room for hesitation, and we all became eager in doing everything we could to strengthen and improve it.

My father continued to write occasional articles. The Quarterly Review received its exposure, as a sequel to that of the Edinburgh. Of his other contributions, the most important were an attack on Southey's Book of the Church, in the fifth number, and a political article in the twelfth. Mr. Austin only contributed one paper, but one of great merit, an argument against primogeniture, in reply to an article then lately published in the Edinburgh Review by McCulloch. Grote also was a contributor only once; all the time he could spare being already taken up with his History of Greece. The article he wrote was on his own subject, and was a very complete exposure and castigation of Mitford. Bingham and Charles Austin continued to write for some time; Fonblanque was a frequent contributor from the third number. Of my particular associates, Ellis was a regular writer up to the ninth number; and about the time when he left off, others of the set began; Eyton Tooke, Graham, and Roebuck. I was myself the most frequent writer of all, having contributed, from the second number to the eighteenth, thirteen articles; reviews of books on history and political economy, or discussions on special political topics, as corn laws, game laws, law of libel. Occasional articles of merit came in from other acquaintances of my father's, and in time, of mine; and some of Mr. Bowring's writers turned out well. On the whole, however, the conduct of the Review was never satisfactory to any of the persons strongly interested in its principles, with whom I came in contact. Hardly ever did a number come out without containing several things extremely offensive to us, either in point of opinion, of taste, or by mere want of ability. The unfavorable judgments passed by my father, Grote, the two Austins, and others, were reechoed with exaggeration by us younger people; and as our youthful zeal rendered us by no means backward in making complaints, we led the two editors a sad life. From my knowledge of what I then was, I have no doubt that we were at least as often wrong as right; and I am very certain that if the Review had been carried on according to our notions (I mean those of the juniors) it would have been no better, perhaps not even so good as it was. But it is worth noting as a fact in the history of Benthamism, that the periodical organ, by which it was best known, was from the first extremely unsatisfactory to those, whose opinions on all subjects it was supposed specially to represent.

Meanwhile, however, the Review made considerable noise in the world, and gave a recognized *status,* in the arena of opinion and discussion, to the Benthamic type of radicalism, out of all proportion to the number of its adherents, and to the personal merits and abilities, at that time, of most of those who could be reckoned among them. It was a time, as is known, of rapidly rising Liberalism. When the fears and animosities accompanying the war with France had been brought to an end, and people had once more a place in their thoughts for home politics, the tide began to set towards reform. The renewed oppression of the Continent by the old reigning families, the countenance apparently given by the English Government to the conspiracy against liberty called the Holy Alliance, and the enormous weight of the national debt and taxation occasioned by so long and costly a war, rendered the government and parliament very unpopular. Radicalism, under the leadership of the Burdetts and Cobbetts, had assumed a character and importance which seriously alarmed the Administration: and their alarm had scarcely been temporarily assuaged by the celebrated Six Acts, when the trial of Queen Caroline roused a still wider and deeper feeling of hatred.[4] Though the outward signs of this hatred passed away with its exciting cause, there arose on all sides a spirit which had never shewn itself before, of opposition to abuses in detail. Mr. Hume's persevering scrutiny of the public expenditure, forcing the House of Commons to a division on every objectionable item in the estimates, had begun to tell with great force on public opinion, and had extorted many minor retrenchments from an unwilling Administration. Political economy had asserted itself with great vigour in public affairs, by the Petition of the Merchants of London for Free Trade, drawn up in 1820 by

[4] The "Six Acts," passed after the Peterloo Massacre in 1819, were measures for the prevention and punishment of sedition. Queen Caroline's "trial" (a scandalous affair in the summer of 1820) was a part of the parliamentary divorce proceedings brought against her by George IV. Popular feeling was entirely on her side.

Mr. Tooke and presented by Mr. Alexander Baring; and by the noble exertions of Ricardo during the few years of his parliamentary life. His writings, following up the impulse given by the Bullion controversy, and followed up in their turn by the expositions and comments of my father and McCulloch (whose writings in the Edinburgh Review during those years were most valuable), had drawn general attention to the subject, making at least partial converts in the Cabinet itself; and Huskisson, supported by Canning, had commenced that gradual demolition of the protective system, which one of their colleagues virtually completed in 1846, though the last vestiges were only swept away by Mr. Gladstone in 1860. Mr. Peel, then Home Secretary, was entering cautiously into the untrodden and peculiarly Benthamic path of Law Reform. At this period, when Liberalism seemed to be becoming the tone of the time, when improvement of institutions was preached from the highest places, and a complete change of the constitution of Parliament was loudly demanded in the lowest, it is not strange that attention should have been roused by the regular appearance in controversy of what seemed a new school of writers, claiming to be the legislators and theorists of this new tendency. The air of strong conviction with which they wrote, when scarcely any one else seemed to have an equally strong faith in as definite a creed; the boldness with which they tilted against the very front of both the existing political parties; their uncompromising profession of opposition to many of the generally received opinions, and the suspicion they lay under of holding others still more heterodox than they professed; the talent and verve of at least my father's articles, and the appearance of a corps behind him sufficient to carry on a review; and finally, the fact that the review was bought and read, made the so called Bentham school in philosophy and politics fill a greater place in the public mind than it had held before, or has ever again held since other equally earnest schools of thought have arisen in England. As I was in the head quarters of it, knew of what it was composed, and as one of the most active of its very small number, might say without undue assumption, *quorum pars magna fui*,[5] it belongs to me more than to most others to give some account of it.

This supposed school, then, had no other existence than what

[5] I was an important element in it (*Aeneid*, II, 6).

was constituted by the fact, that my father's writings and conversation drew round him a certain number of young men who had already imbibed, or who imbibed from him, a greater or smaller portion of his very decided political and philosophical opinions. The notion that Bentham was surrounded by a band of disciples who received their opinions from his lips, is a fable to which my father did justice in his "Fragment on Mackintosh," and which, to all who knew Mr. Bentham's habits of life and manner of conversation, is simply ridiculous. The influence which Bentham exercised was by his writings. Through them he has produced, and is producing, effects on the condition of mankind, wider and deeper, no doubt, than any which can be attributed to my father. He is a much greater name in history. But my father exercised a far greater personal ascendancy. He *was* sought for the vigour and instructiveness of his conversation, and did use it largely as an instrument for the diffusion of his opinions. I have never known any man who could do such ample justice to his best thoughts in colloquial discussion. His perfect command over his great mental resources, the terseness and expressiveness of his language and the moral earnestness as well as intellectual force of his delivery, made him one of the most striking of all argumentative conversers: and he was full of anecdote, a hearty laugher, and when with people whom he liked, a most lively and amusing companion. It was not solely, or even chiefly, in diffusing his merely intellectual convictions, that his power shewed itself: it was still more through the influence of a quality, of which I have only since learnt to appreciate the extreme rarity: that exalted public spirit and regard above all things to the good of the whole, which warmed into life and activity every germ of similar virtue that existed in the minds he came in contact with: the desire he made them feel for his approbation, the shame at his disapproval; the moral support which his conversation and his very existence gave to those who were aiming at the same objects, and the encouragement he afforded to the faint-hearted or desponding among them, by the firm confidence which (though the reverse of sanguine as to the results to be expected in any one particular case) he always felt in the power of reason, the general progress of improvement, and the good which individuals could do by judicious effort.

It was my father's opinions which gave the distinguishing character to the Benthamic or utilitarian propagandism of that time.

They fell singly scattered from him in many directions, but they flowed from him in a continued stream principally in three channels. One was through me, the only mind directly formed by his instructions, and through whom considerable influence was exercised over various young men who became, in their turn, propagandists. A second was through some of the Cambridge cotemporaries of Charles Austin, who, either initiated by him or under the general mental impulse which he gave, had adopted many opinions allied to those of my father, and some of the more considerable of whom afterwards sought my father's acquaintance and frequented his house. Among these may be mentioned Strutt, afterwards Lord Belper, and the present Lord Romilly, with whose eminent father, Sir Samuel, my father had of old been on terms of friendship. The third channel was that of a younger generation of Cambridge undergraduates, cotemporary not with Austin but with Eyton Tooke, who were drawn to that estimable person by affinity of opinions, and introduced by him to my father: the most notable of these was Charles Buller. Various other persons individually received and transmitted a considerable amount of my father's influence: for example, Black (as before mentioned) and Fonblanque: most of these however we accounted only partial allies; Fonblanque, for instance, was always divergent from us on many important points. But indeed there was by no means complete unanimity among any portion of us, nor had any of us adopted implicitly all my father's opinions. For example, although his Essay on Government[6] was regarded probably by all of us as a masterpiece of political wisdom, our adhesion by no means extended to the paragraph of it, in which he maintains that women may consistently with good government, be excluded from the suffrage, because their interest is the same with that of men. From this doctrine, I, and all those who formed my chosen associates, most positively dissented. It is due to my father to say that he denied having intended to affirm that women *should* be excluded, any more than men under the age of forty, concerning whom he maintained, in the very next paragraph, an exactly similar thesis. He was, as he truly said, not discussing whether the suffrage had better be restricted, but only (assuming that it is to be restricted) what is the utmost limit of restriction, which does not necessarily involve a sacrifice of the

[6] In the supplement to the *Encyclopaedia Britannica,* 1820.

securities for good government. But I thought then, as I have always thought since, that the opinion which he acknowledged, no less than that which he disclaimed, is as great an error as any of those against which the Essay was directed; that the interest of women is included in that of men exactly as much and no more, as the interest of subjects is included in that of kings; and that every reason which exists for giving the suffrage to anybody, demands that it should not be withheld from women. This was also the general opinion of the younger proselytes; and it is pleasant to be able to say that Mr. Bentham, on this important point, was wholly on our side.

But though none of us, probably, agreed in every respect with my father, his opinions, as I said before, were the principal element which gave its colour and character to the little group of young men who were the first propagators of what was afterwards called "philosophic radicalism." Their mode of thinking was not characterized by Benthamism in any sense which has relation to Bentham as a chief or guide, but rather by a combination of Bentham's point of view with that of the modern political economy, and with the Hartleian metaphysics. Malthus's population principle was quite as much a banner, and point of union among us, as any opinion specially belonging to Bentham. This great doctrine, originally brought forward as an argument against the indefinite improvability of human affairs, we took up with ardent zeal in the contrary sense, as indicating the sole means of realizing that improvability by securing full employment at high wages to the whole labouring population through a voluntary restriction of the increase of their numbers. The other leading characteristics of the creed, which we held in common with my father, may be stated as follows:

In politics, an almost unbounded confidence in the efficacy of two things: representative government, and complete freedom of discussion. So complete was my father's reliance on the influence of reason over the minds of mankind, whenever it is allowed to reach them, that he felt as if all would be gained if the whole population were taught to read, if all sorts of opinions were allowed to be addressed to them by word and in writing, and if by means of the suffrage they could nominate a legislature to give effect to the opinions they adopted. He thought that when the legislature no longer represented a class interest, it would aim at the general interest, honestly and with adequate wisdom; since the people would be sufficiently under the guidance of educated intelligence, to make in general a good choice of persons to represent them, and having done so, to leave to those whom they had chosen a liberal discretion. Accordingly aristocratic rule, the government of the Few in any of its shapes, being in his eyes the only thing which stood between mankind and an administration of their affairs by the best wisdom to be found among them, was the object of his sternest disapprobation, and a democratic suffrage the principal article of his political creed, not on the ground of liberty, Rights of Man, or any of the phrases, more or less significant, by which, up to that time, democracy had usually been defended, but as the most essential of "securities for good government." In this, too, he held fast only to what he deemed essentials; he was comparatively indifferent to monarchical or republican forms — far more so than Bentham, to whom a king, in the character of "corrupter-general,"[7] appeared necessarily very noxious. Next to aristocracy, an established church, or corporation of priests, as being by position the great depravers of religion, and interested in opposing the progress of the human mind, was the object of his greatest detestation; though he disliked no clergyman personally who did not deserve it, and was on terms of sincere friendship with several. In ethics, his moral feelings were energetic and rigid on all points which he deemed important to human well being, while he was supremely indifferent in opinion (though his indifference did not shew itself in personal conduct) to all those doctrines of the common morality, which he thought had no foundation but in asceticism and priestcraft. He looked forward, for example, to a considerable increase of freedom in the relations between the sexes, though without pretending to define exactly what would be, or ought to be, the precise conditions of that freedom. This opinion was connected in him with no sensuality either of a theoretical or of a practical kind. He anticipated, on the contrary, as one of the beneficial effects of increased freedom, that the imagination would no longer dwell upon the physical relation and its adjuncts, and swell this into one of the principal objects of life; a perversion of the imagination and feelings, which he regarded as one of the deepest seated and most pervading evils in the human mind. In psychology, his fundamental doctrine was the formation of all human character by circumstances,

<hr>

[7] Bentham's term in *Plan of Parliamentary Reform* (1817).

through the universal Principle of Association, and the consequent unlimited possibility of improving the moral and intellectual condition of mankind by education. Of all his doctrines none was more important than this, or needs more to be insisted on: unfortunately there is none which is more contradictory to the prevailing tendencies of speculation, both in his time and since.

These various opinions were seized on with youthful fanaticism by the little knot of young men of whom I was one: and we put into them a sectarian spirit, from which, in intention at least, my father was wholly free. What we (or rather a phantom substituted in the place of us) were sometimes, by a ridiculous exaggeration, called by others, namely a "school," some of us for a time really hoped and aspired to be. The French *philosophes* of the eighteenth century were the example we sought to imitate, and we hoped to accomplish no less results. No one of the set went to so great excesses in this boyish ambition as I did; which might be shewn by many particulars, were it not an useless waste of space and time.

All this, however, is properly only the outside of our existence; or at least, the intellectual part alone, and no more than one side of that. In attempting to penetrate inward, and give any indication of what we were as human beings, I must be understood as speaking only of myself, of whom alone I can speak from sufficient knowledge; and I do not believe that the picture would suit any of my companions without many and great modifications.

I conceive that the description so often given of a Benthamite, as a mere reasoning machine, though extremely inapplicable to most of those who have been designated by that title, was during two or three years of my life not altogether untrue of me. It was perhaps as applicable to me as it can well be to any one just entering into life, to whom the common objects of desire must in general have at least the attraction of novelty. There is nothing very extraordinary in this fact: no youth of the age I then was, can be expected to be more than one thing, and this was the thing I happened to be. Ambition and desire of distinction, I had in abundance; and zeal for what I thought the good of mankind was my strongest sentiment, mixing with and colouring all others. But my zeal was as yet little else, at that period of my life, than zeal for speculative opinions. It had not its root in genuine benevolence, or sympathy with mankind; though these qualities held their due place in my ethical standard. Nor was it connected with any high enthusiasm for ideal nobleness. Yet of this feeling I was imaginatively very susceptible; but there was at that time an intermission of its natural aliment, poetical culture, while there was a superabundance of the discipline antagonistic to it, that of mere logic and analysis. Add to this that, as already mentioned, my father's teachings tended to the under-valuing of feeling. It was not that he was himself cold-hearted or insensible; I believe it was rather from the contrary quality; he thought that feeling could take care of itself; that there was sure to be enough of it if actions were properly cared about. Offended by the frequency with which, in ethical and philosophical controversy, feeling is made the ultimate reason and justification of conduct, instead of being itself called on for a justification, while, in practice, actions, the effect of which on human happiness is mischievous, are defended as being required by feeling, and the character of a person of feeling obtains a credit for desert, which he thought only due to actions, he had a real impatience of attributing praise to feeling, or of any but the most sparing reference to it either in the estimation of persons or in the discussion of things. In addition to the influ-ence which this characteristic in him, had on me and others, we found all the opinions to which we attached most importance, constantly attacked on the ground of feeling. Utility was denounced as cold calculation; political economy as hard-hearted; anti-popula-tion doctrines as repulsive to the natural feelings of mankind. We retorted by the word "sentimentality," which, along with "declama-tion" and "vague generalities," served us as common terms of op-probrium. Although we were generally in the right, as against those who were opposed to us, the effect was that the cultivation of feel-ing (except the feelings of public and private duty) was not in much esteem among us, and had very little place in the thoughts of most of us, myself in particular.[8] What we principally thought of, was to alter people's opinions; to make them believe according to evidence, and know what was their real interest, which when they once knew, they would, we thought, by the instrument of opinion, enforce a regard to it upon one another. While fully rec-ognizing the superior excellence of unselfish benevolence and love of justice, we did not expect the regeneration of mankind from any direct action on those sentiments, but from the effect of educated

[8] In the original MS Mill wrote and then deleted at this point: "And there-fore we had at this time no idea of real culture. In our schemes for improv-ing human affairs we overlooked human beings" (*The Early Draft,* p. 103 n.).

intellect, enlightening the selfish feelings. Although this last is prodigiously important as a means of improvement in the hands of those who are themselves impelled by nobler principles of action, I do not believe that any one of the survivors of the Benthamites or Utilitarians of that day, now relies mainly upon it for the general amendment of human conduct.

From this neglect both in theory and in practice of the cultiva-tion of feeling, naturally resulted among other things an under-valuing of poetry, and of Imagination generally as an element of human nature. It is, or was, part of the popular notion of Ben-thamites, that they are enemies of poetry: this was partly true of Bentham himself; he used to say that "all poetry is misrepresenta-tion":[9] but, in the sense in which he said it, the same might have been said of all impressive speech; of all representation or inculca-tion more oratorical in its character than a sum in arithmetic. An article of Bingham's in the first number of the Westminster Review, in which he offered as an explanation of something which he dis-liked in Moore, that "Mr. Moore *is* a poet, and therefore is *not* a reasoner," did a good deal to attach the notion of hating poetry to the writers in the Review. But the truth was that many of us were great readers of poetry; Bingham himself had been a writer of it, while as regards me (and the same thing might be said of my father), the correct statement would be not that I disliked poetry, but that I was theoretically indifferent to it. I disliked any senti-ments in poetry which I should have disliked in prose; and that included a great deal. And I was wholly blind to its place in human culture, as a means of educating the feelings. But I was always per-sonally very susceptible to some kinds of it. In the most sectarian period of my Benthamism I happened to look into Pope's Essay on Man, and though every opinion in it was contrary to mine, I well remember how powerfully it acted on my imagination. Perhaps at that time poetical composition of any higher type than eloquent discussion in verse, might not have produced a similar effect on me:

---

[9] Cf. Bentham's *The Rationale of Reward* (1825), Book III, ch. I: "In-deed, between poetry and truth there is a natural opposition: false morals, fictitious nature. The poet always stands in need of something false. When he pretends to lay his foundations in truth, the ornaments of his super-structure are fictions; his business consists in stimulating our passions, and exciting our prejudices. Truth, exactitude of every kind, is fatal to poetry. The poet must see everything through coloured media, and strive to make every one else to do the same" (*Works*, II, 253–54).

at all events I seldom gave it an opportunity. This, however, was a mere passing state. Long before I had enlarged in any considerable degree, the basis of my intellectual creed, I had obtained in the natural course of my mental progress, poetic culture of the most valuable kind, by means of reverential admiration for the lives and characters of heroic persons; especially the heroes of philosophy. The same inspiring effect which so many of the benefactors of mankind have left on record that they had experienced from Plutarch's Lives, was produced on me by Plato's pictures of Socrates, and by some modern biographies, above all by Condorcet's Life of Turgot; a book well calculated to rouse the best sort of enthusiasm, since it contains one of the wisest and noblest of lives, delineated by one of the wisest and noblest of men. The heroic virtue of these glorious representatives of the opinions with which I sympathized, deeply affected me, and I perpetually recurred to them as others do to a favorite poet, when needing to be carried up into the more elevated regions of feeling and thought. I may observe by the way that this book cured me of my sectarian follies. The two or three pages beginning "Il regardait toute secte comme nuisible,"[10] and explaining why Turgot always kept himself perfectly distinct from the Encyclopedists, sank deeply into my mind. I left off designating myself and others as Utilitarians, and by the pronoun "we," or any other collective designation, I ceased to *afficher*[11] sectarianism. My real inward sectarianism I did not get rid of till later, and much more gradually.

About the end of 1824, or beginning of 1825, Mr. Bentham, having lately got back his papers on Evidence from M. Dumont (whose Traité des Preuves Judiciaires, grounded on them, was then first completed and published), resolved to have them printed in the original, and bethought himself of me as capable of preparing them for the press; in the same manner as his Book of Fallacies had been recently edited by Bingham. I gladly undertook this task, and it occupied nearly all my leisure for about a year, exclusive of the time afterwards spent in seeing the five large volumes through the press. Mr. Bentham had begun this treatise three times, at considerable intervals, each time in a different manner, and each time without reference to the preceding: two of the three times he had gone over nearly the whole subject. These three masses of manuscript

[10] "He looked on all sects as harmful."
[11] Proclaim publicly.

it was my business to condense into a single treatise; adopting the one last written as the groundwork, and incorporating with it as much of the two others as it had not completely superseded. I had also to unroll such of Bentham's involved and parenthetical sentences, as seemed to overpass by their complexity the measure of what readers were likely to take the pains to understand. It was further Mr. Bentham's particular desire that I should, from myself, endeavour to supply any *lacunæ* which he had left; and at his instance I read, for this purpose, the most authoritative treatises on the English Law of Evidence, and commented on a few of the objectionable points of the English rules, which had escaped Bentham's notice. I also replied to the objections which had been made to some of his doctrines, by reviewers of Dumont's book, and added a few supplementary remarks on some of the more abstract parts of the subject, such as the theory of improbability and impossibility. The controversial part of these editorial additions was written in a more assuming tone, than became one so young and inexperienced as I was: but indeed I had never contemplated coming forward in my own person; and, as an anonymous editor of Bentham, I fell into the tone of my author, not thinking it unsuitable to him or to the subject, however it might be so to me. My name as editor was put to the book after it was printed, at Mr. Bentham's positive desire, which I in vain attempted to persuade him to forego.

The time occupied in this editorial work was extremely well employed in respect to my own improvement. The "Rationale of Judicial Evidence" is one of the richest in matter of all Bentham's productions. The theory of evidence being in itself one of the most important of his subjects, and ramifying into most of the others, the book contains, very fully developed, a great proportion of all his best thoughts: while, among more special things, it comprises the most elaborate exposure of the vices and defects of English law, as it then was, which is to be found in his works; not confined to the law of evidence, but including, by way of illustrative episode, the entire procedure or practice of Westminster Hall. The direct knowledge, therefore, which I obtained from the book, and which was imprinted upon me much more thoroughly than it could have been by mere reading, was itself no small acquisition. But this occupation did for me what might seem less to be expected; it gave a great start to my powers of composition. Everything which I wrote subsequently to this editorial employment, was markedly superior to anything that I had written before it. Bentham's later style, as the world knows, was heavy and cumbersome, from the excess of a good quality, the love of precision, which made him introduce clause within clause into the heart of every sentence, that the reader might receive into his mind all the modifications and qualifications simultaneously with the main proposition: and the habit grew on him until his sentences became, to those not accustomed to them, most laborious reading. But his earlier style, that of the Fragment on Government, Plan of a Judicial Establishment, &c., is a model of liveliness and ease combined with fulness of matter, scarcely ever surpassed: and of this earlier style there were many striking specimens in the manuscripts on Evidence, all of which I endeavoured to preserve. So long a course of this admirable writing had a considerable effect upon my own; and I added to it by the assiduous reading of other writers, both French and English, who combined, in a remarkable degree, ease with force, such as Goldsmith, Fielding, Pascal, Voltaire, and Courier. Through these influences my writing lost the jejuneness of my early compositions; the bones and cartilages began to clothe themselves with flesh, and the style became, at times, lively and almost light.

This improvement was first exhibited in a new field. Mr. Marshall, of Leeds, father of the present generation of Marshalls, the same who was brought into Parliament for Yorkshire when the representation forfeited by Grampound was transferred to it — an earnest parliamentary reformer, and a man of large fortune, of which he made a liberal use, had been much struck with Bentham's Book of Fallacies: and the thought had occurred to him that it would be useful to publish annually the Parliamentary Debates, not in the chronological order of Hansard,[12] but classified according to subjects, and accompanied by a commentary pointing out the fallacies of the speakers. With this intention, he very naturally addressed himself to the editor of the Book of Fallacies; and Bingham, with the assistance of Charles Austin, undertook the editorship. The work was called "Parliamentary History and Review." Its sale was not sufficient to keep it in existence, and it only lasted three years. It excited, however, some attention among parliamentary and political people. The best strength of the party was put forth in it; and its execution did them much more credit, than that

---

[12] *Hansard's Parliamentary Debates,* the official report of the debates of both houses of Parliament, beginning in 1803.

of the Westminster Review had ever done. Bingham and Charles
Austin wrote much in it; as did Strutt, Romilly, and several other
liberal lawyers. My father wrote one article in his best style; the
elder Austin another. Coulson wrote one of great merit. It fell
to my lot to lead off the first number by an article on the principal
topic of the session (that of 1825), the Catholic Association and
the Catholic disabilities. In the second number I wrote an elaborate
Essay on the commercial crisis of 1825 and the Currency Debates.
In the third I had two articles, one on a minor subject, the other on
the Reciprocity principle in commerce, *à propos* of a celebrated
diplomatic correspondence between Canning and Gallatin. These
writings were no longer mere reproductions and applications of the
doctrines I had been taught; they were original thinking, as far as
that name can be applied to old ideas in new forms and connexions:
and I do not exceed the truth in saying that there was a maturity,
and a well-digested character about them, which there had not
been in any of my previous performances. In execution, therefore,
they were not at all juvenile; but their subjects have either gone
by, or have been so much better treated since, that they are entirely
superseded, and should remain buried in the same oblivion with
my contributions to the first dynasty of the Westminster Review.

While thus engaged in writing for the public, I did not neglect
other modes of self-cultivation. It was at this time that I learnt
German; beginning it in the Hamiltonian method,[13] for which purpose I and several of my companions formed a class. For several
years from this period, our social studies assumed a shape which
contributed very much to my mental progress. The idea occurred
to us of carrying on, by reading and conversation, a joint study of
several of the branches of science which we wished to be masters
of. We assembled to the number of a dozen or more. Mr. Grote
lent a room of his house in Threadneedle Street for the purpose,
and his partner Prescott, one of the three original members of the
Utilitarian Society, made one among us. We met two mornings in
every week, from half past eight till ten, at which hour most of
us were called off to our daily occupations. Our first subject was
Political Economy. We chose some systematic treatise as our text-
book; my father's "Elements" being our first choice. One of us
read aloud a chapter, or some smaller portion, of the book. The
discussion was then opened, and any one who had an objection or

[13] A controversial system in which the pupil began at once with word-for-
word translation, ignoring grammar until a later stage of instruction.

other remark to make, made it. Our rule was to discuss thoroughly every point raised, whether great or small, prolonging the discussion until all who took part were satisfied with the conclusion they had individually arrived at; and to follow up every topic of collateral speculation which the chapter or the conversation suggested, never leaving it until we had untied every knot which we found. We repeatedly kept up the discussion of some one point for several weeks, thinking intently on it during the intervals of our meetings, and contriving solutions of the new difficulties which had risen up in the last morning's discussion. When we had finished in this way my father's Elements, we went in the same manner through Ricardo's Principles of Political Economy, and Bailey's Dissertation on Value. These close and vigorous discussions were not only improving in a high degree to those who took part in them, but brought out new views of some topics of abstract Political Economy. The theory of International Values which I afterwards published, emanated from these conversations, as did also the modified form of Ricardo's theory of Profits, laid down in my Essay on Profits and Interest. Those among us with whom new speculations chiefly originated, were Ellis, Graham, and I; though others gave valuable aid to the discussions, especially Prescott and Roebuck, the one by his knowledge, the other by his dialectical acuteness. The theories of International Values and of Profits were excogitated and worked out in about equal proportions by myself and Graham: and if our original project had been executed, my "Essays on some Unsettled Questions of Political Economy" would have been brought out along with some papers of his, under our joint names. But when my exposition came to be written, I found that I had so much overestimated my agreement with him, and he dissented so much from the most original of the two Essays, that on International Values, that I was obliged to consider the theory as now exclusively mine, and it came out as such when published many years later. I may mention that among the alterations which my father made in revising his Elements for the third edition, several were grounded on criticisms elicited by these Conversations; and in particular, he modified his opinions (though not to the extent of our new speculations) on both the points to which I have adverted.

When we had enough of political economy, we took up the syllogistic logic in the same manner, Grote now joining us. Our first text book was Aldrich, but being disgusted with its superficial-ity, we reprinted one of the most finished among the many manuals of the school logic, which my father, a great collector of such books, possessed, the Manuductio ad Logicam of the Jesuit Du Trieu. After finishing this, we took up Whately's Logic, then first republished from the Encyclopædia Metropolitana, and finally the "Computatio sive Logica" of Hobbes. These books, dealt with in our manner, afforded a wide range for original metaphysical speculation: and most of what has been done in the First Book of my System of Logic, to rationalize and correct the principles and distinctions of the school logicians, and to improve the theory of the Import of Propositions, had its origin in these discussions; Graham and I originating most of the novelties, while Grote and others furnished an excellent tribunal or test. From this time I formed the project of writing a book on Logic, though on a much humbler scale than the one I ultimately executed.

Having done with Logic, we launched into analytic psychology, and having chosen Hartley for our text book, we raised Priestley's edition to an extravagant price by searching through London to furnish each of us with a copy. When we had finished Hartley, we suspended our meetings; but, my father's Analysis of the Mind being published soon after, we reassembled for the purpose of reading it. With this our exercises ended. I have always dated from these conversations my own real inauguration as an original and independent thinker. It was also through them that I acquired, or very much strengthened, a mental habit to which I attribute all that I have ever done, or ever shall do, in speculation; that of never accepting half-solutions of difficulties as complete; never abandoning a puzzle, but again and again returning to it until it was cleared up; never allowing obscure corners of a subject to remain unexplored, because they did not appear important; never thinking that I perfectly understood any part of a subject until I understood the whole.

Our doings from 1825 to 1830 in the way of public speaking filled a considerable place in my life during those years, and as they had important effects on my development, something ought to be said of them.

There was for some time in existence a society of Owenites, called the Cooperative Society, which met for weekly public discussions in Chancery Lane. In the early part of 1825, accident brought Roebuck in contact with several of its members, and led to his attending one or two of the meetings and taking part in the debate in opposition to Owenism. Some one of us started the notion of going there in a body and having a general battle: and Charles Austin and some of his friends who did not usually take part in our joint exercises, entered into the project. It was carried out by concert with the principal members of the Society, themselves nothing loth, as they naturally preferred a controversy with opponents to a tame discussion among their own body. The question of population was proposed as the subject of debate: Charles Austin led the case on our side with a brilliant speech, and the fight was kept up by adjournment through five or six weekly meetings before crowded auditories, including along with the members of the Society and their friends, many hearers and some speakers from the Inns of Court. When this debate was ended, another was commenced on the general merits of Owen's system: and the contest altogether lasted about three months. It was a *lutte corps-à-corps*[14] between Owenites and political economists, whom the Owenites regarded as their most inveterate opponents: but it was a perfectly friendly dispute. We who represented political economy had the same objects in view as they had, and took pains to shew it; and the principal champion on their side was a very estimable man, with whom I was well acquainted, Mr. William Thompson, of Cork, author of a book on the Distribution of Wealth, and of an "Appeal" in behalf of women against the passage relating to them in my father's Essay on Government. Ellis, Roebuck, and I, took an active part in the debate, and among those from the Inns of Court who joined in it I remember Charles Villiers. The other side obtained also, on the population question, very efficient support from without. The well known Gale Jones, then an elderly man, made one of his florid speeches; but the speaker with whom I was most struck, though I dissented from nearly every word he said, was Thirlwall, the historian, since Bishop of St. David's, then a Chancery barrister, unknown except by a high reputation for eloquence acquired at the Cambridge Union before the era of Austin and Macaulay. His speech was in answer to one of mine. Before he had uttered ten sentences, I set him down as the best speaker I had ever heard, and I have never since heard any one whom I placed above him.

[14] Hand-to-hand struggle.

The great interest of these debates predisposed some of those who took part in them, to catch at a suggestion thrown out by McCulloch, the political economist, that a society was wanted in London similar to the Speculative Society at Edinburgh, in which Brougham, Horner and others first cultivated public speaking. Our experience at the Cooperative Society seemed to give cause for being sanguine as to the sort of men who might be brought together in London for such a purpose. McCulloch mentioned the matter to several young men of influence to whom he was then giving private lessons in political economy. Some of these entered warmly into the project, particularly George Villiers, afterwards Earl of Clarendon. He and his brothers Hyde and Charles, Romilly, Charles Austin, and I, with some others, met and agreed on a plan. We determined to meet once a fortnight, from November to June, at the Freemason's Tavern, and we had soon a splendid list of members, containing, along with several members of parliament, nearly all the most noted speakers of the Cambridge Union and of the Oxford United Debating Society. It is curiously illustrative of the tendencies of the time that our principal difficulty in recruiting for the Society was to find a sufficient number of Tory speakers. Almost all whom we could press into the service were Liberals, of different orders and degrees. Besides those already named, we had Macaulay, Thirlwall, Praed, Lord Howick, Samuel Wilberforce (afterwards Bishop of Oxford), Charles Poulett Thomson (afterwards Lord Sydenham), Edward and Henry Lytton Bulwer, Fonblanque, and many others whom I cannot now recollect, but who made themselves afterwards more or less conspicuous in public or literary life. Nothing could seem more promising. But when the time for action drew near, and it was necessary to fix on a President, and find somebody to open the first debate, none of our celebrities would consent to perform either office. Of the many who were pressed on the subject, the only one who could be prevailed on was a man of whom I knew very little, but who had taken high honours at Oxford and was said to have acquired a great oratorical reputation there; who some time afterwards became a Tory member of parliament.[15] He accordingly was fixed on, both for filling the President's chair and for making the first speech. The important day arrived; the benches were crowded; all our great

[15] His name was Donald Maclean.

speakers were present, to judge of, but not to help our efforts. The Oxford orator's speech was a complete failure. This threw a damp on the whole concern: the speakers who followed were few, and none of them did their best: the affair was a complete *fiasco;* and the oratorical celebrities we had counted on went away never to return, giving to me at least a lesson in knowledge of the world. This unexpected breakdown altered my whole relation to the project. I had not anticipated taking a prominent part, or speaking much or often, particularly at first; but I now saw that the success of the scheme depended on the new men, and I put my shoulder to the wheel. I opened the second question, and from that time spoke in nearly every debate. It was very uphill work for some time. The three Villiers' and Romilly stuck to us for some time longer, but the patience of all the founders of the Society was at last exhausted, except me and Roebuck. In the season following, 1826/27, things began to mend. We had acquired two excellent Tory speakers, Hayward, and Shee (afterwards Sergeant Shee): the radical side was reinforced by Charles Buller, Cockburn, and others of the second generation of Cambridge Benthamites; and with their and other occasional aid, and the two Tories as well as Roebuck and me for regular speakers, almost every debate was a *bataille rangée*[16] between the "philosophic radicals" and the Tory lawyers; until our conflicts were talked about, and several persons of note and consideration came to hear us. This happened still more in the subsequent seasons, 1828 and 1829, when the Coleridgians, in the persons of Maurice and Sterling, made their appearance in the Society as a second Liberal and even Radical party, on totally different grounds from Benthamism and vehemently opposed to it; bringing into these discussions the general doctrines and modes of thought of the European reaction against the philosophy of the eighteenth century; and adding a third and very important belligerent party to our contests, which were now no bad exponent of the movement of opinion among the most cultivated part of the new generation. Our debates were very different from those of common debating societies, for they habitually consisted of the strongest arguments and most philosophic principles which either side was able to produce, thrown often into close and *serré*[17] confutations of one another. The practice was

---

[16] Pitched battle.
[17] Compact, pressing.

necessarily very useful to us, and eminently so to me. I never, indeed, acquired real fluency, and had always a bad and ungraceful delivery; but I could make myself listened to: and as I always wrote my speeches when, from the feelings involved, or the nature of the ideas to be developed, expression seemed important, I greatly increased my power of effective writing; acquiring not only an ear for smoothness and rhythm, but a practical sense for *telling* sentences, and an immediate criterion of their telling property, by their effect on a mixed audience.

The Society, and the preparation for it, together with the preparation for the morning conversations which were going on simultaneously, occupied the greater part of my leisure; and made me feel it a relief when, in the spring of 1828, I ceased to write for the Westminster. The Review had fallen into difficulties. Though the sale of the first number had been very encouraging, the permanent sale had never, I believe, been sufficient to pay the expenses, on the scale on which the review was carried on. Those expenses had been considerably, but not sufficiently, reduced. One of the editors, Southern, had resigned; and several of the writers, including my father and me, who had been paid like other contributors for our earlier articles, had latterly written without payment. Nevertheless, the original funds were nearly or quite exhausted, and if the Review was to be continued some new arrangement of its affairs had become indispensable. My father and I had several conferences with Bowring on the subject. We were willing to do our utmost for maintaining the Review as an organ of our opinions, but not under Bowring's editorship: while the impossibility of its any longer supporting a paid editor, afforded a ground on which, without affront to him, we could propose to dispense with his services. We, and some of our friends, were prepared to carry on the Review as unpaid writers, either finding among ourselves an unpaid editor, or sharing the editorship among us. But while this negociation was proceeding, with Bowring's apparent acquiescence, he was carrying on another in a different quarter (with Colonel Perronet Thompson), of which we received the first intimation in a letter from Bowring as editor, informing us merely that an arrangement had been made, and proposing to us to write for the next number, with promise of payment. We did not dispute Bowring's right to bring about, if he could, an arrangement more favorable to himself than the one we had proposed; but we thought the concealment which he had practised towards us, while seemingly entering into our own project, an affront: and even had we not thought so, we were indisposed to expend any more of our time and trouble in attempting to write up the Review under his management. Accordingly my father excused himself from writing; though two or three years later, on great pressure, he did write one more political article. As for me, I positively refused. And thus ended my connexion with the original Westminster. The last article which I wrote in it had cost me more labour than any previous; but it was a labour of love, being a defence of the early French Revolutionists against the Tory misrepresentations of Sir Walter Scott, in the introduction to his Life of Napoleon. The number of books which I read for this purpose, making notes and extracts — even the number I had to buy (for in those days there was no public or subscription library trom which books of reference could be taken home), far exceeded the worth of the immediate object; but I had at that time a half formed intention of writing a History of the French Revolution; and though I never executed it, my collections afterwards were very useful to Carlyle for a similar purpose.[18]

---

[18] Carlyle's *The French Revolution* (1837).

CHAPTER V

A CRISIS IN MY MENTAL HISTORY. ONE STAGE ONWARD

FOR some years after this time I wrote very little, and nothing regularly, for publication: and great were the advantages which I derived from the intermission. It was of no common importance to me, at this period, to be able to digest and mature my thoughts for my own mind only, without any immediate call for giving them out in print. Had I gone on writing, it would have much disturbed the important transformation in my opinions and character, which took place during those years. The origin of this transformation, or at least the process by which I was prepared for it, can only be explained by turning some distance back.

From the winter of 1821, when I first read Bentham, and especially from the commencement of the Westminster Review, I had what might truly be called an object in life; to be a reformer of the world. My conception of my own happiness was entirely identified with this object. The personal sympathies I wished for were those of fellow labourers in this enterprise. I endeavoured to pick up as many flowers as I could by the way; but as a serious and permanent personal satisfaction to rest upon, my whole reliance was placed on this: and I was accustomed to felicitate myself on the certainty of a happy life which I enjoyed, through placing my happiness in something durable and distant, in which some progress might be always making, while it could never be exhausted by complete attainment. This did very well for several years, during which the general improvement going on in the world and the idea of myself as engaged with others in struggling to promote it, seemed enough to fill up an interesting and animated existence. But the time came when I awakened from this as from a dream. It was in the autumn of 1826. I was[1] in a dull state of nerves, such as everybody is

[1] In the original MS Mill first wrote: "I was, probably from physical causes (connected perhaps merely with the time of year) . . ." (*The Early Draft*, p. 117 n.). For discussion and interpretation of the mental crisis see the articles by Levi ("The 'Mental Crisis' of John Stuart Mill"), Durham, and Cumming listed in the Select Bibliography.

occasionally liable to; unsusceptible to enjoyment or pleasurable excitement; one of those moods when what is pleasure at other times, becomes insipid or indifferent; the state, I should think, in which converts to Methodism usually are, when smitten by their first "conviction of sin." In this frame of mind it occurred to me to put the question directly to myself, "Suppose that all your objects in life were realized; that all the changes in institutions and opinions which you are looking forward to, could be completely effected at this very instant: would this be a great joy and happiness to you?" And an irrepressible self-consciousness distinctly answered, "No!" At this my heart sank within me: the whole foundation on which my life was constructed fell down. All my happiness was to have been found in the continual pursuit of this end. The end had ceased to charm, and how could there ever again be any interest in the means? I seemed to have nothing left to live for.

At first I hoped that the cloud would pass away of itself; but it did not. A night's sleep, the sovereign remedy for the smaller vexations of life, had no effect on it. I awoke to a renewed consciousness of the woful fact. I carried it with me into all companies, into all occupations. Hardly anything had power to cause me even a few minutes oblivion of it. For some months the cloud seemed to grow thicker and thicker. The lines in Coleridge's "Dejection" — I was not then acquainted with them — exactly describe my case:

> A grief without a pang, void, dark and drear,
> A drowsy, stifled, unimpassioned grief,
> Which finds no natural outlet or relief
> In word, or sigh, or tear.

In vain I sought relief from my favourite books; those memorials of past nobleness and greatness, from which I had always hitherto drawn strength and animation. I read them now without feeling, or with the accustomed feeling *minus* all its charm; and I became persuaded, that my love of mankind, and of excellence for its own sake, had worn itself out. I sought no comfort by speaking to others of what I felt. If I had loved any one sufficiently to make confiding my griefs a necessity, I should not have been in the condition I was. I felt, too, that mine was not an interesting, or in any way respectable distress. There was nothing in it to attract sympathy. Advice, if I had known where to seek it, would have been most precious. The words of Macbeth to the physician often occurred to my thoughts.[2] But there was no one on whom I could build the faintest hope of such assistance. My father, to whom it would have been natural to me to have recourse in any practical difficulties, was the last person to whom, in such a case as this, I looked for help. Everything convinced me that he had no knowledge of any such mental state as I was suffering from, and that even if he could be made to understand it, he was not the physician who could heal it. My education, which was wholly his work, had been conducted without any regard to the possibility of its ending in this result; and I saw no use in giving him the pain of thinking that his plans had failed, when the failure was probably irremediable, and at all events, beyond the power of *his* remedies. Of other friends, I had at that time none to whom I had any hope of making my condition intelligible. It was however abundantly intelligible to myself; and the more I dwelt upon it, the more hopeless it appeared.

My course of study had led me to believe, that all mental and moral feelings and qualities, whether of a good or of a bad kind, were the results of association; that we love one thing and hate another, take pleasure in one sort of action or contemplation, and pain in another sort, through the clinging of pleasurable or painful ideas to those things, from the effect of education or of experience. As a corollary from this, I had always heard it maintained by my father, and was myself convinced, that the object of education should be to form the strongest possible associations of the salutary class; associations of pleasure with all things beneficial to the great whole, and of pain with all things hurtful to it. This doctrine appeared inexpugnable; but it now seemed to me on retrospect, that my teachers had occupied themselves but superficially with the means of forming and keeping up these salutary associations. They seemed to have trusted altogether to the old familiar instruments, praise and blame, reward and punishment. Now I did not doubt that by these means, begun early and applied unremittingly, intense associations of pain and pleasure, especially of pain, might be created, and might produce desires and aversions capable of lasting

[2] Canst thou not minister to a mind diseas'd,
Pluck from the memory a rooted sorrow,
Raze out the written troubles of the brain,
And with some sweet oblivious antidote
Cleanse the stuff'd bosom of that perilous stuff
Which weighs upon the heart?   (V.iii.40–45)

undiminished to the end of life. But there must always be something artificial and casual in associations thus produced. The pains and pleasures thus forcibly associated with things, are not connected with them by any natural tie; and it is therefore, I thought, essential to the durability of these associations, that they should have become so intense and inveterate as to be practically indissoluble, before the habitual exercise of the power of analysis had commenced. For I now saw, or thought I saw, what I had always before received with incredulity — that the habit of analysis has a tendency to wear away the feelings: as indeed it has when no other mental habit is cultivated, and the analysing spirit remains without its natural complements and correctives. The very excellence of analysis (I argued) is that it tends to weaken and undermine whatever is the result of prejudice; that it enables us mentally to separate ideas which have only casually clung together: and no associations whatever could ultimately resist this dissolving force, were it not that we owe to analysis our clearest knowledge of the permanent sequences in nature; the real connexions between Things, not dependent on our will and feelings; natural laws, by virtue of which, in many cases, one thing is inseparable from another in fact; which laws, in proportion as they are clearly perceived and imaginatively realized, cause our ideas of things which are always joined together in Nature, to cohere more and more closely in our thoughts. Analytic habits may thus even strengthen the associations between causes and effects, means and ends, but tend altogether to weaken those which are, to speak familiarly, a *mere* matter of feeling. They are therefore (I thought) favourable to prudence and clearsightedness, but a perpetual worm at the root both of the passions and of the virtues; and above all, fearfully undermine all desires, and all pleasures, which are the effects of association, that is, according to the theory I held, all except the purely physical and organic; of the entire insufficiency of which to make life desirable, no one had a stronger conviction than I had. These were the laws of human nature by which, as it seemed to me, I had been brought to my present state. All those to whom I looked up, were of opinion that the pleasure of sympathy with human beings, and the feelings which made the good of others, and especially of mankind on a large scale, the object of existence, were the greatest and surest sources of happiness. Of the truth of this I was convinced, but to know that a feeling would make me happy if I had it, did not give me the feeling. My education, I thought, had failed to create these feelings in sufficient strength to resist the dissolving influence of analysis, while the whole course of my intellectual cultivation had made precocious and premature analysis the inveterate habit of my mind. I was thus, as I said to myself, left stranded at the commencement of my voyage, with a well equipped ship and a rudder, but no sail; without any real desire for the ends which I had been so carefully fitted out to work for: no delight in virtue or the general good, but also just as little in anything else. The fountains of vanity and ambition seemed to have dried up within me, as completely as those of benevolence. I had had (as I reflected) some gratification of vanity at too early an age: I had obtained some distinction, and felt myself of some importance, before the desire of distinction and of importance had grown into a passion: and little as it was which I had attained, yet having been attained too early, like all pleasures enjoyed too soon, it had made me *blasé* and indifferent to the pursuit. Thus neither selfish nor unselfish pleasures were pleasures to me. And there seemed no power in nature sufficient to begin the formation of my character anew, and create in a mind now irretrievably analytic, fresh associations of pleasure with any of the objects of human desire.

These were the thoughts which mingled with the dry heavy dejection of the melancholy winter of 1826–7. During this time I was not incapable of my usual occupations. I went on with them mechanically, by the mere force of habit. I had been so drilled in a certain sort of mental exercise, that I could still carry it on when all the spirit had gone out of it. I even composed and spoke several speeches at the debating society, how, or with what degree of success I know not. Of four years continual speaking at that society, this is the only year of which I remember next to nothing. Two lines of Coleridge, in whom alone of all writers I have found a true description of what I felt, were often in my thoughts, not at this time (for I had never read them), but in a later period of the same mental malady:

> Work without hope draws nectar in a sieve,
> And hope without an object cannot live.

In all probability my case was by no means so peculiar as I fancied it, and I doubt not that many others have passed through a similar state; but the idiosyncracies of my education had given to the general phenomenon a special character, which made it seem the natural effect of causes that it was hardly possible for time to remove. I frequently asked myself, if I could, or if I was bound to go on living, when life must be passed in this manner. I generally answered to myself, that I did not think I could possibly bear it beyond a year. When, however, not more than half that duration of time had elapsed, a small ray of light broke in upon my gloom. I was reading, accidentally, Marmontel's Memoirs, and came to the passage which relates his father's death, the distressed position of the family, and the sudden inspiration by which he, then a mere boy, felt and made them feel that he would be everything to them — would supply the place of all that they had lost. A vivid conception of the scene and its feelings came over me, and I was moved to tears. From this moment my burthen grew lighter. The oppression of the thought that all feeling was dead within me, was gone. I was no longer hopeless: I was not a stock or a stone. I had still, it seemed, some of the material out of which all worth of character, and all capacity for happiness, are made. Relieved from my ever present sense of irremediable wretchedness, I gradually found that the ordinary incidents of life could again give me some pleasure; that I could again find enjoyment, not intense, but sufficient for cheerfulness, in sunshine and sky, in books, in conversation, in public affairs; and that there was, once more, excitement, though of a moderate kind, in exerting myself for my opinions, and for the public good. Thus the cloud gradually drew off, and I again enjoyed life: and though I had several relapses, some of which lasted many months, I never again was as miserable as I had been.

The experiences of this period had two very marked effects on my opinions and character. In the first place, they led me to adopt a theory of life, very unlike that on which I had before acted, and having much in common with what at that time I certainly had never heard of, the anti-self-consciousness theory of Carlyle.[3] I never, indeed, wavered in the conviction that happiness is the test of all rules of conduct, and the end of life. But I now thought that this end was only to be attained by not making it the direct end. Those only are happy (I thought) who have their minds fixed on some object other than their own happiness; on the happiness of others, on the improvement of mankind, even on some art or pur-

[3] See Carlyle's essay "Characteristics" (1831) and *Sartor Resartus* (1833–34), Book II, ch. IX, "The Everlasting Yea."

suit, followed not as a means, but as itself an ideal end. Aiming thus at something else, they find happiness by the way. The enjoyments of life (such was now my theory) are sufficient to make it a pleasant thing, when they are taken *en passant,* without being made a principal object. Once make them so, and they are immediately felt to be insufficient. They will not bear a scrutinizing examination. Ask yourself whether you are happy, and you cease to be so. The only chance is to treat, not happiness, but some end external to it, as the purpose of life. Let your self-consciousness, your scrutiny, your self-interrogation, exhaust themselves on that; and if otherwise fortunately circumstanced you will inhale happiness with the air you breathe, without dwelling on it or thinking about it, without either forestalling it in imagination, or putting it to flight by fatal questioning. This theory now became the basis of my philosophy of life. And I still hold to it as the best theory for all those who have but a moderate degree of sensibility and of capacity for enjoyment, that is, for the great majority of mankind.

The other important change which my opinions at this time underwent, was that I, for the first time, gave its proper place, among the prime necessities of human well-being, to the internal culture of the individual. I ceased to attach almost exclusive importance to the ordering of outward circumstances, and the training of the human being for speculation and for action. I had now learnt by experience that the passive susceptibilities needed to be cultivated as well as the active capacities, and required to be nourished and enriched as well as guided. I did not, for an instant, lose sight of, or undervalue, that part of the truth which I had seen before; I never turned recreant to intellectual culture, or ceased to consider the power and practice of analysis as an essential condition both of individual and of social improvement. But I thought that it had consequences which required to be corrected, by joining other kinds of cultivation with it. The maintenance of a due balance among the faculties, now seemed to me of primary importance. The cultivation of the feelings became one of the cardinal points in my ethical and philosophical creed. And my thoughts and inclinations turned in an increasing degree towards whatever seemed capable of being instrumental to that object.

I now began to find meaning in the things which I had read or heard about the importance of poetry and art as instruments of human culture. But it was some time longer before I began to know this by personal experience. The only one of the imaginative arts in which I had from childhood taken great pleasure, was music; the best effect of which (and in this it surpasses perhaps every other art) consists in exciting enthusiasm; in winding up to a high pitch those feelings of an elevated kind which are already in the character, but to which this excitement gives a glow and a fervour, which though transitory at its utmost height, is precious for sustaining them at other times. This effect of music I had often experienced; but, like all my pleasurable susceptibilities, it was suspended during the gloomy period. I had sought relief again and again from this quarter, but found none. After the tide had turned, and I was in process of recovery, I had been helped forward by music, but in a much less elevated manner. I at this time first became acquainted with Weber's Oberon,[4] and the extreme pleasure which I drew from its delicious melodies did me good, by shewing me a source of pleasure to which I was as susceptible as ever. The good however was much impaired by the thought, that the pleasure of music (as is quite true of such pleasure as this was, that of mere tune) fades with familiarity, and requires either to be revived by intermittence, or fed by continual novelty. And it is very characteristic both of my then state, and of the general tone of my mind at this period of my life, that I was seriously tormented by the thought of the exhaustibility of musical combinations. The octave consists only of five tones and two semitones, which can be put together in only a limited number of ways, of which but a small proportion are beautiful: most of these, it seemed to me, must have been already discovered, and there could not be room for a long succession of Mozarts and Webers, to strike out as these had done, entirely new and surpassingly rich veins of musical beauty. This source of anxiety may perhaps be thought to resemble that of the philosophers of Laputa, who feared lest the sun should be burnt out.[5] It was, however, connected with the best feature in my character, and the only good point to be found in my very unromantic and in no way honorable distress. For though my dejection, honestly looked at, could not be called other than egotistical, produced by the ruin, as I thought, of my fabric of happiness, yet the destiny

[4] A romantic opera first produced in London in 1826.
[5] *Gulliver's Travels,* Part III, ch. II.

of mankind in general was ever in my thoughts, and could not be separated from my own. I felt that the flaw in my life, must be a flaw in life itself; that the question was, whether, if the reformers of society and government could succeed in their objects, and every person in the community were free and in a state of physical comfort, the pleasures of life, being no longer kept up by struggle and privation, would cease to be pleasures. And I felt that unless I could see my way to some better hope than this for human happiness in general, my dejection must continue; but that if I could see such an outlet, I should then look on the world with pleasure; content as far as I was myself concerned, with any fair share of the general lot.

This state of my thoughts and feelings made the fact of my reading Wordsworth for the first time (in the autumn of 1828) an important event in my life. I took up the collection of his poems from curiosity, with no expectation of mental relief from it, though I had before resorted to poetry with that hope. In the worst period of my depression I had read through the whole of Byron (then new to me) to try whether a poet, whose peculiar department was supposed to be that of the intenser feelings, could rouse any feeling in me. As might be expected, I got no good from this reading, but the reverse. The poet's state of mind was too like my own. His was the lament of a man who had worn out all pleasures, and who seemed to think that life, to all who possess the good things of it, must necessarily be the vapid uninteresting thing which I found it. His Harold and Manfred had the same burthen on them which I had; and I was not in a frame of mind to derive any comfort from the vehement sensual passion of his Giaours, or the sullenness of his Laras. But while Byron was exactly what did not suit my condition, Wordsworth was exactly what did. I had looked into the Excursion two or three years before, and found little in it; and should probably have found as little, had I read it at this time. But the miscellaneous poems, in the two-volume edition of 1815 (to which little of value was added in the latter part of the author's life), proved to be the precise thing for my mental wants at that particular juncture.

In the first place, these poems addressed themselves powerfully to one of the strongest of my pleasurable susceptibilities, the love of rural objects and natural scenery; to which I had been indebted not only for much of the pleasure of my life, but quite recently for relief from one of my longest relapses into depression.[6] In this power of rural beauty over me, there was a foundation laid for taking pleasure in Wordsworth's poetry; the more so, as his scenery lies mostly among mountains, which, owing to my early Pyrenean excursion, were my ideal of natural beauty. But Wordsworth would never have had any great effect on me, if he had merely placed before me beautiful pictures of natural scenery. Scott does this still better than Wordsworth, and a very second-rate landscape does it more effectually than any poet. What made Wordsworth's poems a medicine for my state of mind, was that they expressed, not mere outward beauty, but states of feeling, and of thought coloured by feeling, under the excitement of beauty.[7] They seemed to be the very culture of the feelings, which I was in quest of. In them I seemed to draw from a source of inward joy, of sympathetic and imaginative pleasure, which could be shared in by all human beings; which had no connexion with struggle or imperfection, but would be made richer by every improvement in the physical or social condition of mankind. From them I seemed to learn what would be the perennial sources of happiness, when all the greater evils of life shall have been removed. And I felt myself at once better and happier as I came under their influence. There have certainly been, even in our own age, greater poets than Wordsworth; but poetry of deeper and loftier feeling could not have done for me at that time what his did. I needed to be made to feel that there was real, permanent happiness in tranquil contemplation. Wordsworth taught me this, not only without turning away from, but with a greatly increased interest in, the common feelings and common destiny of human beings. And the delight which these poems gave me, proved that with culture of this sort, there was nothing to dread from the

[6] The original MS has the following deleted continuation: "About Midsummer of that same year 1828 I set out on a short walking tour: for months before I had been in my old state of gloomy dejection though as I have already mentioned not so intense as at first; this continued the greater part of the first day, but the walk by the side of the Thames from Reading to Pangbourne, in one of the loveliest of summer evenings with the western sky in its most splendid colouring before me, and the calm river, rich meadows and wooded hills encompassing me, insensibly changed my state, and except a short interval two days later I had no return of depression during that excursion nor for several months afterwards" (*The Early Draft*, p. 125 n.).

[7] Mill is paraphrasing the fifth paragraph of Wordsworth's Preface to *Lyrical Ballads* (1800).

most confirmed habit of analysis. At the conclusion of the Poems came the famous Ode, falsely called Platonic, "Intimations of Immortality": in which, along with more than his usual sweetness of melody and rhythm, and along with the two passages of grand imagery but bad philosophy so often quoted, I found that he too had had similar experience to mine; that he also had felt that the first freshness of youthful enjoyment of life was not lasting; but that he had sought for compensation, and found it, in the way in which he was now teaching me to find it. The result was that I gradually, but completely, emerged from my habitual depression, and was never again subject to it. I long continued to value Wordsworth less according to his intrinsic merits, than by the measure of what he had done for me. Compared with the greatest poets, he may be said to be the poet of unpoetical natures, possessed of quiet and contemplative tastes. But unpoetical natures are precisely those which require poetic cultivation. This cultivation Wordsworth is much more fitted to give, than poets who are intrinsically far more poets than he.

It so fell out that the merits of Wordsworth were the occasion of my first public declaration of my new way of thinking, and separation from those of my habitual companions who had not undergone a similar change. The person with whom at that time I was most in the habit of comparing notes on such subjects was Roebuck, and I induced him to read Wordsworth, in whom he also at first seemed to find much to admire: but I, like most Wordsworthians, threw myself into strong antagonism to Byron, both as a poet and as to his influence on the character. Roebuck, all whose instincts were those of action and struggle, had, on the contrary, a strong relish and great admiration of Byron, whose writings he regarded as the poetry of human life, while Wordsworth's, according to him, was that of flowers and butterflies. We agreed to have the fight out at our Debating Society, where we accordingly discussed for two evenings the comparative merits of Byron and Wordsworth, propounding and illustrating by long recitations our respective theories of poetry:[8] Sterling also, in a brilliant speech, putting forward his particular theory. This was the first debate on any weighty

[8] The draft of Mill's principal speech in this debate is printed in *John Stuart Mill: Literary Essays*, ed. Edward Alexander (Indianapolis, 1967), pp. 344–55. See also Karl Britton, "J. S. Mill: A Debating Speech on Wordsworth, 1829," *Cambridge Review*, LXXIX (1958), 418–23.

subject in which Roebuck and I had been on opposite sides. The schism between us widened from this time more and more, though we continued for some years longer to be companions. In the beginning, our chief divergence related to the cultivation of the feelings. Roebuck was in many respects very different from the vulgar notion of a Benthamite or Utilitarian.[9] He was a lover of poetry and of most of the fine arts. He took great pleasure in music, in dramatic performances, especially in painting, and himself drew and designed landscapes with great facility and beauty. But he never could be made to see that these things have any value as aids in the formation of character. Personally, instead of being, as Benthamites are supposed to be, void of feeling, he had very quick and strong sensibilities. But, like most Englishmen who have feelings, he found his feelings stand very much in his way. He was much more susceptible to the painful sympathies than to the pleasurable, and looking for his happiness elsewhere, he wished that his feelings should be deadened rather than quickened. And in truth the English character, and English social circumstances, make it so seldom possible to derive happiness from the exercise of the sympathies, that it is not wonderful if they count for little in an Englishman's scheme of life. In most other countries the paramount importance of the sympathies as a constituent of individual happiness is an axiom, taken for granted rather than needing any formal statement; but most English thinkers almost seem to regard them as necessary evils, required for keeping men's actions benevolent and compassionate. Roebuck was, or appeared to be, this kind of Englishman. He saw little good in any cultivation of the feelings, and none at all in cultivating them through the imagination, which he thought was only cultivating illusions. It was in vain I urged on him that the imaginative emotion which an idea when vividly conceived excites in us, is not an illusion but a fact, as real as any of the other qualities of objects; and far from implying anything erroneous and delusive in our mental apprehension of the

9 The brief character of Roebuck that follows is much reduced from the original version (*The Early Draft,* pp. 127–31), a melancholy account of failure in which Roebuck, married and entrapped in "the petty vanities and entanglements of what is called society," gradually became "a panegyrist of England and things English, a conformist to the Church, and in short merged in the common herd of Conservative Liberals." Roebuck himself attributed the schism to his open disapproval of Mill's relationship with Harriet Taylor (see *The Early Draft,* p. 14 and n.).

object, is quite consistent with the most accurate knowledge and most perfect practical recognition of all its physical and intellectual laws and relations. The intensest feeling of the beauty of a cloud lighted by the setting sun, is no hindrance to my knowing that the cloud is vapour of water, subject to all the laws of vapours in a state of suspension; and I am just as likely to allow for, and act on, these physical laws whenever there is occasion to do so, as if I had been incapable of perceiving any distinction between beauty and ugliness.

While my intimacy with Roebuck diminished, I fell more and more into friendly intercourse with our Coleridgian adversaries in the Society, Frederick Maurice and John Sterling, both subsequently so well known, the former by his writings, the latter through the biographies by Hare and Carlyle. Of these two friends, Maurice was the thinker, Sterling the orator, and impassioned expositor of thoughts which, at this period, were almost entirely formed for him by Maurice. With Maurice I had for some time been acquainted through Eyton Tooke, who had known him at Cambridge, and though my discussions with him were almost always disputes, I had carried away from them much that helped to build up my new fabric of thought, in the same way as I was deriving much from Coleridge, and from the writings of Goethe and other German authors which I read during those years. I have so deep a respect for Maurice's character and purposes, as well as for his great mental gifts, that it is with some unwillingness I say anything which may seem to place him on a less high eminence than I would gladly be able to accord to him. But I have always thought that there was more intellectual power wasted in Maurice than in any other of my co-temporaries. Few of them certainly have had so much to waste. Great powers of generalization, rare ingenuity and subtlety, and a wide perception of important and unobvious truths, served him not for putting something better into the place of the worthless heap of received opinions on the great subjects of thought, but for proving to his own mind that the Church of England had known everything from the first, and that all the truths on the ground of which the Church and orthodoxy have been attacked (many of which he saw as clearly as any one) are not only consistent with the Thirty-nine articles, but are better understood and expressed in those articles than by any one who rejects them. I have never been able to find any other explanation of this, than by attributing it to that timidity of conscience, combined with original sensitiveness of temperament, which has so often driven highly gifted men into Romanism from the need of a firmer support than they can find in the independent conclusions of their own judgment. Any more vulgar kind of timidity no one who knew Maurice would ever think of imputing to him, even if he had not given public proof of his freedom from it, by his ultimate collision with some of the opinions commonly regarded as orthodox, and by his noble origination of the Christian Socialist movement. The nearest parallel to him, in a moral point of view, is Coleridge, to whom, in merely intellectual power, apart from poetical genius, I think him decidedly superior. At this time, however, he might be described as a disciple of Coleridge, and Sterling as a disciple of Coleridge and of him. The modifications which were taking place in my old opinions gave me some points of contact with them; and both Maurice and Sterling were of considerable use to my development. With Sterling I soon became very intimate, and was more attached to him than I have ever been to any other man. He was indeed one of the most loveable of men. His frank, cordial, affectionate and expansive character; a love of truth alike conspicuous in the highest things and the humblest; a generous and ardent nature which threw itself with impetuosity into the opinions it adopted, but was as eager to do justice to the doctrines and the men it was opposed to, as to make war on what it thought their errors; and an equal devotion to the two cardinal points of Liberty and Duty, formed a combination of qualities as attractive to me, as to all others who knew him as well as I did. With his open mind and heart, he found no difficulty in joining hands with me across the gulf which as yet divided our opinions. He told me how he and others had looked upon me (from hearsay information) as a "made" or manufactured man, having had a certain impress of opinion stamped on me which I could only reproduce; and what a change took place in his feelings when he found, in the discussion on Wordsworth and Byron, that Wordsworth, and all which that name implies, "belonged" to me as much as to him and his friends. The failure of his health soon scattered all his plans of life, and compelled him to live at a distance from London, so that after the first year or two of our acquaintance we only saw each other at distant intervals. But (as he said himself in one of his letters to Carlyle) when we did meet it was like brothers. Though he was

never, in the full sense of the word, a profound thinker, his openness of mind, and the moral courage in which he greatly surpassed
Maurice, made him outgrow the dominion which Maurice and
Coleridge had once exercised over his intellect; though he retained
to the last a great but discriminating admiration of both, and
towards Maurice a warm affection. Except in that short and transitory phasis of his life, during which he made the mistake of becoming a clergyman, his mind was ever progressive; and the advance
he always seemed to have made when I saw him after an interval,
made me apply to him what Goethe said of Schiller, "Er hatte eine
fürchterliche Fortschreitung."[10] He and I started from intellectual
points almost as wide apart as the poles, but the distance between
us was always diminishing: if I made steps towards some of his
opinions, he, during his short life, was constantly approximating
more and more to several of mine: and if he had lived, and had
health and vigour to prosecute his ever assiduous self-culture, there
is no knowing how much further this spontaneous assimilation
might have proceeded.

After 1829 I withdrew from attendance on the Debating Society.
I had had enough of speech-making, and was glad to carry on my
private studies and meditations without any immediate call for
outward assertion of their results. I found the fabric of my old
and taught opinions giving way in many fresh places, and I never
allowed it to fall to pieces, but was incessantly occupied in weaving
it anew. I never, in the course of my transition, was content to
remain, for ever so short a time, confused and unsettled. When I
had taken in any new idea, I could not rest till I had adjusted its
relation to my old opinions, and ascertained exactly how far its
effect ought to extend in modifying or superseding them.

The conflicts which I had so often had to sustain in defending
the theory of government laid down in Bentham's and my father's
writings, and the acquaintance I had obtained with other schools
of political thinking, made me aware of many things which that
doctrine, professing to be a theory of government in general, ought
to have made room for, and did not. But these things, as yet,

---

[10] "He had an awesome rate of development." Cf. Goethe's remark (in
J. P. Eckermann's *Gespräche mit Goethe,* first published in 1836, entry for
18 January 1825) that "Every week [Schiller] was a different person, and a
more perfected one; each time I saw him again, he seemed to me more
advanced in erudition and judgment."

remained with me rather as corrections to be made in applying the theory to practice, than as defects in the theory. I felt that politics could not be a science of specific experience; and that the accusations against the Benthamic theory of *being* a theory, of proceeding *à priori,* by way of general reasoning, instead of Baconian experiment, shewed complete ignorance of Bacon's principles, and of the necessary conditions of experimental investigation. At this juncture appeared, in the Edinburgh Review, Macaulay's famous attack on my father's Essay on Government. This gave me much to think about. I saw that Macaulay's conception of the logic of politics was erroneous; that he stood up for the empirical mode of treating political phenomena, against the philosophical; that even in physical science, his notion of philosophizing might have recognized Kepler, but would have excluded Newton and Laplace. But I could not help feeling, that though the tone was unbecoming (an error for which the writer, at a later period, made the most ample and honorable amends), there was truth in several of his strictures on my father's treatment of the subject; that my father's premises were really too narrow, and included but a small number of the general truths, on which, in politics, the important consequences depend. Identity of interest between the governing body and the community at large, is not, in any practical sense which can be attached to it, the only thing on which good government depends; neither can this identity of interest be secured by the mere conditions of election. I was not at all satisfied with the mode in which my father met the criticisms of Macaulay. He did not, as I thought he ought to have done, justify himself by saying, "I was not writing a scientific treatise on politics. I was writing an argument for parliamentary reform." He treated Macaulay's argument as simply irrational; an attack upon the reasoning faculty; an example of the saying of Hobbes, that when reason is against a man, a man will be against reason.[11] This made me think that there was really something more fundamentally erroneous in my father's conception of philosophical Method, as applicable to politics, than I had hitherto supposed there was. But I did not at first see clearly what the error might be. At last it flashed upon me all at once in the course of other studies. In the early part of 1830 I had begun to put on paper the ideas on Logic (chiefly on the dis-

[11] Epistle Dedicatory to *Tripos* (a similar remark occurs in *Leviathan,* Part I, ch. XI).

tinctions among Terms, and the import of Propositions) which had been suggested and in part worked out in the morning conversations already spoken of. Having secured these thoughts from being lost, I pushed on into the other parts of the subject, to try whether I could do anything further towards clearing up the theory of Logic generally. I grappled at once with the problem of Induction, postponing that of Reasoning, on the ground that it is necessary to obtain premises before we can reason from them. Now, Induction is mainly a process for finding the causes of effects: and in attempting to fathom the mode of tracing causes and effects in physical science, I soon saw that in the more perfect of the sciences, we ascend, by generalization from particulars, to the tendencies of causes considered singly, and then reason downward from those separate tendencies, to the effect of the same causes when combined. I then asked myself, what is the ultimate analysis of this deductive process; the common theory of the syllogism evidently throwing no light upon it. My practice (learnt from Hobbes and my father) being to study abstract principles by means of the best concrete instances I could find, the Composition of Forces, in dynamics, occurred to me as the most complete example of the logical process I was investigating. On examining, accordingly, what the mind does when it applies the principle of the Composition of Forces, I found that it performs a simple act of addition. It adds the separate effect of the one force to the separate effect of the other, and puts down the sum of these separate effects as the joint effect. But is this a legitimate process? In dynamics, and in all the mathematical branches of physics, it is; but in some other cases, as in chemistry, it is not; and I then recollected that something not unlike this was pointed out as one of the distinctions between chemical and mechanical phenomena, in the introduction to that favorite of my boyhood, Thomson's System of Chemistry. This distinction at once made my mind clear as to what was perplexing me in respect to the philosophy of politics. I now saw, that a science is either deductive or experimental, according as, in the province it deals with, the effects of causes when conjoined, are or are not the sums of the effects which the same causes produce when separate. It followed that politics must be a deductive science. It thus appeared, that both Macaulay and my father were wrong; the one in assimilating the method of philosophizing in politics to the purely experimental method of chemistry; while the other, though right in adopting a deductive method, had made a wrong selection of one, having taken as the type of deduction, not the appropriate process, that of the deductive branches of natural philosophy, but the inappropriate one of pure geometry, which not being a science of causation at all, does not require or admit of any summing-up of effects. A foundation was thus laid in my thoughts for the principal chapters of what I afterwards published on the Logic of the Moral Sciences; and my new position in respect to my old political creed, now became perfectly definite.

If I am asked what system of political philosophy I substituted for that which, as a philosophy, I had abandoned, I answer, no system: only a conviction, that the true system was something much more complex and many sided than I had previously had any idea of, and that its office was to supply, not a set of model institutions, but principles from which the institutions suitable to any given circumstances might be deduced. The influences of European, that is to say, Continental, thought, and especially those of the reaction of the nineteenth century against the eighteenth, were now streaming in upon me. They came from various quarters: from the writings of Coleridge, which I had begun to read with interest even before the change in my opinions; from the Coleridgians with whom I was in personal intercourse; from what I had read of Goethe; from Carlyle's early articles in the Edinburgh and Foreign Reviews, though for a long time I saw nothing in these (as my father saw nothing in them to the last) but insane rhapsody. From these sources, and from the acquaintance I kept up with the French literature of the time, I derived, among other ideas which the general turning upside down of the opinions of European thinkers had brought uppermost, these in particular: That the human mind has a certain order of possible progress, in which some things must precede others, an order which governments and public instructors can modify to some, but not to an unlimited extent: That all questions of political institutions are relative, not absolute, and that different stages of human progress not only *will* have, but *ought* to have, different institutions: That government is always either in the hands, or passing into the hands, of whatever is the strongest power in society, and that what this power is, does not depend on institutions, but institutions on it: That any general theory or philosophy of politics supposes a previous theory of human progress, and that this is the same thing with a philosophy of history. These opinions, true in the main, were held in an exaggerated and violent manner by the thinkers with whom I was now most accustomed to compare notes, and who, as usual with a reaction, ignored that half of the truth which the thinkers of the eighteenth century saw. But though, at one period of my progress, I for some time undervalued that great century, I never joined in the reaction against it, but kept as firm hold of one side of the truth as I took of the other. The fight between the nineteenth century and the eighteenth always reminded me of the battle about the shield, one side of which was white and the other black.[12] I marvelled at the blind rage with which the combatants rushed against one another. I applied to them, and to Coleridge himself, many of Coleridge's sayings about half truths;[13] and Goethe's device, "many-sidedness,"[14] was one which I would most willingly, at this period, have taken for mine.

The writers by whom, more than by any others, a new mode of political thinking was brought home to me, were those of the St. Simonian school in France. In 1829 and 1830 I became acquainted with some of their writings. They were then only in the earlier stages of their speculations. They had not yet dressed out their philosophy as a religion, nor had they organized their scheme of Socialism. They were just beginning to question the principle of hereditary property. I was by no means prepared to go with them even this length; but I was greatly struck with the connected view which they for the first time presented to me, of the natural order of human progress; and especially with their division of all history into organic periods and critical periods. During the organic periods (they said) mankind accept with firm conviction some positive creed, claiming jurisdiction over all their actions, and containing more or less of truth and adaptation to the needs of humanity. Under its influence they make all the progress compatible with the creed, and finally outgrow it; when a period follows

[12] A medieval allegory in which two knights, riding up from opposite directions, first argue and then come to blows over the color or metal of a shield that they see hanging from a tree (it is more often represented as gold on one side, silver on the other). The fight ends when a third knight arrives to show them the difference between the two sides.

[13] In his notes on one of Donne's sermons, Coleridge wrote that no falsehoods are "more dangerous than truths misunderstood" and that "the most mischievous errors on record . . . [have been] half-truths taken as the whole" (*Literary Remains* [1838], III, 145).

[14] Probably Mill is thinking of the idea of self-development expounded in *Wilhelm Meister*.

of criticism and negation, in which mankind lose their old convictions without acquiring any new ones, of a general or authoritative character, except the conviction that the old are false. The period of Greek and Roman polytheism, so long as really believed in by instructed Greeks and Romans, was an organic period, succeeded by the critical or sceptical period of the Greek philosophers. Another organic period came in with Christianity. The corresponding critical period began with the Reformation, has lasted ever since, still lasts, and cannot altogether cease until a new organic period has been inaugurated by the triumph of a yet more advanced creed. These ideas, I knew, were not peculiar to the St. Simonians; on the contrary, they were the general property of Europe, or at least of Germany and France, but they had never, to my knowledge, been so completely systematized as by these writers, nor the distinguishing characteristics of a critical period so powerfully set forth; for I was not then acquainted with Fichte's Lectures on "the Characteristics of the Present Age." In Carlyle, indeed, I found bitter denunciations of an "age of unbelief," and of the present age as such, which I, like most people at that time, supposed to be passionate protests in favour of the old modes of belief. But all that was true in these denunciations I thought that I found more calmly and philosophically stated by the St. Simonians. Among their publications, too, there was one which seemed to me far superior to the rest; in which the general idea was matured into something much more definite and instructive. This was an early work of Auguste Comte,[15] who then called himself, and even announced himself in the title page as, a pupil of Saint-Simon. In this tract M. Comte first put forth the doctrine which he afterwards so copiously illustrated, of the natural succession of three stages in every department of human knowledge: first the theological, next the metaphysical, and lastly, the positive stage; and contended, that social science must be subject to the same law; that the feudal and Catholic system was the concluding phasis of the theological state of the social science, Protestantism the commencement and the doctrines of the French Revolution the consummation of the metaphysical, and that its positive state was yet to come. This doctrine harmonized well with my existing notions, to which it seemed to give a scientific shape. I already regarded the methods of physical

[15] *Système de politique positive* (1823 — not to be confused with Comte's later work by the same title, which Mill mentions in chapter VI).

science as the proper models for political. But the chief benefit
which I derived at this time from the trains of thought suggested by
the St. Simonians and by Comte, was, that I obtained a clearer conception than ever before of the peculiarities of an era of transition
in opinion, and ceased to mistake the moral and intellectual characteristics of such an era, for the normal attributes of humanity. I
looked forward, through the present age of loud disputes but generally weak convictions, to a future which shall unite the best
qualities of the critical with the best qualities of the organic periods;
unchecked liberty of thought, unbounded freedom of individual
action in all modes not hurtful to others; but also, convictions as to
what is right and wrong, useful and pernicious, deeply engraven
on the feelings by early education and general unanimity of sentiment, and so firmly grounded in reason and in the true exigencies
of life, that they shall not, like all former and present creeds, religious, ethical, and political, require to be periodically thrown off
and replaced by others.

M. Comte soon left the St. Simonians, and I lost sight of him and
his writings for a number of years. But the St. Simonians I continued to cultivate. I was kept *au courant* of their progress by one
of their most enthusiastic disciples, M. Gustave d'Eichthal, who
about that time passed a considerable interval in England. I was
introduced to their chiefs, Bazard and Enfantin, in 1830; and as
long as their public teachings and proselytism continued, I read
nearly everything they wrote. Their criticisms on the common doctrines of Liberalism seemed to me full of important truth; and it
was partly by their writings that my eyes were opened to the very
limited and temporary value of the old political economy, which
assumes private property and inheritance as indefeasible facts, and
freedom of production and exchange as the *dernier mot* of social
improvement. The scheme gradually unfolded by the St. Simonians, under which the labour and capital of society would be man-
aged for the general account of the community, every individual
being required to take a share of labour, either as thinker, teacher,
artist, or producer, all being classed according to their capacity,
and remunerated according to their works, appeared to me a far
superior description of Socialism to Owen's. Their aim seemed to
me desirable and rational, however their means might be ineffica-
cious; and though I neither believed in the practicability, nor in the
beneficial operation of their social machinery, I felt that the proc-

lamation of such an ideal of human society could not but tend to give a beneficial direction to the efforts of others to bring society, as at present constituted, nearer to some ideal standard. I honoured them most of all for what they have been most cried down for — the boldness and freedom from prejudice with which they treated the subject of family, the most important of any, and needing more fundamental alterations than remain to be made in any other great social institution, but on which scarcely any reformer has the courage to touch. In proclaiming the perfect equality of men and women, and an entirely new order of things in regard to their relations with one another, the St. Simonians in common with Owen and Fourier have entitled themselves to the grateful remembrance of future generations.

In giving an account of this period of my life, I have only speci fied such of my new impressions as appeared to me, both at the time and since, to be a kind of turning points, marking a definite progress in my mode of thought. But these few selected points give a very insufficient idea of the quantity of thinking which I carried on respecting a host of subjects during these years of transition. Much of this, it is true, consisted in rediscovering things known to all the world, which I had previously disbelieved, or disregarded. But the rediscovery was to me a discovery, giving me plenary possession of the truths not as traditional platitudes but fresh from their source: and it seldom failed to place them in some new light, by which they were reconciled with, and seemed to confirm while they modified, the truths less generally known which lay in my early opinions, and in no essential part of which I at any time wavered. All my new thinking only laid the foundation of these more deeply and strongly, while it often removed misapprehension and confusion of ideas which had perverted their effect. For example, during the later returns of my dejection, the doctrine of what is called Philosophical Necessity weighed on my existence like an incubus. I felt as if I was scientifically proved to be the helpless slave of antecedent circumstances; as if my character and that of all others had been formed for us by agencies beyond our control, and was wholly out of our own power. I often said to myself, what a relief it would be if I could disbelieve the doctrine of the formation of character by circumstances; and remembering the wish of Fox respecting the doctrine of resistance to governments, that it might never be forgotten by kings, nor remembered by subjects, I said that it would be a blessing if the doctrine of necessity could be believed by all *quoad*[16] the characters of others, and disbelieved in regard to their own. I pondered painfully on the subject, till gradually I saw light through it. I perceived, that the word Necessity, as a name for the doctrine of Cause and Effect applied to human action, carried with it a misleading association; and that this association was the operative force in the depressing and paralysing influence which I had experienced. I saw that though our character is formed by circumstances, our own desires can do much to shape those circumstances; and that what is really inspiriting and ennobling in the doctrine of freewill, is the conviction that we have real power over the formation of our own character; that our will, by influencing some of our circumstances, can modify our future habits or capabilities of willing. All this was entirely consistent with the doctrine of circumstances, or rather, was that doctrine itself, properly understood. From that time I drew, in my own mind, a clear distinction between the doctrine of circumstances, and Fatalism; discarding altogether the misleading word Necessity. The theory, which I now for the first time rightly apprehended, ceased altogether to be discouraging, and besides the relief to my spirits, I no longer suffered under the burthen, so heavy to one who aims at being a reformer in opinions, of thinking one doctrine true, and the contrary doctrine morally beneficial. The train of thought which had extricated me from this dilemma, seemed to me, in after years, fitted to render a similar service to others; and it now forms the chapter on Liberty and Necessity in the concluding Book of my "System of Logic."

Again, in politics, though I no longer accepted the doctrine of the Essay on Government as a scientific theory; though I ceased to consider representative democracy as an absolute principle, and regarded it as a question of time, place, and circumstance; though I now looked upon the choice of political institutions as a moral and educational question more than one of material interests, thinking that it ought to be decided mainly by the consideration, what great improvement in life and culture stands next in order for the people concerned, as the condition of their further progress, and what institutions are most likely to promote that; nevertheless this change in the premises of my political philosophy did not alter my

16 With respect to.

practical political creed as to the requirements of my own time and country. I was as much as ever a radical and democrat, for Europe, and especially for England. I thought the predominance of the aristocratic classes, the noble and the rich, in the English Constitution, an evil worth any struggle to get rid of; not on account of taxes, or any such comparatively small inconvenience, but as the great demoralizing agency in the country. Demoralizing, first, because it made the conduct of the government an example of gross public immorality, through the predominance of private over public interests in the State, and the abuse of the powers of legislation for the advantage of classes. Secondly, and in a still greater degree, because the respect of the multitude always attaching itself principally to that which, in the existing state of society, is the chief passport to power; and under English institutions, riches, hereditary or acquired, being the almost exclusive source of political importance; riches, and the signs of riches, were almost the only things really respected, and the life of the people was mainly devoted to the pursuit of them. I thought, that while the higher and richer classes held the power of government, the instruction and improvement of the mass of the people were contrary to the self interest of those classes, because tending to render the people more powerful for throwing off the yoke: but if the democracy obtained a large, and perhaps the principal, share in the governing power, it would become the interest of the opulent classes to promote their education, in order to ward off really mischievous errors, and especially those which would lead to unjust violations of property. On these grounds I was not only as ardent as ever for democratic institutions, but earnestly hoped that Owenite, St. Simonian, and all other anti-property doctrines might spread widely among the poorer classes; not that I thought those doctrines true, or desired that they should be acted on, but in order that the higher classes might be made to see that they had more to fear from the poor when uneducated, than when educated.

In this frame of mind the French Revolution of July[17] found me. It roused my utmost enthusiasm, and gave me, as it were, a new existence. I went at once to Paris, was introduced to Lafayette, and laid the groundwork of the intercourse I afterwards kept up with several of the active chiefs of the extreme popular party.

[17] 1830.

After my return I entered warmly, as a writer, into the political discussions of the time; which soon became still more exciting, by the coming in of Lord Grey's ministry, and the proposing of the Reform Bill.[18] For the next few years I wrote copiously in newspapers. It was about this time that Fonblanque, who had for some time written the political articles in the Examiner, became the proprietor and editor of the paper. It is not forgotten with what verve and talent, as well as fine wit, he carried it on, during the whole period of Lord Grey's ministry, and what importance it assumed as the principal representative, in the newspaper press, of radical opinions. The distinguishing character of the paper was given to it entirely by his own articles, which formed at least three fourths of all the original writing contained in it: but of the remaining fourth I contributed during those years a much larger share than any one else. I wrote nearly all the articles on French subjects, including a weekly summary of French politics, often extending to considerable length; together with many leading articles on general politics, commercial and financial legislation, and any miscellaneous subjects in which I felt interested, and which were suitable to the paper, including occasional reviews of books. Mere newspaper articles on the occurrences or questions of the moment gave no opportunity for the development of any general mode of thought; but I attempted, in the beginning of 1831, to embody in a series of articles, headed "The Spirit of the Age," some of my new opinions, and especially to point out in the character of the present age, the anomalies and evils characteristic of the transition from a system of opinions which had worn out, to another only in process of being formed. These articles were, I fancy, lumbering in style, and not lively or striking enough to be at any time acceptable to newspaper readers; but had they been far more attractive, still, at that particular moment, when great political changes were impending, and engrossing all minds, these discussions were ill timed, and missed fire altogether. The only effect which I know to have been produced by them, was that Carlyle, then living in a secluded part of Scotland, read them in his solitude, and saying to himself (as he afterwards told me) "here is a new Mystic," enquired on coming to London that autumn respecting their authorship; an enquiry

[18] Lord Grey's Whig ministry lasted from 1830 to 1834. The Reform Bill was passed in June 1832.

which was the immediate cause of our becoming personally acquainted.

I have already mentioned Carlyle's earlier writings as one of the channels through which I received the influences which enlarged my early narrow creed; but I do not think that those writings, by themselves, would ever have had any effect on my opinions. What truths they contained, though of the very kind which I was already receiving from other quarters, were presented in a form and vesture less suited than any other to give them access to a mind trained as mine had been. They seemed a haze of poetry and German metaphysics, in which almost the only clear thing was a strong animosity to most of the opinions which were the basis of my mode of thought; religious scepticism, utilitarianism, the doctrine of circumstances, and the attaching any importance to democracy, logic, or political economy. Instead of my having been taught anything, in the first instance, by Carlyle, it was only in proportion as I came to see the same truths, through media more suited to my mental constitution, that I recognized them in his writings. Then, indeed, the wonderful power with which he put them forth made a deep impression upon me, and I was during a long period one of his most fervent admirers; but the good his writings did me, was not as philosophy to instruct, but as poetry to animate. Even at the time when our acquaintance commenced, I was not sufficiently advanced in my new modes of thought, to appreciate him fully; a proof of which is, that on his shewing me the manuscript of Sartor Resartus, his best and greatest work, which he had just then finished, I made little of it; though when it came out about two years afterwards in Fraser's Magazine, I read it with enthusiastic admiration and the keenest delight.[19] I did not seek and cultivate Carlyle less on account of the fundamental differences in our philosophy. He soon found out that I was not "another mystic," and when for the sake of my own integrity I wrote to him a distinct profession of all those

---

[19] In the original MS Mill wrote and then (following his wife's markings) deleted at this point: "In this part of my life I was in such a state of reaction against sectarianism of thought or feeling, that those in whom I recognized any kind of superiority I did not judge or criticize at all; I estimated them by that side of their qualities or achievements by which they were admirable and valuable to me, while whatever I saw that seemed criticizable was not a *per contra* to be deducted, but was simply uncounted and disregarded" (*The Early Draft,* p. 145 n.).

of my opinions which I knew he most disliked, he replied that the chief difference between us was that I "was as yet consciously nothing of a mystic."[20] I do not know at what period he gave up the expectation that I was destined to become one; but though both his and my opinions underwent in subsequent years considerable changes, we never approached much nearer to each other's modes of thought than we were in the first years of our acquaintance. I did not, however, deem myself a competent judge of Carlyle. I felt that he was a poet, and that I was not; that he was a man of intuition, which I was not; and that as such, he not only saw many things long before me, which I could only, when they were pointed out to me, hobble after and prove, but that it was highly probable he could see many things which were not visible to me even after they were pointed out. I knew that I could not see round him, and could never be certain that I saw over him;[21] and I never presumed to judge him with any definiteness, until he was interpreted to me by one greatly the superior of us both[22] — who was more a poet than he, and more a thinker than I — whose own mind and nature included his, and infinitely more.

Among the persons of intellect whom I had known of old, the one with whom I had now most points of agreement was the elder Austin. I have mentioned that he always set himself in opposition to our early sectarianism; and latterly he had, like myself, come under new influences. Having been appointed Professor of Jurisprudence in the London University (now University College), he had lived for some time at Bonn to study for his Lectures; and the influences of German literature and of the German character and state of society had made a very perceptible change in his views of life. His personal disposition was much softened; he was less militant and polemic; his tastes had begun to turn themselves towards the poetic and contemplative. He attached much less importance than formerly to outward changes, unless accompanied by a better cultivation of the inward nature. He had a strong distaste for the general meanness of English life, the absence of enlarged thoughts

[20] For Mill's profession of opinions see the letter of 12 January 1834 in *Earlier Letters,* ed. Mineka, *Collected Works,* XII, 204–209. Carlyle's reply is in *Letters of Thomas Carlyle to John Stuart Mill, John Sterling and Robert Browning,* ed. Alexander Carlyle (London, 1923), pp. 90–96.

[21] Cf. *Sartor Resartus,* Book II, ch. I, "what you see, yet cannot see over, is as good as infinite."

[22] Harriet Taylor, subsequently Mill's wife.

and unselfish desires, the low objects on which the faculties of all classes of the English are intent. Even the kind of public interests which Englishmen care for, he held in very little esteem. He thought that there was more practical good government, and (which is true enough) infinitely more care for the education and mental improvement of all ranks of the people, under the Prussian monarchy, than under the English representative government: and he held, with the French Economistes, that the real security for good government is "un peuple éclairé,"[23] which is not always the fruit of popular institutions, and which if it could be had without them, would do their work better than they. Though he approved of the Reform Bill, he predicted, what in fact occurred, that it would not produce the great immediate improvements in government, which many expected from it. The men, he said, who could do these great things, did not exist in the country. There were many points of sympathy between him and me, both in the new opinions he had adopted and in the old ones which he retained. Like me, he never ceased to be an utilitarian, and with all his love of the Germans, and enjoyment of their literature, never became in the smallest degree reconciled to the innate-principle metaphysics. He cultivated more and more a kind of German religion, a religion of poetry and feeling with little if anything of positive dogma; while, in politics (and here it was that I most differed with him) he acquired an indifference, bordering on contempt, for the progress of popular institutions: though he rejoiced in that of Socialism, as the most effectual means of compelling the powerful classes to educate the people, and to impress on them the only real means of permanently improving their material condition, a limitation of their numbers. Neither was he, at this time, fundamentally opposed to Socialism in itself, as an ultimate result of improvement. He professed great disrespect for what he called "the universal principles of human nature of the political economists," and insisted on the evidence which history and daily experience afford of the "extraordinary pliability of human nature" (a phrase which I have somewhere borrowed from him); nor did he think it possible to set any positive bounds to the moral capabilities which might unfold themselves in mankind, under an enlightened direction of social and educational influences. Whether he retained all these opinions to

23 An enlightened people.

the end of life I know not. Certainly the modes of thinking of
his later years and especially of his last publication were much
more Tory in their general character, than those which he held
at this time.[24]

My father's tone of thought and feeling, I now felt myself at a
great distance from: greater, indeed, than a full and calm explanation and reconsideration on both sides, might have shewn to exist
in reality. But my father was not one with whom calm and full
explanations on fundamental points of doctrine could be expected,
at least with one whom he might consider as, in some sort, a
deserter from his standard. Fortunately we were almost always in
strong agreement on the political questions of the day, which engrossed a large part of his interest and of his conversation. On
those matters of opinion on which we differed, we talked little. He
knew that the habit of thinking for myself, which his mode of
education had fostered, sometimes led me to opinions different
from his, and he perceived from time to time that I did not always
tell him *how* different. I expected no good, but only pain to both
of us, from discussing our differences: and I never expressed them
but when he gave utterance to some opinion or feeling repugnant
to mine, in a manner which would have made it disingenuousness
on my part to remain silent.

It remains to speak of what I wrote during these years, which,
independently of my contributions to newspapers, was considerable. In 1830 and 1831 I wrote the five Essays since published
under the title of "Essays on some Unsettled Questions of Political
Economy," almost as they now stand, except that in 1833 I partially rewrote the fifth Essay. They were written with no immediate
purpose of publication; and when, some years later, I offered them
to a publisher, he declined them. They were only printed in 1844,
after the success of the "System of Logic." I also resumed my
speculations on this last subject, and puzzled myself, like others
before me, with the great paradox of the discovery of new truths
by general reasoning. As to the fact, there could be no doubt. As
little could it be doubted, that all reasoning is resolvable into syllo-

[24] The original MS contains at this point a severely critical paragraph
on Austin's wife, who is described as having, among other faults, "a very
mischievous tongue" (*The Early Draft,* pp. 147–48). Like Roebuck (see
p. 91 n. in the present volume), Mrs. Austin was still living when Mill
revised this part of the draft and copied it into the Columbia MS.

gisms, and that in every syllogism the conclusion is actually contained and implied in the premises. How, being so contained and implied, it could be new truth, and how the theorems of geometry, so different, in appearance, from the definitions and axioms, could be all contained in these, was a difficulty which no one, I thought, had sufficiently felt, and which at all events no one had succeeded in clearing up. The explanations offered by Whately and others, though they might give a temporary satisfaction, always, in my mind, left a mist still hanging over the subject. At last, when reading a second or third time the chapters on Reasoning in the second volume of Dugald Stewart, interrogating myself on every point, and following out as far as I knew how, every topic of thought which the book suggested, I came upon an idea of his respecting the use of axioms in ratiocination, which I did not remember to have before noticed, but which now, in meditating on it, seemed to me not only true of axioms, but of all general propositions whatever, and to be the key of the whole perplexity. From this germ grew the theory of the Syllogism propounded in the second Book of the Logic; which I immediately fixed by writing it out. And now, with greatly increased hope of being able to produce a work on Logic, of some originality and value, I proceeded to write the First Book, from the rough and imperfect draft I had already made. What I now wrote became the basis of that part of the subsequent Treatise; except that it did not contain the Theory of Kinds, which was a later addition, suggested by otherwise inextricable difficulties which met me in my first attempt to work out the subject of some of the concluding chapters of the Third Book. At the point which I have now reached I made a halt, which lasted five years. I had come to the end of my tether; I could make nothing satisfactory of Induction, at this time. I continued to read any book which seemed to promise light on the subject, and appropriated, as well as I could, the results; but for a long time I found nothing which seemed to open to me any very important vein of meditation.

In 1832 I wrote several papers for the first series of Tait's Magazine, and one for a quarterly periodical called the Jurist, which had been founded and for a short time carried on by a set of friends, all lawyers and law reformers, with several of whom I was acquainted. The paper in question is the one on the rights and duties of the State respecting Corporation and Church Property, now standing first among the collected "Dissertations and Discussions";

where one of my articles in Tait, "The Currency Juggle," also appears. In the whole mass of what I wrote previous to these, there is nothing of sufficient permanent value to justify reprinting. The paper in the Jurist, which I still think a very complete discussion of the rights of the State over Foundations, shewed both sides of my opinions, asserting as firmly as I should have done at any time, the doctrine that all endowments are national property, which the government may and ought to control; but not, as I should once have done, condemning endowments in themselves, and proposing that they should be taken to pay off the national debt. On the contrary, I urged strenuously the importance of having a provision for education, not dependent on the mere demand of the market, that is, on the knowledge and discernment of average parents, but calculated to establish and keep up a higher standard of instruction than is likely to be spontaneously demanded by the buyers of the article. All these opinions have been confirmed and strengthened by the whole course of my subsequent reflections.

CHAPTER VI

COMMENCEMENT OF THE MOST VALUABLE
FRIENDSHIP OF MY LIFE. MY FATHER'S DEATH.
WRITINGS AND OTHER PROCEEDINGS UP TO 1840

IT was at the period of my mental progress which I have now reached that I formed the friendship which has been the honour and chief blessing of my existence, as well as the source of a great part of all that I have attempted to do, or hope to effect hereafter, for human improvement. My[1] first introduction to the lady who, after a friendship of twenty years, consented to become my wife, was in 1830, when I was in my twenty-fifth and she in her twenty-third year. With her husband's family it was the renewal of an old acquaintanceship. His grandfather lived in the next house to my father's in Newington Green, and I had sometimes when a boy been invited to play in the old gentleman's garden. He was a fine specimen of the old Scotch puritan; stern, severe, and powerful, but very kind to children, on whom such men make a lasting impression. Although it was years after my introduction to Mrs. Taylor before my acquaintance with her became at all intimate or confidential, I very soon felt her to be the most admirable person I had ever known. It is not to be supposed that she was, or that any one, at the age at which I first saw her, could be, all that she afterwards became. Least of all could this be true of her, with whom self-improvement, progress in the highest and in all senses, was a law of her nature; a necessity equally from the ardour with which she sought it, and from the spontaneous tendency of faculties which could not receive an impression or an experience without making it the source or the occasion of an accession of wisdom. Up to the time when I first saw her, her rich and powerful nature had chiefly unfolded itself according to the received type of feminine genius. To her outer circle she was a beauty and a wit, with an air of natural distinction, felt by all who approached her: to the inner, a

[1] For Mill's considerably longer original version of this passage, which his wife helped him revise and condense, see *The Early Draft*, pp. 191–200. On their relationship, and especially on the much-debated question of her influence on his thought, see the works by Hayek, Pappe, Mineka, and Robson ("Harriet Taylor and John Stuart Mill") listed in the Select Bibliography, and *The Early Draft*, pp. 22–28.

woman of deep and strong feeling, of penetrating and intuitive intelligence, and of an eminently meditative and poetic nature. Married at a very early age, to a most upright, brave, and honourable
man, of liberal opinions and good education, but without the intellectual or artistic tastes which would have made him a companion
for her — though a steady and affectionate friend, for whom she
had true esteem and the strongest affection through life, and whom
she most deeply lamented when dead; shut out by the social disabilities of women from any adequate exercise of her highest
faculties in action on the world without; her life was one of inward
meditation, varied by familiar intercourse with a small circle of
friends, of whom one only (long since deceased)[2] was a person of
genius, or of capacities of feeling or intellect kindred with her
own, but all had more or less of alliance with her in sentiments and
opinions. Into this circle I had the good fortune to be admitted,
and I soon perceived that she possessed in combination, the
qualities which in all other persons whom I had known I had been
only too happy to find singly. In her, complete emancipation
from every kind of superstition (including that which attributes a
pretended perfection to the order of nature and the universe), and
an earnest protest against many things which are still part of the
established constitution of society, resulted not from the hard intellect but from strength of noble and elevated feeling, and co-
existed with a highly reverential nature. In general spiritual characteristics, as well as in temperament and organisation, I have often
compared her, as she was at this time, to Shelley: but in thought
and intellect, Shelley, so far as his powers were developed in his
short life, was but a child compared with what she ultimately became. Alike in the highest regions of speculation and in the smallest
practical concerns of daily life, her mind was the same perfect instrument, piercing to the very heart and marrow of the matter;
always seizing the essential idea or principle. The same exactness
and rapidity of operation, pervading as it did her sensitive as well
as her mental faculties, would with her gifts of feeling and imagination have fitted her to be a consummate artist, as her fiery and
tender soul and her vigorous eloquence would certainly have made
her a great orator, and her profound knowledge of human nature
and discernment and sagacity in practical life, would in the times

2 The musical composer Eliza Flower.

when such a *carrière*[3] was open to women, have made her eminent
among the rulers of mankind. Her intellectual gifts did but minister
to a moral character at once the noblest and the best balanced
which I have ever met with in life. Her unselfishness was not that
of a taught system of duties, but of a heart which thoroughly
identified itself with the feelings of others, and often went to excess
in consideration for them, by imaginatively investing their feelings
with the intensity of its own. The passion of justice might have
been thought to be her strongest feeling, but for her boundless gen-
erosity, and a lovingness ever ready to pour itself forth upon any
or all human beings who were capable of giving the smallest feeling
in return. The rest of her moral characteristics were such as naturally accompany these qualities of mind and heart: the most
genuine modesty combined with the loftiest pride; a simplicity and
sincerity which were absolute, towards all who were fit to receive
them; the utmost scorn of whatever was mean and cowardly, and
a burning indignation at everything brutal or tyrannical, faithless or
dishonorable in conduct and character; while making the broadest
distinction between *mala in se* and mere *mala prohibita* — between
acts giving evidence of intrinsic badness in feeling and character,
and those which are only violations of conventions either good or
bad, violations which whether in themselves right or wrong, are
capable of being committed by persons in every other respect loveable or admirable.

To be admitted into any degree of mental intercourse with a
being of these qualities, could not but have a most beneficial influence on my developement; though the effect was only gradual,
and many years elapsed before her mental progress and mine went
forward in the complete companionship they at last attained. The
benefit I received was far greater than any which I could hope to
give; though to her, who had at first reached her opinions by the
moral intuition of a character of strong feeling, there was doubtless
help as well as encouragement to be derived from one who had
arrived at many of the same results by study and reasoning: and in
the rapidity of her intellectual growth, her mental activity, which
converted everything into knowledge, doubtless drew from me, as
it did from other sources, many of its materials. What I owe, even
intellectually, to her, is, in its detail, almost infinite; of its general

[3] Course, career.

character, a few words will give some, though a very imperfect, idea. With those who, like all the best and wisest of mankind, are dissatisfied with human life as it is, and whose feelings are wholly identified with its radical amendment, there are two main regions of thought. One is the region of ultimate aims; the constituent elements of the highest realizable ideal of human life. The other is that of the immediately useful and practically attainable. In both these departments I have acquired more from her teaching, than from all other sources taken together. And, to say truth, it is in these two extremes principally, that real certainty lies. My own strength lay wholly in the uncertain and slippery intermediate region, that of theory, or moral and political science: respecting the conclusions of which, in any of the forms in which I have received or originated them, whether as political economy, analytic psychology, logic, philosophy of history, or anything else, it is not the least of my intellectual obligations to her that I have derived from her a wise scepticism, which, while it has not hindered me from following out the honest exercise of my thinking faculties to whatever conclusions might result from it, has put me on my guard against holding or announcing those conclusions with a degree of confidence which the nature of such speculations does not warrant, and has kept my mind not only open to admit, but prompt to welcome and eager to seek, even on the questions on which I have most meditated, any prospect of clearer perceptions and better evidence. I have often received praise, which in my own right I only partially deserve, for the greater practicality which is supposed to be found in my writings, compared with those of most thinkers who have been equally addicted to large generalizations. The writings in which this quality has been observed, were not the work of one mind, but of the fusion of two, one of them as preeminently practical in its judgments and perceptions of things present, as it was high and bold in its anticipations for a remote futurity.

At the present period, however, this influence was only one among many which were helping to shape the character of my future development: and even after it became, I may truly say, the presiding principle of my mental progress, it did not alter the path, but only made me move forward more boldly and at the same time more cautiously in the same course. The only actual revolution which has ever taken place in my modes of thinking, was already complete. My new tendencies had to be confirmed in some respects, moderated in others: but the only substantial changes of opinion that were yet to come, related to politics, and consisted, on one hand, in a greater approximation, so far as regards the ultimate prospects of humanity, to a qualified Socialism, and on the other, a shifting of my political ideal from pure democracy, as commonly understood by its partisans, to the modified form of it, which is set forth in my "Considerations on Representative Government."

This last change, which took place very gradually, dates its commencement from my reading, or rather study, of M. de Tocqueville's "Democracy in America," which fell into my hands immediately after its first appearance. In that remarkable work, the excellencies of Democracy were pointed out in a more conclusive, because a more specific manner than I had ever known them to be even by the most enthusiastic democrats; while the specific dangers which beset Democracy, considered as the government of the numerical majority, were brought into equally strong light, and subjected to a masterly analysis, not as reasons for resisting what the author considered as an inevitable result of human progress, but as indications of the weak points of popular government, the defences by which it needs to be guarded, and the correctives which must be added to it in order that while full play is given to its beneficial tendencies, those which are of a different nature may be neutralized or mitigated. I was now well prepared for speculations of this character, and from this time onward my own thoughts moved more and more in the same channel, though the consequent modifications in my practical political creed were spread over many years, as would be shewn by comparing my first review of "Democracy in America," written and published in 1835, with the one in 1840 (reprinted in the "Dissertations"), and this last, with the "Considerations on Representative Government."

A collateral subject on which also I derived great benefit from the study of Tocqueville, was the fundamental question of Centralization. The powerful philosophic analysis which he applied to American and to French experience, led him to attach the utmost importance to the performance of as much of the collective business of society, as can safely be so performed, by the people themselves, without any intervention of the executive government, either to supersede their agency, or to dictate the manner of its exercise. He viewed this practical political activity of the individual citizen, not only as one of the most effectual means of training the social feelings and practical intelligence of the people, so important in themselves and so indispensable to good government, but also as the specific counteractive to some of the characteristic infirmities of Democracy, and a necessary protection against its degenerating into the only despotism of which in the modern world there is real danger — the absolute rule of the head of the executive over a congregation of isolated individuals, all equals but all slaves. There was, indeed, no immediate peril from this source on the British side of the channel, where nine tenths of the internal business which elsewhere devolves on the government, was transacted by agencies independent of it; where Centralization was, and is, the subject not only of rational disapprobation, but of unreasoning prejudice; where jealousy of Government interference was a blind feeling preventing or resisting even the most beneficial exertion of legis- lative authority to correct the abuses of what pretends to be local self-government, but is, too often, selfish mismanagement of local interests, by a jobbing and *borné*[4] local oligarchy. But the more certain the public were to go wrong on the side opposed to Cen- tralization, the greater danger was there lest philosophic reformers should fall into the contrary error, and overlook the mischiefs of which they had been spared the painful experience. I was myself, at this very time, actively engaged in defending important measures, such as the great Poor Law Reform of 1834, against an irrational clamour grounded on the Anti-Centralization prejudice: and had it not been for the lessons of Tocqueville, I do not know that I might not, like many reformers before me, have been hurried into the excess opposite to that which, being the one prevalent in my own country, it was generally my business to combat. As it is, I have steered carefully between the two errors, and whether I have or have not drawn the line between them exactly in the right place, I have at least insisted with equal emphasis upon the evils on both sides, and have made the means of reconciling the advantages of both, a subject of serious study.

In the meanwhile had taken place the election of the first Re- formed Parliament, which included several of the most notable of my Radical friends and acquaintances; Grote, Roebuck, Buller, Sir William Molesworth, John and Edward Romilly, and several

4 Narrow-minded.

more; besides Warburton, Strutt, and others, who were in parliament already. Those who thought themselves, and were called by their friends, the philosophic radicals, had now, it seemed, a fair opportunity, in a more advantageous position than they had ever before occupied, for shewing what was in them; and I, as well as my father, founded great hopes on them. These hopes were destined to be disappointed. The men were honest, and faithful to their opinions, as far as votes were concerned; often in spite of much discouragement. When measures were proposed, flagrantly at variance with their principles, such as the Irish Coercion Bill, or the Canada coercion in 1837, they came forward manfully, and braved any amount of hostility and prejudice rather than desert the right. But on the whole they did very little to promote any opinions; they had little enterprise, little activity; they left the lead of the radical portion of the House to the old hands, to Hume and O'Connell. A partial exception must be made in favour of one or two of the younger men; and in the case of Roebuck, it is his title to permanent remembrance, that in the very first year during which he sat in Parliament he originated (or reoriginated after the unsuccessful attempt of Mr. Brougham) the parliamentary movement for National Education; and that he was the first to commence, and for years carried on almost alone, the contest for the self-government of the Colonies. Nothing, on the whole equal to these two things, was done by any other individual, even of those from whom most was expected. And now, on a calm retrospect, I can perceive that the men were less in fault than we supposed, and that we had expected too much from them.[5] They were in unfavourable circumstances. Their lot was cast in the ten years of inevitable reaction, when the Reform excitement being over, and

[5] Mill had not yet achieved this calm retrospect when he first drafted the *Autobiography*. In the original MS he specifically names Grote as the man whom they looked to for leadership: "Nobody disappointed my father and me more than Grote because no one else had so much in his power. We had long known him fainthearted, ever despairing of success, thinking all obstacles gigantic; but the Reform Bill excitement seemed for a time to make a new man of him: he had grown hopeful, and seemed as if he could almost become energetic. When brought face to face however with an audience opposed to his opinions, when called on to beat up against the stream, he was found wanting. . . . If his courage and energy had been equal to the circumstances, or to his knowledge and abilities, the history of those ten years of relapse into Toryism might have been very different" (*The Early Draft*, p. 155).

the few legislative improvements which the public really called for having been rapidly effected, power gravitated back in its natural direction, to those who were for keeping things as they were; when the public mind desired rest, and was less disposed than at any other period since the peace, to let itself be moved by attempts to work up the reform feeling into fresh activity in favour of new things. It would have required a great political leader, which no one is to be blamed for not being, to have effected really great things by parliamentary discussion when the nation was in this mood. My father and I had hoped that some competent leader might arise; some man of philosophic attainments and popular talents, who could have put heart into the many younger or less distinguished men that would have been ready to join him — could have made them available, to the extent of their talents, in bringing advanced ideas before the public — could have used the House of Commons as a rostra or a teacher's chair for instructing and impelling the public mind; and would either have forced the Whigs to receive their measures from him, or have taken the lead of the Reform party out of their hands. Such a leader there would have been, if my father had been in Parliament. For want of such a man, the instructed Radicals sank into a mere *côté gauche*[6] of the Whig party. With a keen, and as I now think, an exaggerated sense of the possibilities which were open to the Radicals if they made even ordinary exertion for their opinions, I laboured from this time till 1839, both by personal influence with some of them, and by writings, to put ideas into their heads and purpose into their hearts. I did some good with Charles Buller, and some with Sir William Molesworth; both of whom did valuable service, but were unhappily cut off almost in the beginning of their usefulness. On the whole, however, my attempt was vain. To have had a chance of succeeding in it, required a different position from mine. It was a task only for one who, being himself in Parliament, could have mixed with the radical members in daily consultation, could himself have taken the initiative, and instead of urging others to lead, could have summoned them to follow.

What I could do by writing, I did. During the year 1833 I continued working in the Examiner with Fonblanque, who at that time was zealous in keeping up the fight for radicalism against the Whig

6 Left wing.

ministry. During the session of 1834 I wrote comments on passing events, of the nature of newspaper articles (under the title "Notes on the Newspapers"), in the Monthly Repository, a magazine conducted by Mr. Fox, well known as a preacher and political orator, and subsequently as member of parliament for Oldham; with whom I had lately become acquainted, and for whose sake chiefly I wrote in his Magazine. I contributed several other articles to this periodical, the most considerable of which (on the theory of poetry) is reprinted in the "Dissertations." Altogether, the writings (independently of those in newspapers) which I published from 1832 to 1834, amount to a large volume. This, however, includes abstracts of several of Plato's Dialogues, with introductory remarks, which, though not published until 1834, had been written several years earlier; and which I afterwards, on various occasions, found to have been read, and their authorship known, by more people than were aware of anything else which I had written, up to that time. To complete the tale of my writings at this period, I may add that in 1833, at the request of Bulwer, who was just then completing his "England and the English" (a work, at that time, greatly in advance of the public mind), I wrote for him a critical account of Bentham's philosophy, a small part of which he incorporated in his text, and printed the rest (with an honorable acknowledgment) as an Appendix. In this, along with the favorable, a part also of the unfavourable side of my estimation of Bentham's doctrines, considered as a complete philosophy, was for the first time put into print.

But an opportunity soon offered by which, as it seemed, I might have it in my power to give more effectual aid, and at the same time, stimulus, to the "philosophic radical" party, than I had done hitherto. One of the projects occasionally talked of between my father and me, and some of the parliamentary and other Radicals who frequented his house, was the foundation of a periodical organ of philosophic radicalism, to take the place which the Westminster Review had been intended to fill: and the scheme had gone so far as to bring under discussion the pecuniary contributions which could be looked for, and the choice of an editor. Nothing however came of it for some time: but in the summer of 1834 Sir William Molesworth, himself a laborious student, and a precise and metaphysical thinker capable of aiding the cause by his pen as well as by his purse, spontaneously proposed to establish a Review, provided I would consent to be the real, if I could not be the ostensible, editor. Such a proposal was not to be refused; and the review was founded, at first under the title of the London Review, and afterwards under that of the London and Westminster, Molesworth having bought the Westminster from its proprietor General Thompson, and merged the two into one. In the years between 1834 and 1840 the conduct of this review occupied the greater part of my spare time. In the beginning, it did not, as a whole, by any means represent my opinions. I was under the necessity of conceding much to my inevitable associates. The Review was established to be the representative of the "philosophic radicals," with most of whom I was now at issue on many essential points, and among whom I could not even claim to be the most important individual. My father's cooperation as a writer we all deemed indispensable, and he wrote largely in it until prevented by his last illness. The subjects of his articles, and the strength and decision with which his opinions were expressed in them, made the Review at first derive its tone and colouring from him much more than from any of the other writers. I could not exercise editorial control over his articles, and I was sometimes obliged to sacrifice to him portions of my own. The old Westminster Review doctrines, but little modified, thus formed the staple of the review; but I hoped, by the side of these, to introduce other ideas and another tone, and to obtain for my own shade of opinion a fair representation, along with those of other members of the party. With this end chiefly in view, I made it one of the peculiarities of the work that every article should bear an initial, or some other signature, and be held to express the opinions solely of the individual writer; the editor being only responsible for its being worth publishing, and not in conflict with the objects for which the Review was set on foot. I had an opportunity of putting in practice my scheme of conciliation between the old and the new "philosophic radicalism" by the choice of a subject for my own first contribution. Professor Sedgwick, a man of eminence in a particular walk of natural science, but who should not have trespassed into philosophy, had lately published his Discourse on the Studies of Cambridge, which had as its most prominent feature an intemperate assault on analytic psychology and utilitarian ethics, in the form of an attack on Locke and Paley. This had excited great indignation in my father and others, which I thought it fully deserved. And here, I imagined, was an opportu-

nity of at the same time repelling an unjust attack, and inserting
into my defence of Hartleianism and Utilitarianism a number of
the opinions which constituted my view of those subjects, as distinguished from that of my old associates. In this I partially succeeded, though my relation to my father would have made it painful
to me in any case, and impossible in a review for which he wrote,
to speak out my whole mind on the subject at this time.

I am, however, inclined to think that my father was not so much
opposed as he seemed, to the modes of thought in which I believed
myself to differ from him; that he did injustice to his own opinions
by the unconscious exaggerations of an intellect emphatically polemical; and that when thinking without an adversary in view, he
was willing to make room for a great portion of the truths he
seemed to deny. I have frequently observed that he made large
allowance in practice for considerations which seemed to have no
place in his theory. His "Fragment on Mackintosh," which he
wrote and published about this time, although I greatly admired
some parts of it, I read as a whole with more pain than pleasure;
yet on reading it again, long after, I found little in the opinions it
contains, but what I think in the main just; and I can even sympa-
thize in his disgust at the *verbiage* of Mackintosh, though his asper-
ity towards it went not only beyond what was judicious, but beyond
what was even fair. One thing which I thought, at the time, of good
augury, was the very favorable reception he gave to Tocqueville's
"Democracy in America." It is true, he said and thought much
more about what Tocqueville said in favour of Democracy, than
about what he said of its disadvantages. Still, his high appreciation
of a book which was at any rate an example of a mode of treating
the question of government almost the reverse of his — wholly
inductive and analytical, instead of purely ratiocinative — gave me
great encouragement. He also approved of an article which I published in the first number following the junction of the two reviews,
the Essay reprinted in the Dissertations under the title "Civilization"; into which I threw many of my new opinions, and criticized
rather emphatically the mental and moral tendencies of the time,
on grounds and in a manner which I certainly had not learnt from
him.

All speculation, however, on the possible future developments of
my father's opinions, and on the probabilities of permanent cooperation between him and me in the promulgation of our thoughts,

was doomed to be cut short. During the whole of 1835 his health had been declining: his symptoms became unequivocally those of pulmonary consumption, and after lingering to the last stage of debility, he died on the 23rd of June 1836. Until the last few days of his life there was no apparent abatement of intellectual vigour; his interest in all things and persons that had interested him through life was undiminished, nor did the approach of death cause the smallest wavering (as in so strong and firm a mind it was impossible that it should) in his convictions on the subject of religion. His principal satisfaction, after he knew that his end was near, seemed to be the thought of what he had done to make the world better than he found it; and his chief regret in not living longer, that he had not had time to do more.

His place is an eminent one in the literary, and even in the political history of his country; and it is far from honourable to the generation which has benefitted by his worth, that he is so seldom mentioned, and, compared with men far his inferiors, so little remembered. This is probably to be ascribed mainly to two causes. In the first place, the thought of him merges too much in the deservedly superior fame of Bentham. Yet he was anything but Bentham's mere follower or disciple. Precisely because he was himself one of the most original thinkers of his time, he was one of the earliest to appreciate and adopt the most important mass of original thought which had been produced by the generation preceding him. His mind and Bentham's were essentially of different construction. He had not all Bentham's high qualities, but neither had Bentham all his. It would, indeed, be ridiculous to claim for him the praise of having accomplished for mankind such splendid services as Bentham's. He did not revolutionize — or rather create — one of the great departments of human thought. But, leaving out of the reckoning all that portion of his labours in which he benefitted by what Bentham had done, and counting only what he achieved in a province in which Bentham had done nothing, that of analytic psychology, he will be known to posterity as one of the greatest names in that most important branch of speculation, on which all the moral and political sciences ultimately rest, and will mark one of the essential stages in its progress. The other reason, which has made his fame less than he deserved, is that notwithstanding the great number of his opinions which, partly through his own efforts, have now been generally adopted, there was on the whole a marked opposition between his spirit and that of the present time. As Brutus was called the last of the Romans,[7] so was he the last of the eighteenth century: he continued its tone of thought and sentiment into the nineteenth (though not unmodified nor unimproved), partaking neither in the good nor in the bad influences of the reaction against the eighteenth century, which was the great characteristic of the first half of the nineteenth. The eighteenth century was a great age, an age of strong and brave men, and he was a fit companion for its strongest and bravest. By his writings and his personal influence he was a great centre of light to his generation. During his later years he was quite as much the head and leader of the intellectual radicals in England, as Voltaire was of the *philosophes* of France. It is only one of his minor merits, that he was the originator of all sound statesmanship in regard to the subject of his largest work, India. He wrote on no subject which he did not enrich with valuable thought, and excepting the "Elements of Political Economy," a very useful book when first written, but which has now for some time finished its work, it will be long before any of his books will be wholly superseded, or will cease to be instructive reading to students of their subjects. In the power of influencing by mere force of mind and character, the convictions and purposes of others, and in the strenuous exertion of that power to promote freedom and progress, he left, as far as my knowledge extends, no equal among men, and but one among women.[8]

Though acutely sensible of my own inferiority in the qualities by which he acquired his personal ascendancy, I had now to try what it might be possible for me to accomplish without him; and the Review was the instrument on which I built my chief hopes of establishing a useful influence over the liberal and democratic section of the public mind. Deprived of my father's aid, I was also exempted from the restraints and retinences by which that aid had been purchased. I did not feel that there was any other radical writer or politician to whom I was bound to defer, further than consisted with my own opinions: and having the complete confidence of Molesworth, I resolved henceforth to give full scope to my own opinions and modes of thought, and to open the Review

7 In *Julius Caesar* (V.iii.99), it is Brutus who uses these words to refer to Titinius and Cassius.
8 Mill's wife.

widely to all writers who were in sympathy with Progress as I understood it, even though I should lose by it the support of my former associates. Carlyle, consequently, became from this time a frequent writer in the Review; Sterling, soon after, an occasional one; and though each individual article continued to be the expression of the private sentiments of its writer, the general tone conformed in some tolerable degree to my opinions. For the conduct of the Review, under and in conjunction with me, I associated with myself a young Scotchman of the name of Robertson, who had some ability and information, much industry, and an active scheming head, full of devices for making the Review more saleable, and on whose capacities in that direction I founded a good deal of hope: insomuch that when Molesworth, in the beginning of 1837, became tired of carrying on the Review at a loss, and desirous of getting rid of it (he had done *his* part honourably, and at no small pecuniary cost), I, very imprudently for my own pecuniary interest, and very much from reliance on Robertson's devices, determined to continue it at my own risk, until his plans should have had a fair trial. The devices were good, and I never had any reason to change my opinion of them. But I do not believe that any devices would have made a radical and democratic review defray its expenses, including a paid editor or sub editor, and a liberal payment to writers. I myself and several frequent contributors gave our labour gratuitously, as we had done for Molesworth; but the paid contributors continued to be remunerated on the usual scale of the Edinburgh and Quarterly Reviews; and this could not be done from the proceeds of the sale.

In the same year, 1837, and in the midst of these occupations, I resumed the Logic. I had not touched my pen on the subject for five years, having been stopped and brought to a halt on the threshold of Induction. I had gradually discovered that what was mainly wanting, to overcome the difficulties of that branch of the subject, was a comprehensive and at the same time accurate view of the whole circle of physical science, which I feared it would take me a long course of study to acquire; since I knew not of any book, or other guide, that would spread out before me the generalities and processes of the sciences, and I apprehended that I should have no choice but to extract them for myself, as I best could, from the details. Happily for me, Dr. Whewell, early in this year, published his History of the Inductive Sciences. I read it with eagerness, and found in it a considerable approximation to what I wanted. Much, if not most, of the philosophy of the work appeared open to objection; but the materials were there, for my own thoughts to work upon: and the author had given to those materials that first degree of elaboration, which so greatly facilitates and abridges the subsequent labour. I had now obtained what I had been waiting for. Under the impulse given me by the thoughts excited by Dr. Whewell, I read again Sir J. Herschel's Discourse on the Study of Natural Philosophy; and I was able to measure the progress my mind had made, by the great help I now found in this work, though I had read and even reviewed it several years before with little profit. I now set myself vigorously to work out the subject in thought and in writing. The time I bestowed on this had to be stolen from occupations more urgent. I had just two months to spare, at this period, in the intervals of writing for the Review. In these two months I completed the first draft of about a third, the most difficult third, of the book. What I had before written I estimate at another third, so that only one third remained. What I wrote at this time consisted of the remainder of the doctrine of Reasoning (the theory of Trains of Reasoning, and Demonstrative Science), and the greater part of the Book on Induction. When this was done, I had, as it seemed to me, untied all the really hard knots, and the completion of the book had become only a question of time. Having got thus far, I had to leave off in order to write two articles for the next number of the Review. When these were written, I returned to the subject, and now for the first time fell in with Comte's Cours de Philosophie Positive, or rather with the two volumes of it which were all that had at that time been published.

My theory of Induction was substantially completed before I knew of Comte's book; and it is perhaps well that I came to it by a different road from his, since the consequence has been that my treatise contains, what his certainly does not, a reduction of the inductive process to strict rules and to a scientific test, such as the Syllogism is for ratiocination. Comte is always precise and profound on the methods of investigation, but he does not even attempt any exact definition of the conditions of proof: and his writings shew that he never attained a just conception of them. This, however, was specifically the problem which, in treating of Induction, I had proposed to myself. Nevertheless, I gained much from Comte, with which to enrich my chapters in the subsequent rewriting: and his book was of essential service to me in some of the parts which still remained to be thought out. As his subsequent .olumes successively made their appearance, I read them with avidity, but, when he reached the subject of Social Science, with varying feelings. The fourth volume disappointed me: it contained those of his opinions on social subjects with which I most disagree. But the fifth, containing the connected view of history, rekindled all my enthusiasm; which the sixth (or concluding) volume did not materially abate. In a merely logical point of view, the only leading conception for which I am indebted to him is that of the Inverse Deductive Method, as the one chiefly applicable to the complicated subjects of History and Statistics: a process differing from the more common form of the Deductive Method in this, that instead of arriving at its conclusions by general reasoning and verifying them by specific experience (as is the natural order in the deductive branches of physical science), it obtains its generalizations by a collation of specific experience, and verifies them by ascertaining whether they are such as would follow from known general principles. This was an idea entirely new to me when I found it in Comte: and but for him I might not soon (if ever) have arrived at it.

I had been long an ardent admirer of Comte's writings before I had any communication with himself; nor did I ever, to the last, see him in the body. But for some years we were frequent correspondents, until our correspondence became controversial, and our zeal cooled. I was the first to slacken correspondence; he was the first to drop it. I found, and he probably found likewise, that I could do no good to his mind, and that all the good he could do to mine, he did by his books. This would never have led to discontinuance of intercourse, if the differences between us had been on matters of simple doctrine. But they were chiefly on those points of opinion which blended in both of us with our strongest feelings, and determined the entire direction of our aspirations. I had fully agreed with him when he maintained that the mass of mankind, including even their rulers in all the practical departments of life, must, from the necessity of the case, accept most of their opinions on political and social matters, as they do on physical, from the authority of those who have bestowed more study on those subjects than they generally have it in their power to do. This lesson had been strongly impressed on me by the early work of Comte, to which I have adverted. And there was nothing in his great Treatise which I admired more than his remarkable exposition of the benefits which the nations of modern Europe have historically derived from the separation, during the middle ages, of temporal and spiritual power, and the distinct organization of the latter. I agreed with him that the moral and intellectual ascendancy, once exercised by priests, must in time pass into the hands of philosophers, and will naturally do so when they become sufficiently unanimous, and in other respects worthy to possess it. But when he exaggerated this line of thought into a practical system, in which philosophers were to be organized into a kind of corporate hierarchy, invested with almost the same spiritual supremacy (though without any secular power) once possessed by the Catholic church; when I found him relying on this spiritual authority as the only security for good government, the sole bulwark against practical oppression, and expecting that by it a system of despotism in the state and despotism in the family would be rendered innocuous and beneficial; it is not surprising, that while as logicians we were nearly at one, as sociologists we could travel together no further. M. Comte lived to carry out these doctrines to their extremest consequences, by planning, in his last work, the "Système de Politique Positive," the completest system of spiritual and temporal despotism, which ever yet emanated from a human brain, unless possibly that of Ignatius Loyola: a system by which the yoke of general opinion, wielded by an organized body of spiritual teachers and rulers, would be made supreme over every action, and as far as is in human possibility, every thought, of every member of the community, as well in the things which regard only himself, as in those which concern the interests of others. It is but just to say that this work is a considerable improvement, in many points of feeling, over Comte's previous writings on the same subjects: but as an accession to social philosophy, the only value it seems to me to possess consists in putting an end to the notion that no effectual moral authority can be maintained over society without the aid of religious belief; for Comte's work recognizes no religion except that of Humanity, yet it leaves an irresistible conviction that any moral beliefs, concurred in by the community generally, may be brought to bear upon the whole conduct and lives of its individual members with an energy and potency truly alarming to think of. The book stands a monumental warning to thinkers on society and politics, of what happens when once men lose sight, in their speculations, of the value of Liberty and of Individuality.

To return to myself: the Review engrossed, for some time longer, nearly all the time I could devote to authorship, or to thinking with authorship in view. The articles from the London and Westminster Review which are reprinted in the "Dissertations" are scarcely a fourth part of those I wrote. In the conduct of the Review I had two principal objects. One was to free philosophic radicalism from the reproach of sectarian Benthamism. I desired, while retaining the precision of expression, the definiteness of meaning, the contempt of declamatory phrases and vague generalities, which were so honorably characteristic both of Bentham and of my father, to give a wider basis and a more free and genial character to Radical speculations; to shew that there was a Radical philosophy, better and more complete than Bentham's, while recognizing and incorporating all of Bentham's which is permanently valuable. In this first object I, to a certain extent, succeeded. The other thing I attempted, was to stir up the educated Radicals, in and out of Parliament, to exertion, and induce them to make themselves, what I thought by using the proper means, they might become — a powerful party capable of taking the government of the country, or at least of dictating the terms on which they should share it with the Whigs. This attempt was from the first chimerical: partly because the time was unpropitious, the Reform fervour being in its period of ebb, and the Tory influences powerfully rallying; but, still more, because, as Austin so truly said, "the country did not contain the men." Among the Radicals in Parliament there were several qualified to be useful members of an enlightened Radical party, but none capable of forming and leading such a party. The exhortations I addressed to them found no response. One occasion did present itself when there seemed to be room for a bold and successful stroke for Radicalism. Lord Durham had left the ministry, by reason, as was thought, of their not being sufficiently liberal; he afterwards accepted from them the task of ascertaining and removing the causes of the Canadian rebellion: he had shewn a disposition to surround himself at the outset with Radical advisers; one of his earliest measures, a good measure both in intention and in effect, having been disapproved and reversed by the Government at home, he had resigned his post, and placed himself openly in a position of quarrel with the ministers. Here was a possible chief for a Radical party in the person of a man of importance, who was hated by the Tories, and had just been injured by the Whigs. Any one who had the most elementary notions of party tactics, must have attempted to make something of such an opportunity. Lord Durham was bitterly attacked from all sides, inveighed against by enemies, given up by timid friends; while those who would willingly have defended him did not know what to say. He appeared to be returning a defeated and discredited man. I had followed the Canadian events from the beginning; I had been one of the prompters of his prompters; his policy was almost exactly what mine would have been, and I was in a position to defend it. I wrote and published a manifesto in the Review, in which I took the very highest ground in his behalf, claiming for him not mere acquittal, but praise and honour. Instantly a number of other writers took up the tone. I believe there was a portion of truth in what Lord Durham, soon after, with polite exaggeration, said to me — that to this article might be ascribed the almost triumphal reception which he met with on his arrival in England. I believe it to have been the word in season, which, at a critical moment, does much to decide the result; the touch which determines whether a stone, set in motion at the top of an eminence, shall roll down on one side or on the other. All hopes connected with Lord Durham as a politician soon vanished; but with regard to Canadian, and generally to colonial policy, the cause was gained: Lord Durham's report, written by Charles Buller, partly under the inspiration of Wakefield, began a new era; its recommendations, extending to complete internal self-government, were in full operation in Canada within two or three years, and have been since extended to nearly all the other colonies, of European race, which have any claim to the character of important communities. And I may say that in successfully upholding the reputation of Lord Durham and his advisers at the most important moment, I contributed materially to this result.

One other case occurred during my conduct of the Review, which similarly illustrated the effect of taking a prompt initiative. I believe that the early success and reputation of Carlyle's French Revolution, were considerably accelerated by what I wrote about it in the Review. Immediately on its publication, and before the commonplace critics, all whose rules and modes of judgment it set at defiance, had time to preoccupy the public with their disapproval of it, I wrote and published a review of the book, hailing it as one of those productions of genius which are above all rules, and are a law to themselves. Neither in this case nor in that of Lord Durham do I ascribe the impression, which I think was produced by what I wrote, to any particular merit of execution: indeed, in at least one of the cases (the article on Carlyle) I do not think the execution was good. And in both instances, I am persuaded that anybody, in a position to be read, who had expressed the same opinion at the same precise time, and had made any tolerable statement of the just grounds for it, would have produced the same effect. But, after the complete failure of my hopes of putting a new life into radical politics by means of the Review, I am glad to look back on these two instances of success in an honest attempt to do immediate service to things and persons that deserved it.

After the last hope of the formation of a Radical party had disappeared, it was time for me to stop the heavy expenditure of time and money which the Review cost me. It had to some extent answered my personal purpose, as a vehicle for my opinions. It had enabled me to express in print much of my altered mode of thought, and to separate myself in a marked manner from the narrower Benthamism of my early writings. This was done by the general tone of all I wrote, including various purely literary articles, but especially by the two papers (reprinted in the Dissertations) which attempted a philosophical estimate of Bentham and of Coleridge. In the first of these, while doing full justice to the merits of Bentham, I pointed out what I thought the errors and deficiencies of his philosophy. The substance of this criticism I still think perfectly just; but I have sometimes doubted whether it was right to publish it at that time. I have often felt that Bentham's philosophy, as an instrument of progress, has been to some extent discredited before it had done its work, and that to lend a hand towards lowering its reputation was doing more harm than service to improvement. Now however when a counter-reaction appears to be setting in towards what is good in Benthamism, I can look with more satisfaction on this criticism of its defects, especially as I have myself balanced it by vindications of the fundamental principles of Bentham's philosophy, which are reprinted along with it in the same collection. In the essay on Coleridge I attempted to characterize the European reaction against the negative philosophy of the eighteenth century: and here, if the effect only of this one paper were to be considered, I might be thought to have erred by giving undue prominence to the favourable side, as I had done in the case of Bentham to the unfavourable. In both cases, the impetus with which I had detached myself from what was untenable in the doctrines of Bentham and of the eighteenth century, may have carried me, though in appearance rather than in reality, too far on the contrary side. But as far as relates to the article on Coleridge, my defence is, that I was writing for Radicals and Liberals, and it was my business to dwell most on that in writers of a different school, from the knowledge of which they might derive most improvement.

The number of the Review which contained the paper on Coleridge, was the last which was published during my proprietorship. In the spring of 1840 I made over the Review to Mr. Hickson, who had been a frequent and very useful unpaid contributor under my management; only stipulating that the change should be marked by a resumption of the old name, that of Westminster Review. Under that name Mr. Hickson conducted it for ten years, on the plan of dividing among contributors only the net proceeds of the Review, giving his own labour as writer and editor gratuitously. Under the difficulty in obtaining writers, which arose from this low scale of payment, it is highly creditable to him that he was able to maintain, in some tolerable degree, the character of the Review as an organ of radicalism and progress. I did not cease altogether to write for the Review, but continued to send it occasional contributions, not, however, exclusively; for the greater circulation of the Edinburgh Review induced me from this time to offer articles to it also when I had anything to say for which it appeared to be a suitable vehicle. And the concluding volumes of "Democracy in America" having just then come out, I inaugurated myself as a contributor to the Edinburgh by the article on that work, which heads the second volume of the "Dissertations."

CHAPTER VII

GENERAL VIEW OF THE REMAINDER
OF MY LIFE

FROM this time, what is worth relating of my life will come into a very small compass; for I have no further mental changes to tell of, but only, as I hope, a continued mental progress; which does not admit of a consecutive history, and the results of which, if real, will be best found in my writings. I shall therefore greatly abridge the chronicle of my subsequent years.

The first use I made of the leisure which I gained by disconnecting myself from the Review, was to finish the Logic. In July and August 1838 I had found an interval in which to execute what was still undone of the original draft of the Third Book. In working out the logical theory of those laws of nature which are not laws of Causation, nor corollaries from such laws, I was led to recognize Kinds as realities in nature, and not mere distinctions for convenience; a light which I had not obtained when the First Book was written, and which made it necessary for me to modify and enlarge several chapters of that Book. The Book on Language and Classification, and the chapter on the Classification of Fallacies, were drafted in the autumn of the same year; the remainder of the work in the summer and autumn of 1840. From April following to the end of 1841, my spare time was devoted to a complete rewriting of the book from its commencement. It is in this way that all my books have been composed. They were always written at least twice over; a first draft of the entire work was completed to the very end of the subject, then the whole begun again *de novo;* but incorporating, in the second writing, all sentences and parts of sentences of the old draft, which appeared as suitable to my purpose as anything which I could write in lieu of them. I have found great advantages in this system of double redaction. It combines, better than any other mode of composition, the freshness and vigour of the first conception, with the superior precision and completeness resulting from prolonged thought. In my own case, moreover, I have found that the patience necessary for a careful elaboration of the details of exposition and expression, costs much less effort after the entire subject has been once gone through, and the substance of all that I find to say has in some manner, however imperfect, been got upon paper. The only thing which I am careful, in the first draft, to make as perfect as I am able, is the arrangement. If that is bad, the whole thread on which the ideas string themselves becomes twisted; thoughts placed in a wrong connexion are not expounded in a manner that suits the right, and a first draft with this original vice is next to useless as a foundation for the final treatment.

During the rewriting of the Logic, Dr. Whewell's Philosophy of the Inductive Sciences made its appearance; a circumstance fortunate for me, as it gave me what I greatly desired, a full treatment of the subject by an antagonist, and enabled me to present my ideas with greater clearness and emphasis as well as fuller and more varied development, in defending them against definite objections, and confronting them distinctly with an opposite theory. The controversies with Dr. Whewell, as well as much matter derived from Comte, were first introduced into the book in the course of the rewriting.

At the end of 1841, the book being ready for press, I offered it to Murray, who kept it until too late for publication that season, and then refused it, for reasons which could just as well have been given at first. But I have had no cause to regret a rejection which led to my offering it to Mr. Parker, by whom it was published in the spring of 1843. My original expectations of success were extremely limited. Archbishop Whately had indeed rehabilitated the name of Logic, and the study of the forms, rules, and fallacies of Ratiocination; and Dr. Whewell's writings had begun to excite an interest in the other part of my subject, the theory of Induction. A treatise, however, on a matter so abstract, could not be expected to be popular; it could only be a book for students, and students on such subjects were not only (at least in England) few, but addicted chiefly to the opposite school of metaphysics, the ontological and "innate principles" school. I therefore did not expect that the book would have many readers, or approvers; and looked for little practical effect from it, save that of keeping the tradition unbroken of what I thought a better philosophy. What hopes I had of exciting any immediate attention, were mainly grounded on the polemical propensities of Dr. Whewell; who, I thought, from observation of his conduct in other cases, would probably do something to bring the book into notice, by replying, and that promptly, to the attack on his opinions. He did reply, but not till 1850, just in time for me to answer him in the third edition. How the book came to have, for a work of the kind, so much success, and what sort of persons compose the bulk of those who have bought, I will not venture to say read, it, I have never thoroughly understood. But taken in conjunction with the many proofs which have since been given of a revival of speculation, speculation too of a free kind, in many quarters, and above all (where at one time I should have least expected it) in the Universities, the fact becomes partially intelligible. I have never indulged the illusion that the book had made any considerable impression on philosophical opinion. The German, or *à priori* view of human knowledge, and of the knowing faculties, is likely for some time longer (though it may be hoped in a diminishing degree) to predominate among those who occupy themselves with such enquiries, both here and on the Continent. But the "System of Logic" supplies what was much wanted, a text-book of the opposite doctrine — that which derives all knowledge from experience, and all moral and intellectual qualities principally from the direction given to the associations. I make as humble an estimate as anybody of what either an analysis of logical processes, or any possible canons of evidence, can do by themselves, towards guiding or rectifying the operations of the understanding. Combined with other requisites, I certainly do think them of great use; but whatever may be the practical value of a true philosophy of these matters, it is hardly possible to exaggerate the mischiefs of a false one. The notion that truths external to the mind may be known by intuition or consciousness, independently of observation and experience, is, I am persuaded, in these times, the great intellectual support of false doctrines and bad institutions. By the aid of this theory, every inveterate belief and every intense feeling, of which the origin is not remembered, is enabled to dispense with the obligation of justifying itself by reason, and is erected into its own all-sufficient voucher and justification. There never was such an instrument devised for consecrating all deep seated prejudices. And the chief strength of this false philosophy in morals, politics, and religion, lies in the appeal which it is accustomed to make to the evidence of mathematics and of the cognate branches of physical science. To expel it from these, is to drive it from its stronghold: and because this had never been effectually done, the intuitive school, even after what my father had written in his Analysis of the Mind, had in appearance, and as far as published writings were concerned, on the whole the best of the argument. In attempting to clear up the real nature of the evidence of mathematical and physical truths, the "System of Logic" met the intuition philosophers on ground on which they had previously been deemed unassailable; and gave its own explanation, from experience and association, of that peculiar character of what are called necessary truths, which is adduced as proof that their evidence must come from a deeper source than experience. Whether this has been done effectually, is still *sub judice;* and even then, to deprive a mode of thought so strongly rooted in human prejudices and partialities, of its mere speculative support, goes but a very little way towards overcoming it; but though only a step, it is a quite indispensable one; for since, after all, prejudice can only be successfully combated by philosophy, no way can really be made against it permanently until it has been shewn not to have philosophy on its side.

Being now released from any active concern in temporary politics, and from any literary occupation involving personal communication with contributors and others, I was enabled to indulge the inclination, natural to thinking persons when the age of boyish vanity is once past, for limiting my own society to a very few persons. General society, as now carried on in England, is so insipid an affair, even to the persons who make it what it is, that it is kept up for any reason rather than the pleasure it affords. All serious discussion on matters on which opinions differ, being considered ill bred, and the national deficiency in liveliness and sociability having prevented the cultivation of the art of talking agreeably on trifles, in which the French of the last century so much excelled, the sole attraction of what is called society to those who are not at the top of the tree, is the hope of being aided to climb a little higher in it; while to those who are already at the top, it is chiefly a compliance with custom, and with the supposed requirements of their station. To a person of any but a very common order in thought or feeling, such society, unless he has personal objects to serve by it, must be supremely unattractive: and most people, in the present day, of any really high class of intellect, make their contact with it so slight, and at such long intervals, as to be almost considered as retiring from it altogether. Those persons of any mental superiority who do otherwise, are, almost without exception, greatly deteriorated by it. Not to mention loss of time, the tone of their feelings is lowered: they become less in earnest about those of their opinions respecting which they must remain silent in the society they frequent: they come to look upon their most elevated objects as unpractical, or, at least, too remote from realization to be more than a vision, or a theory; and if, more fortunate than most, they retain their higher principles unimpaired, yet with respect to the persons and affairs of their own day they insensibly adopt the modes of feeling and judgment in which they can hope for sympathy from the company they keep. A person of high intellect should never go into unintellectual society unless he can enter it as an apostle; yet he is the only person with high objects, who can safely enter it at all. Persons even of intellectual aspirations had much better, if they can, make their habitual associates of at least their equals, and as far as possible, their superiors, in knowledge, intellect, and elevation of sentiment. Moreover, if the character is formed, and the mind made up, on the few cardinal points of human opinion, agreement of conviction and feeling on these, has been felt in all times to be an essential requisite of anything worthy the name of friendship, in a really earnest mind. All these circumstances united, made the number very small of those whose society, and still more whose intimacy, I now voluntarily sought.

Among these, by far the principal was the incomparable friend of whom I have already spoken. At this period she lived mostly, with one young daughter, in a quiet part of the country, and only occasionally in town, with her first husband, Mr. Taylor. I visited her equally in both places; and was greatly indebted to the strength of character which enabled her to disregard the false interpretations liable to be put on the frequency of my visits to her while living generally apart from Mr. Taylor, and on our occasionally travelling together, though in all other respects our conduct during those years gave not the slightest ground for any other supposition than the true one, that our relation to each other at that time was one of strong affection and confidential intimacy only. For though we did not consider the ordinances of society binding on a subject so entirely personal, we did feel bound that our conduct should be such as in no degree to bring discredit on her husband, nor therefore on herself.[1]

In this third period (as it may be termed) of my mental progress,[2] which now went hand in hand with hers, my opinions gained equally in breadth and depth. I understood more things, and those which I had understood before, I now understood more thoroughly. I had now completely turned back from what there had been of excess in my reaction against Benthamism. I had, at the height of that reaction, certainly become much more indulgent to the common opinions of society and the world, and more willing to be content with seconding the superficial improvement which had begun to take place in those common opinions, than became one whose convictions, on so many points, differed fundamentally from them. I was much more inclined, than I can now approve, to put in abeyance the more decidedly heretical part of my opinions, which I now look upon as almost the only ones, the assertion of which tends in any way to regenerate society. But in addition to this, our opinions were now far *more* heretical than mine had been in the days of my most extreme Benthamism. In those days I had seen little further than the old school of political economists into the possibilities of fundamental improvement in social arrangements. Private property as now understood, and inheritance, appeared to me as to them, the *dernier mot* of legislation: and I looked no further than to mitigating the inequalities consequent on these institutions, by getting rid of primogeniture and entails. The notion that it was possible to go further than this in removing the injustice — for injustice it is whether admitting of a complete remedy or not — involved in the fact that some are born to riches and the vast

[1] The original MS continues the sentence: "and we disdained, as every person not a slave of his animal appetites must do, the abject notion that the strongest and tenderest friendship cannot exist between a man and a woman without a sensual relation, or that any impulses of that lower character cannot be put aside when regard for the feelings of others, or even when only prudence and personal dignity require it" (*The Early Draft,* p. 171).

[2] A canceled passage in the original MS clarifies the three periods: "The success of the Logic led to the publication in 1844 of the Political Economy Essays . . . . With this terminates what may be termed the second period of my writings; reckoning the old Westminster Review period as the first. The 'Principles of Political Economy' and all subsequent writings belong to a third and different stage of my mental progress, which was essentially characterized by the predominating influence of my wife's intellect and character" (*The Early Draft,* p. 169 n.).

majority to poverty, I then reckoned chimerical; and only hoped
that by universal education, leading to voluntary restraint on population, the portion of the poor might be made more tolerable. In
short, I was a democrat, but not the least of a Socialist. We were
now much less democrats than I had been, because so long as
education continues to be so wretchedly imperfect, we dreaded the
ignorance and especially the selfishness and brutality of the mass:
but our ideal of ultimate improvement went far beyond Democracy,
and would class us decidedly under the general designation of
Socialists. While we repudiated with the greatest energy that
tyranny of society over the individual which most Socialistic sys-
tems are supposed to involve, we yet looked forward to a time when
society will no longer be divided into the idle and the industrious;
when the rule that they who do not work shall not eat, will be
applied not to paupers only, but impartially to all; when the division of the produce of labour, instead of depending, as in so great
a degree it now does, on the accident of birth, will be made by
concert, on an acknowledged principle of justice; and when it will
no longer either be, or be thought to be, impossible for human
beings to exert themselves strenuously in procuring benefits which
are not to be exclusively their own, but to be shared with the
society they belong to. The social problem of the future we considered to be, how to unite the greatest individual liberty of action,
with a common ownership in the raw material of the globe, and an
equal participation of all in the benefits of combined labour. We
had not the presumption to suppose that we could already foresee,
by what precise form of institutions these objects could most effectually be attained, or at how near or how distant a period they
would become practicable. We saw clearly that to render any such
social transformation either possible or desirable, an equivalent
change of character must take place both in the uncultivated herd
who now compose the labouring masses, and in the immense majority of their employers. Both these classes must learn by practice
to labour and combine for generous, or at all events for public and
social purposes, and not, as hitherto, solely for narrowly interested
ones. But the capacity to do this has always existed in mankind,
and is not, nor is ever likely to be, extinct. Education, habit, and
the cultivation of the sentiments will make a common man dig or
weave for his country, as readily as fight for his country. True
enough, it is only by slow degrees, and a system of culture pro-

longed through successive generations, that men in general can be brought up to this point. But the hindrance is not in the essential constitution of human nature. Interest in the common good is at present so weak a motive in the generality, not because it can never be otherwise, but because the mind is not accustomed to dwell on it as it dwells from morning till night on things which tend only to personal advantage. When called into activity as only self interest now is, by the daily course of life, and spurred from behind by the love of distinction and the fear of shame, it is capable of producing, even in common men, the most strenuous exertions as well as the most heroic sacrifices. The deeprooted selfishness which forms the general character of the existing state of society, is *so* deeply rooted, only because the whole course of existing institutions tends to foster it; modern institutions in some respects more than ancient, since the occasions on which the individual is called on to do anything for the public without receiving its pay, are far less frequent in modern life, than in the smaller commonwealths of antiquity. These considerations did not make us overlook the folly of premature attempts to dispense with the inducements of private interest in social affairs, while no substitute for them has been or can be provided: but we regarded all existing institutions and social arrangements as being (in a phrase I once heard from Austin) "merely provisional," and we welcomed with the greatest pleasure and interest all socialistic experiments by select individuals (such as the Cooperative Societies), which, whether they succeeded or failed, could not but operate as a most useful education of those who took part in them, by cultivating their capacity of acting upon motives pointing directly to the general good, or making them aware of the defects which render them and others incapable of doing so.

In the "Principles of Political Economy," these opinions were promulgated, less clearly and fully in the first edition, rather more so in the second, and quite unequivocally in the third. The difference arose partly from the change of times, the first edition having been written and sent to press before the French Revolution of 1848, after which the public mind became more open to the reception of novelties in opinion, and doctrines appeared moderate which would have been thought very startling a short time before. In the first edition the difficulties of Socialism were stated so strongly, that the tone was on the whole that of opposition to it.

In the year or two which followed, much time was given to the study of the best Socialistic writers on the Continent, and to meditation and discussion on the whole range of topics involved in the controversy: and the result was that most of what had been written on the subject in the first edition was cancelled, and replaced by arguments and reflexions which represent a more advanced opinion.

The Political Economy was far more rapidly executed than the Logic, or indeed than anything of importance which I had previously written. It was commenced in the autumn of 1845, and was ready for the press before the end of 1847. In this period of little more than two years there was an interval of six months during which the work was laid aside, while I was writing articles in the Morning Chronicle (which unexpectedly entered warmly into my purpose) urging the formation of peasant properties on the waste lands of Ireland. This was during the period of the famine, the winter of 1846/47, when the stern necessities of the time seemed to afford a chance of gaining attention for what appeared to me the only mode of combining relief to immediate destitution with permanent improvement of the social and economical condition of the Irish people. But the idea was new and strange; there was no English precedent for such a proceeding: and the profound ignorance of English politicians and the English public concerning all social phenomena not generally met with in England (however common elsewhere) made my endeavours an entire failure. Instead of a great operation on the waste lands, and the conversion of cottiers[3] into proprietors, Parliament passed a Poor Law for maintaining them as paupers: and if the nation has not since found itself in inextricable difficulties from the joint operation of the old evils and the quack remedy, it is indebted for its deliverance to that most unexpected and surprising fact, the depopulation of Ireland, commenced by famine, and continued by emigration.

The rapid success of the Political Economy shewed that the public wanted, and were prepared for such a book. Published early in 1848, an edition of a thousand copies was sold in less than a year. Another similar edition was published in the spring of 1849; and a third, of 1250 copies, early in 1852. It was, from the first, continually cited and referred to as an authority, because it was not a book merely of abstract science, but also of application, and treated

[3] Irish peasants who rented small plots of land by the year.

Political Economy not as a thing by itself, but as a fragment of a greater whole; a branch of Social Philosophy, so interlinked with all the other branches, that its conclusions, even in its own peculiar province, are only true conditionally, subject to interference and counteraction from causes not directly within its scope: while to the character of a practical guide it has no pretension, apart from other classes of considerations. Political Economy, in truth, has never pretended to give advice to mankind with no lights but its own; though people who knew nothing *but* political economy (and therefore knew that ill) have taken upon themselves to advise, and could only do so by such lights as they had. But the numerous sentimental enemies of political economy, and its still more numerous interested enemies in sentimental guise, have been very successful in gaining belief for this among other unmerited imputations against it. And the "Principles" having, in spite of the freedom of many of its opinions, become for the present the most popular treatise on the subject, has helped to disarm the enemies of so important a study. The amount of its worth as an exposition of the science, and the value of the different applications which it suggests, others of course must judge.

For a considerable time after this, I published no work of magnitude; though I still occasionally wrote in periodicals, and my correspondence (much of it with persons quite unknown to me) on subjects of public interest, swelled to a considerable bulk. During these years I wrote or commenced various Essays, for eventual publication, on some of the fundamental questions of human and social life, with regard to several of which I have already much exceeded the severity of the Horatian precept.[4] I continued to watch with keen interest the progress of public events. But it was not, on the whole, very encouraging to me. The European reaction after 1848, and the success of an unprincipled usurper in December 1851,[5] put an end, as it seemed, to all present hope for freedom or social improvement in France and the Continent. In England, I had seen and continued to see many of the opinions of my youth obtain general recognition, and many of the reforms in

[4] Probably *Satires*, I, i, 106–107, "modus in rebus . . .": "There is a measure in things — fixed bounds beyond and short of which it is not proper to go." In several passages (most notably in *Satires*, I, iv) Horace condemns the fault of too readily reciting one's writings in public.

[5] Louis Napoleon, who became emperor of the French as Napoleon III in the following year.

institutions, for which I had through life contended, either effected
or in course of being so. But these changes had been attended
with much less benefit to human well being than I should formerly
have anticipated, because they had produced very little improvement in that which all real amelioration in the lot of mankind depends on, their intellectual and moral state: and it might even be
questioned if the various causes of deterioration which had been at
work in the meanwhile, had not more than counterbalanced the
tendencies to improvement. I had learnt from experience that
many false opinions may be exchanged for true ones, without in the
least altering the habits of mind of which false opinions are the
result. The English public, for example, are quite as raw and un-
discerning on subjects of political economy since the nation has
been converted to free trade, as they were before; and are still
further from having acquired better habits of thought and feeling,
or being in any way better fortified against error, on subjects of a
more elevated character. For, though they have thrown off certain
errors, the general discipline of their minds, intellectually and
morally, is not altered. I am now convinced, that no great improvements in the lot of mankind are possible, until a great change
takes place in the fundamental constitution of their modes of
thought. The old opinions in religion, morals, and politics, are so
much discredited in the more intellectual minds as to have lost
the greater part of their efficacy for good, while they have still life
enough in them to be a powerful obstacle to the growing up of any
better opinions on those subjects. When the philosophic minds of
the world can no longer believe its religion, or can only believe it
with modifications amounting to an essential change of its character, a transitional period commences, of weak convictions, para-
lysed intellects, and growing laxity of principle, which cannot
terminate until a renovation has been effected in the basis of their
belief, leading to the evolution of some faith, whether religious or
merely human, which they can really believe: and when things are
in this state, all thinking or writing which does not tend to promote such a renovation, is of very little value beyond the moment.
Since there was little in the apparent condition of the public mind,
indicative of any tendency in this direction, my view of the immediate prospects of human improvement was not sanguine. More
recently a spirit of free speculation has sprung up, giving a more
encouraging prospect of the gradual mental emancipation of En-

gland; and, concurring with the renewal, under better auspices, of the movement for political freedom in the rest of Europe, has given to the present condition of human affairs a more hopeful aspect.

Between the time of which I have now spoken, and the present, took place the most important events of my private life. The first of these was my marriage, in April 1851, to the lady whose incomparable worth had made her friendship the greatest source to me both of happiness and of improvement, during many years in which we never expected to be in any closer relation to one another. Ardently as I should have aspired to this complete union of our lives at any time in the course of my existence at which it had been practicable, I, as much as my wife, would far rather have foregone that privilege for ever, than have owed it to the premature death of one for whom I had the sincerest respect, and she the strongest affection. That event however having taken place in July 1849, it was granted to me to derive from that evil my own greatest good, by adding to the partnership of thought, feeling, and writing which had long existed, a partnership of our entire existence. For seven and a half years that blessing was mine; for seven and a half only! I can say nothing which could describe, even in the faintest manner, what that loss was and is. But because I know that she would have wished it, I endeavour to make the best of what life I have left, and to work on for her purposes with such diminished strength as can be derived from thoughts of her, and communion with her memory.

During the years which intervened between the commencement of my married life and the catastrophe which closed it, the principal occurrences of my outward existence (unless I count as such a first attack of the family disease, and a consequent journey of more than six months for the recovery of health, in Italy, Sicily, and Greece) had reference to my position in the India House. In 1856 I was promoted to the rank of chief of the office in which I had served for upwards of thirty-three years. The appointment, that of Examiner of India Correspondence, was the highest, next to that of Secretary, in the East India Company's home service, involving the general superintendance of all the correspondence with the Indian Governments, except the military, naval, and financial. I held this office as long as it continued to exist, being a little more than two years; after which it pleased Parliament, in other words Lord

Palmerston, to put an end to the East India Company as a branch of the government of India under the Crown, and convert the administration of that country into a thing to be scrambled for by the second and third class of English parliamentary politicians. I was the chief manager of the resistance which the Company made to their own political extinction. To the letters and petitions I wrote for them, and the concluding chapter of my treatise on Representative Government, I must refer for my opinions on the folly and mischief of this ill-considered change. Personally I considered myself a gainer by it, as I had given enough of my life to India, and was not unwilling to retire on the liberal compensation granted. After the change was consummated, Lord Stanley, the first Secretary of State for India, made me the honorable offer of a seat in the Council, and the proposal was subsequently renewed by the Council itself, on the first occasion of its having to supply a vacancy in its own body. But the conditions of Indian government under the new system made me anticipate nothing but useless vexation and waste of effort from any participation in it: and nothing that has since happened has had any tendency to make me regret my refusal.

During the two years which immediately preceded the cessation of my official life, my wife and I were working together at the "Liberty." I had first planned and written it as a short essay, in 1854. It was in mounting the steps of the Capitol,[6] in January 1855, that the thought first arose of converting it into a volume. None of my writings have been either so carefully composed, or so sedulously corrected as this. After it had been written as usual twice over, we kept it by us, bringing it out from time to time and going through it *de novo,* reading, weighing and criticizing every sentence. Its final revision was to have been a work of the winter of 1858/59, the first after my retirement, which we had arranged to pass in the South of Europe. That hope and every other were frustrated by the most unexpected and bitter calamity of her death — at Avignon, on our way to Montpellier, from a sudden attack of pulmonary congestion.

Since then, I have sought for such alleviation as my state admitted of, by the mode of life which most enabled me to feel her still near me. I bought a cottage as close as possible to the place

[6] The Capitol in Rome, where (as Mill surely remembered) Gibbon also first thought of writing *The Decline and Fall of the Roman Empire.*

where she is buried, and there her daughter (my fellow-sufferer and now my chief comfort) and I, live constantly during a great portion of the year. My objects in life are solely those which were hers; my pursuits and occupations those in which she shared, or sympathized, and which are indissolubly associated with her. Her memory is to me a religion, and her approbation the standard by which, summing up as it does all worthiness, I endeavour to regulate my life.

In resuming my pen some years after closing the preceding narrative,[7] I am influenced by a desire not to leave incomplete the record, for the sake of which chiefly this biographical sketch was undertaken, of the obligations I owe to those who have either contributed essentially to my own mental developement or had a direct share in my writings and in whatever else of a public nature I have done. In the preceding pages, this record, so far as it relates to my wife, is not so detailed and precise as it ought to be; and since I lost her, I have had other help, not less deserving and requiring acknowledgment.

When two persons have their thoughts and speculations completely in common; when all subjects of intellectual or moral interest are discussed between them in daily life, and probed to much greater depths than are usually or conveniently sounded in writings intended for general readers; when they set out from the same principles and arrive at their conclusions by processes pursued jointly, it is of little consequence in respect to the question of originality which of them holds the pen; the one who contributes least to the composition may contribute most to the thought; the writings which result are the joint product of both, and it must often be impossible to disentangle their respective parts and affirm that this belongs to one and that to the other. In this wide sense, not only during the years of our married life, but during many of the years of confidential friendship which preceded, all my published writings were as much her work as mine; her share in them constantly increasing as years advanced. But in certain cases, what belongs to her can be distinguished, and specially identified. Over and above the general influence which her mind had over mine, the most valuable ideas and features in these joint productions — those which have been most fruitful of

---

[7] Mill is now writing in the winter of 1869–70.

important results, and have contributed most to the success and reputation of the works themselves — originated with her; were emanations from her mind, my part in them being no greater than in any of the thoughts which I found in previous writers, and made my own only by incorporating them with my own system of thought. During the greater part of my literary life I have performed the office in relation to her, which from a rather early period I had considered as the most useful part that I was qualified to take in the domain of thought, that of an interpreter of original thinkers, and mediator between them and the public; for I had always a humble opinion of my own powers as an original thinker, except in abstract science (logic, metaphysics, and the theoretic principles of political economy and politics), but thought myself much superior to most of my contemporaries in willingness and ability to learn from everybody; as I found hardly any one who made such a point of examining what was said in defence of all opinions, however new or however old, in the conviction that even if they were errors there might be a substratum of truth underneath them, and that in any case the discovery of what it was that made them plausible, would be a benefit to truth. I had, in consequence, marked out this as a sphere of usefulness in which I was under a special obligation to make myself active: the more so, as the acquaintance I had formed with the ideas of the Coleridgians, of the German thinkers, and of Carlyle, all of them fiercely opposed to the mode of thought in which I had been brought up, had convinced me that along with much error they possessed much truth, which was veiled from minds otherwise capable of receiving it by the transcendental and mystical phraseology in which they were accustomed to shut it up and from which they neither cared, nor knew how, to disengage it; and I did not despair of separating the truth from the error and expressing it in terms which would be intelligible and not repulsive to those on my own side in philosophy. Thus prepared, it will easily be believed that when I came into close intellectual communion with a person of the most eminent faculties, whose genius, as it grew and unfolded itself in thought, continually struck out truths far in advance of me, but in which I could not, as I had done in those others, detect any mixture of error, the greatest part of my mental growth consisted in the assimilation of those truths, and the most valuable part of my intellectual work was in building the bridges and clearing the paths which connected them with my general system of thought.[8]

The first of my books in which her share was conspicuous was the "Principles of Political Economy." The "System of Logic" owed little to her except in the minuter matters of composition, in which respect my writings, both great and small, have largely benefitted by her accurate and clear-sighted criticism.[9] The chapter

[8] The steps in my mental growth for which I was indebted to her were far from being those which a person wholly uninformed on the subject would probably suspect. It might be supposed, for instance, that my strong convictions on the complete equality in all legal, political, social and domestic relations, which ought to exist between men and women, may have been adopted or learnt from her. This was so far from being the fact, that those convictions were among the earliest results of the application of my mind to political subjects, and the strength with which I held them was, as I believe, more than anything else, the originating cause of the interest she felt in me. What is true is, that until I knew her, the opinion was, in my mind, little more than an abstract principle. I saw no more reason why women should be held in legal subjection to other people, than why men should. I was certain that their interests required fully as much protection as those of men, and were quite as little likely to obtain it without an equal voice in making the laws by which they are to be bound. But that perception of the vast practical bearings of women's disabilities which found expression in the book on the Subjection of Women, was acquired mainly through her teaching. But for her rare knowledge of human nature and comprehension of moral and social influences, though I should doubtless have held my present opinions I should have had a very insufficient perception of the mode in which the consequences of the inferior position of women intertwine themselves with all the evils of existing society and with all the difficulties of human improvement. I am indeed painfully conscious how much of her best thoughts on the subject I have failed to reproduce, and how greatly that little treatise falls short of what would have been if she had put on paper her entire mind on this question, or had lived to revise and improve, as she certainly would have done, my imperfect statement of the case (Mill's note).

[9] The only person from whom I received any direct assistance in the preparation of the "System of Logic" was Mr. Bain, since so justly celebrated for his philosophical writings. He went carefully through the manuscript before it was sent to press, and enriched it with a great number of additional examples and illustrations from science; many of which, as well as some detached remarks of his own in confirmation of my logical views, I inserted nearly in his own words.

My obligations to Comte were only to his writings — to the part which had then been published of his "Cours de Philosophie Positive": and as has been seen from what I have said in the Narrative, the amount of these obligations is far less than has sometimes been asserted. The first volume, which contains all the fundamental doctrines of the book, was substantially complete before I had seen Comte's treatise. I derived from him many valuable thoughts, conspicuously in the chapter on Hypotheses and in the view

of the Political Economy which has had a greater influence on opinion than all the rest, that on "the Probable Future of the Labouring Classes," is entirely due to her: in the first draft of the book, that chapter did not exist. She pointed out the need of such a chapter, and the extreme imperfection of the book without it: she was the cause of my writing it; and the more general part of the chapter, the statement and discussion of the two opposite theories respecting the proper condition of the labouring classes, was wholly an exposition of her thoughts, often in words taken from her own lips. The purely scientific part of the Political Economy I did not learn from her; but it was chiefly her influence that gave to the book that general tone by which it is distinguished from all previous expositions of Political Economy that had any pretension to being scientific, and which has made it so useful in conciliating minds which those previous expositions had repelled. This tone consisted chiefly in making the proper distinction between the laws of the Production of Wealth, which are real laws of nature, dependent on the properties of objects, and the modes of its Distribution, which, subject to certain conditions, depend on human will. The common run of political economists confuse these together, under the designation of economic laws, which they deem incapable of being defeated or modified by human effort; ascribing the same necessity to things dependent on the unchangeable conditions of our earthly existence, and to those which, being but the necessary consequences of particular social arrangements, are merely coextensive with these. Given certain institutions and customs, wages, profits, and rent will be determined by certain causes; but this class of political economists drop the indispensable presupposition, and argue that these causes must by an inherent necessity, against which no human means can avail, determine the shares which fall, in the division of the produce, to labourers, capitalists, and landlords. The "Principles of Political Economy" yielded to none of its predecessors in aiming at the scientific appreciation of the action of these causes, under the conditions which they presuppose; but it set the example of not treating those condi-

---

taken of the logic of algebra: but it is only in the concluding Book, on the Logic of the Moral Sciences, that I owe to him any radical improvement in my conception of the application of logical methods. This improvement I have stated and characterized in a former part of the present Memoir (Mill's note).

tions as final. The economic generalisations which depend, not on necessities of nature but on those combined with the existing arrangements of society, it deals with only as provisional, and as liable to be much altered by the progress of social improvement. I had indeed partially learnt this view of things from the thoughts awakened in me by the speculations of the Saint-Simonians; but it was made a living principle pervading and animating the book by my wife's promptings. This example illustrates well the general character of what she contributed to my writings. What was abstract and purely scientific was generally mine; the properly human element came from her: in all that concerned the application of philosophy to the exigencies of human society and progress, I was her pupil, alike in boldness of speculation and cautiousness of practical judgment. For, on the one hand, she was much more courageous and farsighted than without her I should have been, in anticipations of an order of things to come, in which many of the limited generalizations now so often confounded with universal principles will cease to be applicable. Those parts of my writings and especially of the Political Economy which contemplate possibilities in the future such as, when affirmed by Socialists, have in general been fiercely denied by political economists, would, but for her, either have been absent, or the suggestions would have been made much more timidly and in a more qualified form. But while she thus rendered me bolder in speculation on human affairs, her practical turn of mind, and her almost unerring estimate of practical obstacles, repressed in me all tendencies that were really visionary. Her mind invested all ideas in a concrete shape, and formed to itself a conception of how they would actually work: and her knowledge of the existing feelings and conduct of mankind was so seldom at fault, that the weak point in any unworkable suggestion seldom escaped her.[10]

The "Liberty" was more directly and literally our joint produc-

---

[10] A few dedicatory lines, acknowledging what the book owed to her, were prefixed to some of the presentation copies of the Political Economy on its first publication. Her dislike of publicity alone prevented their insertion in the other copies of the work (Mill's note). The dedication was the following: "To Mrs. John Taylor as the most eminently qualified of all persons known to the author either to originate or to appreciate speculations on social improvement, this attempt to explain and diffuse ideas many of which were first learned from herself, is with the highest respect and regard dedicated" (Hayek, *John Stuart Mill and Harriet Taylor*, p. 122).

tion than anything else which bears my name, for there was not a sentence of it that was not several times gone through by us together, turned over in many ways, and carefully weeded of any faults, either in thought or expression, that we detected in it. It is in consequence of this that, although it never underwent her final revision, it far surpasses, as a mere specimen of composition, anything which has proceeded from me either before or since. With regard to the thoughts, it is difficult to identify any particular part or element as being more hers than all the rest. The whole mode of thinking of which the book was the expression, was emphatically hers. But I also was so thoroughly imbued with it that the same thoughts naturally occurred to us both. That I was thus penetrated with it, however, I owe in a great degree to her. There was a moment in my mental progress when I might easily have fallen into a tendency towards over-government, both social and political; as there was also a moment when, by reaction from a contrary excess, I might have become a less thorough radical and democrat than I am. In both these points as in many others, she benefitted me as much by keeping me right where I was right, as by leading me to new truths and ridding me of errors. My great readiness and eagerness to learn from everybody, and to make room in my opinions for every new acquisition by adjusting the old and the new to one another, might, but for her steadying influence, have seduced me into modifying my early opinions too much. She was in nothing more valuable to my mental development than by her just measure of the relative importance of different considerations, which often protected me from allowing to truths I had only recently learnt to see, a more important place in my thoughts than was properly their due.

The "Liberty" is likely to survive longer than anything else that I have written (with the possible exception of the "Logic"), because the conjunction of her mind with mine has rendered it a kind of philosophic text-book of a single truth, which the changes progressively taking place in modern society tend to bring out into ever stronger relief: the importance, to man and society, of a large variety in types of character, and of giving full freedom to human nature to expand itself in innumerable and conflicting directions. Nothing can better shew how deep are the foundations of this truth, than the great impression made by the exposition of it at a time which, to superficial observation, did not seem to stand much in need of such a lesson. The fears we expressed lest the inevitable growth of social equality and of the government of public opinion should impose on mankind an oppressive yoke of uniformity in opinion and practice, might easily have appeared chimerical to those who looked more at present facts than at tendencies; for the gradual revolution that is taking place in society and institutions has thus far been decidedly favourable to the development of new opinions, and has procured for them a much more unprejudiced hearing than they previously met with. But this is a feature belonging to periods of transition, when old notions and feelings have been unsettled and no new doctrines have yet succeeded to their ascendancy. At such times people of any mental activity, having given up many of their old beliefs, and not feeling quite sure that those they still retain can stand unmodified, listen eagerly to new opinions. But this state of things is necessarily transitory: some particular body of doctrine in time rallies the majority round it, organizes social institutions and modes of action conformably to itself, education impresses this new creed upon the new generations without the mental processes that have led to it, and by degrees it acquires the very same power of compression, so long exercised by the creeds of which it had taken the place. Whether this noxious power will be exercised depends on whether mankind have by that time become aware that it cannot be exercised without stunting and dwarfing human nature. It is then that the teachings of the "Liberty" will have their greatest value. And it is to be feared that they will retain that value a long time.

As regards originality, it has of course no other than that which every thoughtful mind gives to its own mode of conceiving and expressing truths which are common property. The leading thought of the book is one which, though in many ages confined to insulated thinkers, mankind have probably at no time since the beginning of civilisation been entirely without. To speak only of the last few generations, it is distinctly contained in the vein of important thought respecting education and culture spread through the European mind by the labours and genius of Pestalozzi. The unqualified championship of it by Wilhelm von Humboldt is referred to in the book; but he by no means stood alone in his own country. During the early part of the present century, the doctrine of the rights of individuality, and the claim of the moral nature to develope itself in its own way, was pushed by a whole school of

German authors even to exaggeration; and the writings of Goethe, the most celebrated of all German authors, though not belonging to that or to any other school, are penetrated throughout by views of morals and of conduct in life, often in my opinion not defensible, but which are incessantly seeking whatever defence they admit of in the theory of the right and duty of self-development. In our own country, before the book "on Liberty" was written, the doctrine of Individuality had been enthusiastically asserted, in a stile of vigorous declamation sometimes reminding one of Fichte, by Mr. William Maccall, in a series of writings of which the most elaborate is entitled "Elements of Individualism." And a remarkable American, Mr. Warren, had framed a System of Society, on the foundation of "the Sovereignty of the Individual," had obtained a number of followers, and had actually commenced the formation of a Village Community (whether it now exists I know not)[11] which, though bearing a superficial resemblance to some of the projects of Socialists, is diametrically opposite to them in principle, since it recognises no authority whatever in Society over the individual, except to enforce equal freedom of development for all individualities. As the book which bears my name claimed no originality for any of its doctrines, and was not intended to write their history, the only author who had preceded me in their assertion of whom I thought it appropriate to say anything, was Humboldt, who furnished the motto to the work; although in one passage I borrowed from the Warrenites their phrase, the sovereignty of the individual. It is hardly necessary here to remark that there are abundant differences in detail, between the conception of the doctrine by any of the predecessors I have mentioned, and that set forth in the book.

After my irreparable loss one of my earliest cares was to print and publish the treatise, so much of which was the work of her whom I had lost, and consecrate it to her memory. I have made no alteration or addition to it, nor shall I ever. Though it wants the last touch of her hand, no substitute for that touch shall ever be attempted by mine.

The political circumstances of the time induced me shortly after to complete and publish a pamphlet ("Thoughts on Parliamentary Reform"), part of which had been written some years previously

[11] Josiah Warren's community, Modern Times, on Long Island, lasted from the early 1850's to about 1862.

on the occasion of one of the abortive Reform Bills and had at the time been approved and revised by her. Its principal features were, hostility to the Ballot (a change of opinion in both of us, in which she rather preceded me) and a claim of representation for minorities; not however at that time going beyond the cumulative vote proposed by Mr. Garth Marshall. In finishing the pamphlet for publication with a view to the discussions on the Reform Bill of Lord Derby's and Mr. Disraeli's Government in 1859, I added a third feature, a plurality of votes, to be given, not to property, but to proved superiority of education. This recommended itself to me, as a means of reconciling the irresistible claim of every man or woman to be consulted, and to be allowed a voice, in the regulation of affairs which vitally concern them, with the superiority of weight justly due to opinions grounded on superiority of knowledge. The suggestion however was one which I had never discussed with my almost infallible counsellor, and I have no evidence that she would have concurred in it. As far as I have been able to observe, it has found favour with nobody; all who desire any sort of inequality in the electoral vote, desiring it in favour of property and not of intelligence or knowledge. If it ever overcomes the strong feeling which exists against it, this will only be after the establishment of a systematic National Education by which the various grades of politically valuable acquirement may be accurately defined and authenticated. Without this it will always remain liable to strong, possibly conclusive, objections; and with this, it would perhaps not be needed.

It was soon after the publication of "Thoughts on Parliamentary Reform" that I became acquainted with Mr. Hare's admirable system of Personal Representation, which, in its present shape, was then for the first time published. I saw in this great practical and philosophical idea, the greatest improvement of which the system of representative government is susceptible; an improvement which, in the most felicitous manner, exactly meets and cures the grand, and what before seemed the inherent, defect of the representative system; that of giving to a numerical majority all power, instead of only a power proportional to its numbers, and enabling the strongest party to exclude all weaker parties from making their opinions heard in the assembly of the nation, except through such opportunity as may be given to them by the accidentally unequal distribution of opinions in different localities.

To these great evils nothing more than very imperfect palliatives had seemed possible; but Mr. Hare's system affords a radical cure. This great discovery, for it is no less, in the political art, inspired me, as I believe it has inspired all thoughtful persons who have adopted it, with new and more sanguine hopes respecting the prospects of human society; by freeing the form of political institutions towards which the whole civilised world is manifestly and irresistibly tending, from the chief part of what seemed to qualify or render doubtful its ultimate benefits. Minorities, so long as they remain minorities, are, and ought to be, outvoted; but under arrangements which enable any assemblage of voters, amounting to a certain number, to place in the legislature a representative of its own choice, minorities cannot be suppressed. Independent opinions will force their way into the council of the nation and make themselves heard there, a thing which often cannot happen in the existing forms of representative democracy; and the legislature instead of being weeded of individual peculiarities and entirely made up of men who simply represent the creed of great political or religious parties, will comprise a large proportion of the most eminent individual minds in the country placed there without reference to party by voters who appreciate their individual eminence. I can understand that persons, otherwise intelligent, should, for want of sufficient examination, be repelled from Mr. Hare's plan by what they think the complex nature of its machinery. But any one who does not feel the want which the scheme is intended to supply; any one who throws it over as a mere theoretical subtlety or crotchet, tending to no valuable purpose, and unworthy of the attention of practical men, may be pronounced an incompetent statesman, unequal to the politics of the future. I mean, unless he is a minister, or aspires to become one: for we are quite accustomed to a minister's continuing to profess unqualified hostility to an improvement almost to the very day when his conscience or his interest induces him to take it up as a public measure and carry it.

Had I met with Mr. Hare's system before the publication of my pamphlet, I should have given an account of it there. Not having done so, I wrote an article in Fraser's Magazine (reprinted in my miscellaneous writings) principally for that purpose, though I included in it, along with Mr. Hare's book, a review of two other productions on the question of the day; one of them a pamphlet by

my early friend Mr. John Austin, who had in his old age become an enemy of all further parliamentary reform; the other an
able and ingenious though partially erroneous work by Mr. Lorimer.[12]

In the course of the same summer I fulfilled a duty particularly
incumbent upon me, that of helping (by an article in the Edinburgh Review) to make known Mr. Bain's profound treatise on
the Mind, just then completed by the publication of its second
volume.[13] And I carried through the press a selection of my
minor writings, forming the first two volumes of "Dissertations and
Discussions." The selection had been made during my wife's lifetime, but the revision, in concert with her, with a view to republi-
cation, had been barely commenced; and when I had no longer the
guidance of her judgment I despaired of pursuing it further, and
republished the papers as they were, with the exception of striking
out such passages as were no longer in accordance with my opinions. My literary work of the year terminated with an essay in
Fraser's magazine (afterwards republished in the third volume of
"Dissertations and Discussions") entitled "a Few Words on Non-
Intervention." I was prompted to write this paper by a desire,
while vindicating England from the imputations commonly brought
against her on the Continent of a peculiar selfishness in matters of
foreign policy, to warn Englishmen of the colour given to this im-
putation by the low tone in which English statesmen are accustomed to speak of English policy as concerned only with English
interests, and by the conduct of Lord Palmerston at that particular
time in opposing the Suez Canal. And I took the opportunity of
expressing ideas which had long been in my mind (some of them
generated by my Indian experience and others by the international
questions which then greatly occupied the European public) respecting the true principles of international morality and the legitimate modifications made in it by difference of times and circumstances; a subject I had already to some extent discussed in the
vindication of the French Provisional Government of 1848 against
the attacks of Lord Brougham and others which I published at the

[12] The works were Thomas Hare's *A Treatise on the Election of Repre-
sentatives, Parliamentary and Municipal* (1859), Austin's *A Plea for the
Constitution* (1859), and James Lorimer's *Political Progress Not Necessarily
Democratic* (1857).

[13] *The Emotions and the Will* (1859). The earlier volume was *The Senses
and the Intellect* (1855).

time in the Westminster Review and which is reprinted in the "Dissertations."

I had now settled, as I believed for the remainder of my existence, into a purely literary life; if that can be called literary which continued to be occupied in a preeminent degree with politics, and not merely with theoretical, but practical politics, although a great part of the year was spent at a distance of many hundred miles[14] from the chief seat of the politics of my own country, to which, and primarily for which, I wrote. But in truth, the modern facilities of communication have not only removed all the disadvantages, to a political writer in tolerably easy circumstances, of distance from the scene of political action, but have converted them into advantages. The immediate and regular receipt of newspapers and periodicals keeps him *au courant* of even the most temporary politics, and gives him a much more correct view of the state and progress of opinion than he could acquire by personal contact with individuals: for every one's social intercourse is more or less limited to particular sets or classes, whose impressions and no others reach him through that channel; and experience has taught me that those who give their time to the absorbing claims of what is called society, not having leisure to keep up a large acquaintance with the organs of opinion, remain much more ignorant of the general state either of the public mind, or of the active and instructed part of it, than a recluse who reads the newspapers need be. There are, no doubt, disadvantages in too long a separation from one's country — in not occasionally renewing one's impressions of the light in which men and things appear when seen from a position in the midst of them; but the deliberate judgment formed at a distance, and undisturbed by inequalities of perspective, is the most to be depended on, even for application to practice. Alternating between the two positions I combined the advantages of both. And, though the inspirer of my best thoughts was no longer with me, I was not alone: she had left a daughter — my stepdaughter, Miss Helen Taylor, the inheritor of much of her wisdom, and of all her nobleness of character, whose ever growing and ripening talents from that day to this have been devoted to the same great purposes, and have already made her name better and more widely known than was that of her mother, though far less so than I predict that if

[14] In Avignon.

she lives, it is destined to become. Of the value of her direct cooperation with me, something will be said hereafter: of what I owe in
the way of instruction to her great powers of original thought and
soundness of practical judgment, it would be a vain attempt to give
an adequate idea. Surely no one ever before was so fortunate, as,
after such a loss as mine, to draw another such prize in the lottery
of life — another companion, stimulator, adviser, and instructor of
the rarest quality. Whoever, either now or hereafter, may think of
me and of the work I have done, must never forget that it is the
product not of one intellect and conscience but of three, the least
considerable of whom, and above all the least original, is the one
whose name is attached to it.

The work of the years 1860 and 1861 consisted chiefly of two
treatises, only one of which was intended for immediate publication. This was the "Considerations on Representative Government," a connected exposition of what, by the thoughts of many
years, I had come to regard as the best form of a popular constitution. Along with as much of the general theory of government as
is necessary to support this particular portion of its practice, the
volume contains my matured views of the principal questions which
occupy the present age, within the province of purely organic institutions, and raises by anticipation some other questions to which
growing necessities will sooner or later compel the attention both
of theoretical and of practical politicians. The chief of these last
is the distinction between the function of making laws, for which
a numerous popular assembly is radically unfit, and that of getting
good laws made, which is its proper duty, and cannot be satisfac-
torily fulfilled by any other authority: and the consequent need of
a Legislative Commission, as a permanent part of the constitution
of a free country; consisting of a small number of highly trained
political minds on whom, when Parliament has determined that a
law shall be made, the task of making it should be devolved; Parliament retaining the power of passing or rejecting the bill when
drawn up, but not of altering it otherwise than by sending proposed
amendments to be dealt with by the Commission. The question
here raised respecting the most important of all public functions,
that of legislation, is a particular case of the great problem of modern political organization, stated I believe for the first time in its
full extent by Bentham, though in my opinion not always satisfac-
torily resolved by him; the combination of complete popular control

over public affairs with the greatest attainable perfection of skilled agency.

The other treatise written at this time is the one which was published some years later under the title of "The Subjection of Women." It was written at my daughter's suggestion that there might, in any event, be in existence a written exposition of my opinions on that great question, as full and conclusive as I could make it. The intention was to keep this among other unpublished papers, improving it from time to time if I was able, and to publish it at the time when it should seem likely to be most useful. As ultimately published it was enriched with some important ideas of my daughter's, and passages of her writing. But in what was of my own composition, all that is most striking and profound belongs to my wife; coming from the fund of thought which had been made common to us both, by our innumerable conversations and discussions on a topic which filled so large a place in our minds.

Soon after this time I took from their repository a portion of the unpublished papers which I had written during the last years of our married life, and shaped them, with some additional matter, into the little work entitled "Utilitarianism"; which was first published in three parts, in successive numbers of Fraser's Magazine, and afterwards reprinted in a volume.

Before this however the state of public affairs had become extremely critical, by the commencement of the American civil war. My strongest feelings were engaged in this struggle, which, I felt from the beginning, was destined to be a turning point, for good or evil, of the course of human affairs for an indefinite duration. Having been a deeply interested observer of the Slavery quarrel in America, during the many years that preceded the open breach, I knew that it was in all its stages an aggressive enterprise of the slave owners to extend the territory of slavery; under the combined influences of pecuniary interest, domineering temper, and the fanaticism of a class for its class privileges, influences so fully and powerfully depicted in the admirable work of my friend Professor Cairnes, "The Slave Power." Their success, if they succeeded, would be a victory of the powers of evil which would give courage to the enemies of progress and damp the spirits of its friends all over the civilised world, while it would create a formidable military power grounded on the worst and most anti-social form of the tyranny of men over men, and by destroying for a long time the prestige of the great democratic republic would give to all the privileged classes of Europe a false confidence, probably only to be extinguished in blood. On the other hand, if the spirit of the North was sufficiently roused to carry the war to a successful termination, and if that termination did not come too soon and too easily, I foresaw, from the laws of human nature and the experience of revolutions, that when it did come it would in all probability be thorough: that the bulk of the Northern population, whose conscience had as yet been awakened only to the point of resisting the further extension of slavery, but whose fidelity to the Constitution of the United States made them disapprove of any attempt by the Federal Government to interfere with slavery in the States where it already existed, would acquire feelings of another kind when the Constitution had been shaken off by armed rebellion, would determine to have done for ever with the accursed thing, and would join their banner with that of the noble body of Abolitionists, of whom Garrison was the courageous and single minded apostle, Wendell Phillips the eloquent orator, and John Brown the voluntary martyr.[15] Then, too, the whole mind of the United States would be let loose from its bonds, no longer corrupted by the supposed necessity of apologising to foreigners for the most flagrant of all possible violations of the free principles of their Constitution, while the tendency of a fixed state of society to stereotype a set of national opinions would be at least temporarily checked and the national mind would become more open to the recognition of whatever was bad in either the institutions or the customs of the people. These hopes, so far as related to Slavery, have been completely, and in other respects are in course of being progressively realized. Foreseeing from the first this double set of consequences from the success or failure of the rebellion, it may be imagined with what feelings I contemplated the rush of nearly the whole upper and middle classes of my own country, even those who passed for Liberals, into a furious pro-Southern partisanship: the working classes, and some of the literary and scientific men, being almost the sole exceptions to the general frenzy. I never before felt so keenly how little permanent improvement had reached the minds of our influential classes and of what small value were the liberal opinions they had got into the habit of

---

[15] The saying of this true hero, after his capture, that he was worth more for hanging than for any other purpose, reminds one, by its combination of wit, wisdom, and self devotion, of Sir Thomas More (Mill's note).

professing. None of the Continental Liberals committed the same frightful mistake. But the generation which had extorted negro emancipation from our West India planters had passed away; another had succeeded which had not learnt by many years of discussion and exposure to feel strongly the enormities of slavery; and the inattention habitual with Englishmen to whatever is going on in the world outside their own island, made them profoundly ignorant of all the antecedents of the struggle, insomuch that it was not generally believed in England, for the first year or two of the war, that the quarrel was one of slavery. There were men of high principle and unquestionable liberality of opinion who thought it a dispute about tariffs, or assimilated it to the cases in which they were accustomed to sympathise, of a people struggling for independence.

It was my obvious duty to be one of the small minority who protested against this perverted state of public opinion. I was not the first to protest. It ought to be remembered to the honour of Mr. Hughes and of Mr. Ludlow, that they, by writings published at the very beginning of the struggle, began the protestation. Mr. Bright followed in one of the most powerful of his speeches, followed by others not less striking. I was on the point of adding my words to theirs when there occurred, towards the end of 1861, the seizure of the Southern envoys on board a British vessel, by an officer of the United States. Even English forgetfulness has not yet had time to lose all remembrance of the explosion of feeling in England which then burst forth, the expectation, prevailing for some weeks, of war with the United States, and the warlike preparations actually commenced on this side. While this state of things lasted there was no chance of a hearing for anything favourable to the American cause; and moreover I agreed with those who thought the act unjustifiable and such as to require that England should demand its disavowal. When the disavowal came, and the alarm of war was over, I wrote, in January 1862, the paper, in Fraser's Magazine, entitled "The Contest in America." And I shall always feel grateful to my daughter that her urgency prevailed on me to write it when I did: for we were then on the point of setting out for a journey of some months in Greece and Turkey, and but for her, I should have deferred writing till our return. Written and published when it was, the paper helped to encourage those Liberals who had felt overborne by the tide of illiberal opinion, and to form in favour of the good cause a nucleus of opinion which increased gradually, and after the success of the North began to seem probable, rapidly. When we returned from our journey I wrote a second article, a review of Professor Cairnes' book published in the Westminster Review. England is paying the penalty, in many uncomfortable ways, of the durable resentment which her ruling classes stirred up in the United States by their ostentatious wishes for the ruin of America as a nation; they have reason to be thankful that a few, if only a few known writers and speakers, standing firmly by the Americans in the time of their greatest difficulty, effected a partial diversion of these bitter feelings, and made Great Britain not altogether odious to the Americans.

This duty having been performed, my principal occupation for the next two years was on subjects not political. The publication of Mr. Austin's Lectures on Jurisprudence after his decease, gave me an opportunity of paying a deserved tribute to his memory and at the same time expressing some thoughts on a subject on which, in my old days of Benthamism, I had bestowed much study. But the chief product of those years was the Examination of Sir William Hamilton's Philosophy. His Lectures, published in 1860 and 1861, I had read towards the end of the latter year, with a half formed intention of giving an account of them in a Review, but I soon found that this would be idle, and that justice could not be done to the subject in less than a volume. I had then to consider whether it would be advisable that I myself should attempt such a performance. On consideration, there seemed to be strong reasons for doing so. I was greatly disappointed with the Lectures. I read them, certainly, with no prejudice against Sir W. Hamilton. I had up to that time deferred the study of his Notes to Reid on account of their unfinished state, but I had not neglected his "Discussions in Philosophy"; and though I knew that his general mode of treating the facts of mental philosophy differed from that of which I most approved, yet his vigorous polemic against the later Transcendentalists, and his strenuous assertion of some important principles, especially the Relativity of human knowledge, gave me many points of sympathy with his opinions, and made me think that genuine psychology had considerably more to gain than to lose by his authority and reputation. His Lectures and the Dissertations on Reid dispelled this illusion: and even the Discussions, read by the light which these threw on them, lost much of their value. I found that the points of apparent agreement between his opinions and mine were more verbal than real; that the important philosophical principles which I had thought he recognised, were so explained away by him as to mean little or nothing, or were continually lost sight of, and doctrines entirely inconsistent with them were taught in nearly every part of his philosophical writings. My estimation of him was therefore so far altered, that instead of regarding him as occupying a kind of intermediate position between the two rival philosophies, holding some of the principles of both, and supplying to both powerful weapons of attack and defence, I now looked upon him as one of the pillars, and in this country from his high philosophical reputation the chief pillar, of that one of the two which seemed to me to be erroneous.

Now, the difference between these two schools of philosophy, that of Intuition, and that of Experience and Association, is not a mere matter of abstract speculation; it is full of practical consequences, and lies at the foundation of all the greatest differences of practical opinion in an age of progress. The practical reformer has continually to demand that changes be made in things which are supported by powerful and widely spread feelings, or to question the apparent necessity and indefeasibleness of established facts; and it is often an indispensable part of his argument to shew, how those powerful feelings had their origin, and how those facts came to seem necessary and indefeasible. There is therefore a natural hostility between him and a philosophy which discourages the explanation of feelings and moral facts by circumstances and association, and prefers to treat them as ultimate elements of human nature; a philosophy which is addicted to holding up favourite doctrines as intuitive truths, and deems intuition to be the voice of Nature and of God, speaking with an authority higher than that of our reason. In particular, I have long felt that the prevailing tendency to regard all the marked distinctions of human character as innate, and in the main indelible, and to ignore the irresistible proofs that by far the greater part of those differences, whether between individuals, races, or sexes, are such as not only might but naturally would be produced by differences in circumstances, is one of the chief hindrances to the rational treatment of great social questions, and one of the greatest stumbling blocks to human improvement. This tendency has its source in the intuitional metaphysics which characterized the reaction of the nineteenth century against the eighteenth, and it is a tendency so agreeable to human indolence, as well as to conservative interests generally, that unless attacked at the very root, it is sure to be carried to even a greater length than is really justified by the more moderate forms of the intuitional philosophy. That philosophy, not always in its moderate forms, had ruled the thought of Europe for the greater part of a century. My father's Analysis of the Mind, my own Logic, and Professor Bain's great treatise, had attempted to reintroduce a better mode of philosophizing, latterly with quite as much success as could be expected; but I had for some time felt that the mere contrast of the two philosophies was not enough, that there ought to be a hand-to-hand fight between them, that controversial as well as expository writings were needed, and that the time was come when such controversy would be useful. Considering then the writings and fame of Sir W. Hamilton as the great fortress of the intuitional philosophy in this country, a fortress the more formidable from the imposing character, and the in many respects great personal merits and mental endowments, of the man, I thought it might be a real service to philosophy to attempt a thorough examination of all his most important doctrines, and an estimate of his general claims to eminence as a philosopher. And I was confirmed in this resolution by observing that in the writings of at least one, and him one of the ablest, of Sir W. Hamilton's followers, his peculiar doctrines were made the justification of a view of religion which I hold to be profoundly immoral — that it is our duty to bow down in worship before a Being whose moral attributes are affirmed to be unknowable by us, and to be perhaps extremely different from those which, when we are speaking of our fellow-creatures, we call by the same names.

As I advanced in my task, the damage to Sir W. Hamilton's reputation became greater than I at first expected, through the almost incredible multitude of inconsistencies which shewed themselves on comparing different passages with one another. It was my business however to shew things exactly as they were, and I did not flinch from it. I endeavoured always to treat the philosopher whom I criticized with the most scrupulous fairness; and I knew that he had abundance of disciples and admirers to correct me if I ever unintentionally did him injustice. Many of them accordingly have answered me, more or less elaborately; and they have pointed out oversights and misunderstandings, though few in number, and mostly very unimportant in substance. Such of those as had (to my knowledge) been pointed out before the publication of the latest edition (at present the third) have been corrected there, and the remainder of the criticisms have been, as far as seemed necessary, replied to. On the whole, the book has done its work: it has shewn the weak side of Sir W. Hamilton, and has reduced his too great philosophical reputation within more moderate bounds; and by some of its discussions, as well as by two expository chapters, on the notions of Matter and of Mind, it has perhaps thrown additional light on some of the disputed questions in the domain of psychology and metaphysics.

After the completion of the book on Hamilton, I applied myself to a task which a variety of reasons seemed to render specially incumbent upon me; that of giving an account, and forming an estimate, of the doctrines of Auguste Comte. I had contributed more than any one else to make his speculations known in England. In consequence chiefly of what I had said of him in my Logic, he had readers and admirers among thoughtful men on this side of the Channel at a time when his name had not yet, in France, emerged from obscurity. So unknown and unappreciated was he at the time when my Logic was written and published, that to criticise his weak points might well appear superfluous, while it was a duty to give as much publicity as one could to the important contributions he had made to philosophic thought. At the time however at which I have now arrived, this state of affairs had entirely changed. His name at least was known almost universally, and the general character of his doctrines very widely. He had taken his place in the estimation both of friends and opponents, as one of the conspicuous figures in the thought of the age. The better parts of his speculations had made great progress in working their way into those minds, which by their previous culture and tendencies, were fitted to receive them: and under cover of those better parts those of a worse character, greatly developed and added to in his later writings, had also made some way, having obtained active and enthusiastic adherents, some of them of no inconsiderable personal merit, in England, France, and other countries. These causes not only made it desirable that some one should undertake the task of sifting what is good from what is bad in M. Comte's speculations, but seemed to impose on myself in particular a special obligation to make the attempt. This I accordingly did in two Essays, published in successive numbers of the Westminster Review, and reprinted in a small volume under the title "Auguste Comte and Positivism."

The writings which I have now mentioned, together with a small number of papers in periodicals which I have not deemed worth preserving, were the whole of the products of my activity as a writer during the years from 1859 to 1865. In the early part of the last mentioned year, in compliance with a wish frequently expressed to me by working men, I published cheap People's Editions of those of my writings which seemed the most likely to find readers among the working classes; viz. Principles of Political Economy, Liberty, and Representative Government. This was a considerable sacrifice of my pecuniary interest, especially as I resigned all idea of deriving profit from the cheap editions, and after ascertaining from my publishers the lowest price which they thought would remunerate them on the usual terms of an equal division of profits, I gave up my half share to enable the price to be fixed still lower. To the credit of Messrs. Longman they fixed, unasked, a certain number of years after which the copyright and stereotype plates were to revert to me, and a certain number of copies after the sale of which I should receive half of any further profit. This number of copies (which in the case of the Political Economy was 10,000) has for some time been exceeded, and the People's Editions have begun to yield me a small but unexpected pecuniary return, though very far from an equivalent for the diminution of profit from the Library Editions.

In this summary of my outward life I have now arrived at the period at which my tranquil and retired existence as a writer of books was to be exchanged for the less congenial occupation of a member of the House of Commons. The proposal made to me, early in 1865, by some electors of Westminster, did not present the idea to me for the first time. It was not even the first offer I had received, for, more than ten years previous, in consequence of my opinions on the Irish Land question, Mr. Lucas and Mr. Duffy, in the name of the popular party in Ireland, offered to bring me into Parliament for an Irish County, which they could easily have done: but the incompatibility of a seat in Parliament with the office I then held in the India House, precluded even consideration of the proposal. After I had quitted the India House, several of my friends would gladly have seen me a member of Parliament; but there seemed no probability that the idea would ever take any practical shape. I was convinced that no numerous or influential portion of any electoral body, really wished to be represented by a person of my opinions; and that one who possessed no local connexion or popularity, and who did not choose to stand as the mere organ of a party, had small chance of being elected anywhere unless through the expenditure of money. Now it was, and is, my fixed conviction, that a candidate ought not to incur one farthing of expense for undertaking a public duty. Such of the lawful expenses of an election as have no special reference to any particular candidate ought to be borne as a public charge, either by the State or by the locality. What has to be done by the supporters of each candidate in order to bring his claims properly before the constituency, should be done by unpaid agency, or by voluntary subscription. If members of the electoral body, or others, are willing to subscribe money of their own for the purpose of bringing by lawful means into Parliament some one who they think would be useful there, no one is entitled to object: but that the expense, or any part of it, should fall on the candidate, is fundamentally wrong; because it amounts, in reality, to buying his seat. Even on the most favourable supposition as to the mode in which the money is expended, there is a legitimate suspicion that any one who gives money for leave to undertake a public trust, has other than public ends to promote by it; and (a consideration of the greatest importance) the cost of elections, when borne by the candidates, deprives the nation of the services, as members of Parliament, of all who cannot or will not afford to incur a heavy expense. I do not say that, so long as there is scarcely a chance for an independent candidate to come into Parliament without complying with this vicious practice, it must always be morally wrong in him to spend money, provided that no part of it is either directly or indirectly employed in corruption. But, to justify it, he ought to be very certain that he can be of more use to his country as a member of Parliament than in any other mode which is open to him; and this assurance, in my own case, I did not feel. It was by no means clear to me that I could do more to advance the public objects which had a claim on my exertions from the benches of the House of Commons, than from the simple position of a writer. I felt, therefore, that I ought not to seek election to Parliament, much less to expend any money in procuring it.

But the conditions of the question were considerably altered when a body of electors sought me out, and spontaneously offered to bring me forward as their candidate. If it should appear, on explanation, that they persisted in this wish, knowing my opinions, and accepting the only conditions on which I could conscientiously serve, it was questionable whether this was not one of those calls upon a member of the community by his fellow citizens, which he was scarcely justified in rejecting. I therefore put their disposition to the proof by one of the frankest explanations ever tendered, I should think, to an electoral body by a candidate. I wrote in reply to the offer a letter for publication,[16] saying that I had no personal wish to be a member of parliament, that I thought a candidate ought neither to canvass nor to incur any expense, and that I could not consent to do either. I said further that if elected I could not undertake to give any of my time and labour to their local interests. With respect to general politics, I told them without reserve what I thought on a number of important subjects on which they had asked my opinion; and one of these being the suffrage, I made known to them, among other things, my conviction (as I was bound to do, since I intended, if elected, to act on it) that women were entitled to representation in Parliament on the same terms with men. It was the first time, doubtless, that such a doctrine had ever been mentioned to electors; and the fact that I was elected after proposing it, gave the start to the movement which has since become so vigorous in favour of women's suffrage. Nothing, at the time, appeared more unlikely than that a candidate (if candidate I could be called) whose professions and conduct set so completely at defiance all ordinary notions of electioneering, should nevertheless be elected. A well known literary man, who was also a man of society, was heard to say, that the Almighty himself would have no chance of being elected on such a programme. I strictly adhered to it, neither spending money nor canvassing, nor did I take any personal part in the election until about a week preceding the day of nomination, when I attended a few public meetings to state my principles and give to any questions which the electors might exercise their just right of putting to me for their own guidance, answers as plain and unreserved as my Address. On one subject only, my religious opinions, I announced from the beginning that I would

16 In the *Daily News*, 23 March 1865.

answer no questions; a determination which appeared to be completely approved by those who attended the meetings. My frankness on all other subjects on which I was interrogated, evidently
did me far more good than my answers, whatever they might be,
did harm. Among the proofs I received of this, one is too remarkable not to be recorded. In the pamphlet "Thoughts on Parliamentary Reform" I had said, rather bluntly, that the working classes,
though differing from those of some other countries in being
ashamed of lying, are yet generally liars. This passage some opponent got printed in a placard, which was handed to me at a meeting,
chiefly composed of the working classes, and I was asked whether
I had written and published it. I at once answered "I did."
Scarcely were these two words out of my mouth, when vehement
applause resounded through the whole meeting. It was evident that
the working people were so accustomed to expect equivocation and
evasion from those who sought their suffrages, that when they
found, instead of that, a direct avowal of what was likely to be
disagreeable to them, instead of being offended they concluded at
once that this was a person whom they could trust. A more striking
instance never came under my notice of what, I believe, is the
experience of those who best know the working classes — that the
most essential of all recommendations to their favour is that of
complete straightforwardness; its presence outweighs in their minds
very strong objections, while no amount of other qualities will make
amends for its apparent absence. The first working man who spoke
after the incident I have mentioned (it was Mr. Odger) said, that
the working classes had no desire not to be told of their faults; they
wanted friends, not flatterers, and felt under obligation to any one
who told them of anything in themselves which he sincerely believed to require amendment. And to this the meeting heartily
responded.

Had I been defeated in the election, I should still have had no
reason to regret the contact it had brought me into with large bodies
of my countrymen; which not only gave me much new experience,
but enabled me to scatter my political opinions rather widely, and
by making me known in many quarters where I had never before
been heard of, increased the number of my readers and the pre-
sumable influence of my writings. These latter effects were of
course produced in a still greater degree, when, as much to my
own surprise as to that of any one, I was returned to Parliament

by a majority of some hundreds over my Conservative competitor.

I was a member of the House during the three sessions of the Parliament which passed the Reform Bill; during which time Parliament was necessarily my main occupation, except during the recess. I was a tolerably frequent speaker, sometimes of prepared speeches, sometimes extemporaneously. But my choice of occasions was not such as I should have made if my leading object had been parliamentary influence. When I had gained the ear of the House, which I did by a successful speech on Mr. Gladstone's Reform Bill, the idea I proceeded on was that when anything was likely to be as well done, or sufficiently well done, by other people, there was no necessity for me to meddle with it. As I therefore, in general, reserved myself for work which no others were likely to do, a great proportion of my appearances were on points on which the bulk of the Liberal party, even the advanced portion of it, either were of a different opinion from mine, or were comparatively indifferent. Several of my speeches, especially one against the motion for the abolition of capital punishment, and another in favour of resuming the right of seizing enemies' goods in neutral vessels, were opposed to what then was, and probably still is, regarded as the advanced liberal opinion. My advocacy of women's suffrage, and of Personal Representation, were at the time looked upon by many as whims of my own, but the great progress since made by those opinions, and especially the zealous response made from almost all parts of the kingdom to the demand for women's suffrage, fully justified the timeliness of those movements, and have made what was undertaken as a moral and social duty, a personal success. Another duty which was particularly incumbent on me as one of the Metropolitan Members, was the attempt to obtain a Municipal Government for the Metropolis: but on that subject the indifference of the House of Commons was such that I found hardly any help or support within its walls. On this subject, however, I was the organ of an active and intelligent body of persons outside, with whom and not with me the scheme originated, who carried on all the agitation on the subject and drew up the Bills. My part was to bring in Bills already prepared, and to sustain the discussion of them during the short time they were allowed to remain before the House; after having taken an active part in the work of a Committee presided over by Mr. Ayrton, which sat through the greater part of the Session of 1866 to take evidence on the subject. The very different position in which the question now stands (1870) may justly be attributed to the preparation which went on during those years, and which produced but little visible effect at the time; but all questions on which there are strong private interests on one side, and only the public good on the other, have a similar period of incubation to go through.

The same idea, that the use of my being in Parliament was to do work which others were not able or not willing to do, made me think it my duty to come to the front in defence of advanced Liberalism on occasions when the obloquy to be encountered was such as most of the advanced Liberals in the House, preferred not to incur. My first vote in the House was in support of an amendment in favour of Ireland, moved by an Irish member and for which only five English and Scotch votes were given, including my own: the other four were Mr. Bright, Mr. McLaren, Mr. T. B. Potter and Mr. Hadfield. And the second speech I delivered[17] was on the bill to prolong the suspension of the Habeas Corpus in Ireland. In denouncing, on this occasion, the English mode of governing Ireland, I did no more than the general opinion of England now admits to have been just; but the anger against Fenianism was then in all its freshness; any attack on what Fenians attacked was looked upon as an apology for them; and I was so unfavourably received by the House, that more than one of my friends advised me (and my own judgment agreed with the advice) to wait, before speaking again, for the favourable opportunity that would be given by the first great debate on the Reform Bill. During this silence, many flattered themselves that I had turned out a failure, and that they should not be troubled with me any more. Perhaps their uncomplimentary comments may, by the force of reaction, have helped to make my speech on the Reform Bill the success it was. My position in the House was further improved by a speech in which I insisted on the duty of paying off the National Debt before our coal supplies are exhausted, and by an ironical reply to some of the Tory leaders who had quoted against me certain passages of my writings

---

[17] The first was in answer to Mr. Lowe's reply to Mr. Bright on the Cattle Plague Bill, and was thought at the time to have helped to get rid of a provision in the Government measure which would have given to landholders a second indemnity, after they had already been once indemnified for the loss of some of their cattle by the increased selling price of the remainder (Mill's note).

and called me to account for others, especially for one in my "Considerations on Representative Government" which said that the Conservative party was by the law of its composition the stupidest party. They gained nothing by drawing attention to this passage, which up to that time had not excited any notice, but the *sobriquet* of "the stupid party" stuck to them for a considerable time afterwards. Having now no longer any apprehension of not being listened to, I confined myself, as I have since thought, too much, to occasions on which my services seemed specially needed, and abstained more than enough from speaking on the great party questions. With the exception of Irish questions, and those which concerned the working classes, a single speech on Mr. Disraeli's Reform Bill was nearly all that I contributed to the great decisive debates of the last two of my three sessions.

I have, however, much satisfaction in looking back to the part I took on the two classes of subjects just mentioned. With regard to the working classes, the chief topic of my speech on Mr. Gladstone's Reform Bill was the assertion of their claims to the suffrage. A little later, after the resignation of Lord Russell's ministry and the succession of a Tory Government, came the attempt of the working classes to hold a meeting in Hyde Park, their exclusion by the police, and the breaking down of the park railing by the crowd. Though Mr. Beales and the leaders of the working men had retired under protest before this took place, a scuffle ensued in which many innocent persons were maltreated by the police, and the exasperation of the working men was extreme. They shewed a determination to make another attempt at a meeting in the Park, to which many of them would probably have come armed; the Government made military preparations to resist the attempt, and something very serious seemed impending. At this crisis I really believe that I was the means of preventing much mischief. I had in my place in Parliament taken the side of the working men, and strongly censured the conduct of the Government. I was invited, with several other Radical members, to a conference with the leading members of the Council of the Reform League; and the task fell chiefly upon myself of persuading them to give up the Hyde Park project, and hold their meeting elsewhere. It was not Mr. Beales and Colonel Dickson who needed persuading; on the contrary, it was evident that those gentlemen had already exerted their influence in the same direction, thus far without success. It was the working men who held out: and so bent were they on their original scheme that I was obliged to have recourse to *les grands moyens*.[18] I told them that a proceeding which would certainly produce a collision with the military, could only be justifiable on two conditions: if the position of affairs had become such that a revolution was desirable, and if they thought themselves able to accomplish one. To this argument after considerable discussion they at last yielded: and I was able to inform Mr. Walpole that their intention was given up. I shall never forget the depth of his relief or the warmth of his expressions of gratitude. After the working men had conceded so much to me, I felt bound to comply with their request that I would attend and speak at their meeting at the Agricultural Hall: the only meeting called by the Reform League which I ever attended. I had always declined being a member of the League, on the avowed ground that I did not agree in its programme of manhood suffrage and the ballot: from the ballot I dissented entirely; and I could not consent to hoist the flag of manhood suffrage, even on the assurance that the exclusion of women was not intended to be implied; since if one goes beyond what can be immediately carried and professes to take one's stand on a principle, one should go the whole length of the principle. I have entered thus particularly into this matter because my conduct on this occasion gave great displeasure to the Tory and Tory-Liberal press, who have charged me ever since with having shewn myself, in the trials of public life, intemperate and passionate. I do not know what they expected from me; but they had reason to be thankful to me if they knew from what I had in all probability preserved them. And I do not believe it could have been done, at that particular juncture, by any one else. No other person, I believe, had at that moment the necessary influence for restraining the working classes, except Mr. Gladstone and Mr. Bright, neither of whom was available: Mr. Gladstone, for obvious reasons; Mr. Bright, because he was out of town.

When, some time later, the Tory Government brought in a bill to prevent public meetings in the Parks, I not only spoke strongly in opposition to it, but formed one of a number of advanced Liberals, who, aided by the very late period of the Session, succeeded in defeating the Bill by what is called talking it out. It has not since been renewed.

[18] Extreme measures.

On Irish affairs also I felt bound to take a decided part. I was one of the foremost in the deputation of Members of Parliament who prevailed on Lord Derby to spare the life of the condemned Fenian insurgent, General Burke. The Church question was so vigorously handled by the leaders of the party, in the session of 1868, as to require no more from me than an emphatic adhesion; but the land question was by no means in so advanced a position: the superstitions of landlordism had up to that time been little challenged, especially in Parliament, and the backward state of the question, so far as concerned the Parliamentary mind, was evidenced by the extremely mild measure brought in by Lord Russell's Government in 1866, which nevertheless could not be carried. On that bill I delivered one of my most careful speeches, in which I attempted to lay down some of the principles of the subject, in a manner calculated less to stimulate friends, than to conciliate and convince opponents. The engrossing subject of Parliamentary Reform prevented either this bill, or one of a similar character brought in by Lord Derby's Government, from being carried through. They never got beyond the second reading. Meanwhile the signs of Irish disaffection had become much more decided; the demand for complete separation between the two countries had assumed a menacing aspect, and there were few who did not feel that if there was still any chance of reconciling Ireland to British connexion, it could only be by the adoption of much more thorough reforms in the territorial and social relations of the country, than had yet been contemplated. The time seemed to me to have come when it would be useful to speak out my whole mind; and the result was my pamphlet "England and Ireland," which was written in the winter of 1867, and published shortly before the commencement of the session of 1868. The leading features of the pamphlet were on the one hand an argument to shew the undesirableness, for Ireland as well as England, of separation between the countries, and on the other, a proposal for settling the land question by giving to the existing tenants a permanent tenure at a fixed rent, to be assessed after due enquiry by the State.

The pamphlet was not popular, except in Ireland, as I did not expect it to be. But, if no measure short of that which I proposed would do full justice to Ireland, or afford a prospect of conciliating the mass of the Irish people, the duty of proposing it was imperative; while if on the other hand, there was any intermediate course

which had a claim to a trial, I well knew that to propose something
which would be called extreme was the true way not to impede but
to facilitate a more moderate experiment. It is most improbable
that a measure conceding so much to the tenantry as Mr. Gladstone's Irish Land Bill, would have been proposed by a Government, or could have been carried through Parliament, unless the
British public had been led to perceive that a case might be made,
and perhaps a party formed, for a measure considerably stronger.
It is the character of the British people, or at least of the higher
and middle classes who pass muster for the British people, that to
induce them to approve of any change it is necessary that they
should look upon it as a middle course: they think every proposal
extreme and violent unless they hear of some other proposal going
still farther, upon which their antipathy to extreme views may dis-
charge itself. So it proved in the present instance; my proposal was
condemned, but any scheme of Irish Land reform, short of mine,
came to be thought moderate by comparison. I may observe that
the attacks made on my plan usually gave a very incorrect idea of
its nature. It was usually discussed as a proposal that the State
should buy up the land and become the universal landlord; though
in fact it only offered to each individual landlord this as an alternative, if he liked better to sell his estate than to retain it on the new
conditions; and I fully anticipated that most landlords would continue to prefer the position of landowners to that of Government
annuitants, and would retain their existing relation to their tenants,
often on more indulgent terms than the full rents on which the
compensation to be given them by Government would have been
based. This and many other explanations I gave in a speech on
Ireland, in the debate on Mr. Maguire's Resolution, early in the
session of 1868. A corrected report of this speech, together with
my speech on Mr. Fortescue's Bill, has been published (not by me,
but with my permission) in Ireland.

Another public duty, of a most serious kind, it was my lot to
have to perform, both in and out of Parliament, during these years.
A disturbance in Jamaica, provoked in the first instance by injustice, and exaggerated by rage and panic into a premeditated rebellion, had been the motive or excuse for taking hundreds of innocent lives by military violence or by sentence of what were called
courts martial, continuing for weeks after the brief disturbance had

been put down; with many added atrocities of destruction of property, flogging women as well as men, and a great display of the brutal recklessness which generally prevails when fire and sword are let loose. The perpetrators of these deeds were defended and applauded in England by the same kind of people who had so long upheld negro slavery: and it seemed at first as if the British nation was about to incur the disgrace of letting pass without even a protest, excesses of authority as revolting as any of those for which, when perpetrated by the instruments of other governments, Englishmen can hardly find terms sufficient to express their abhorrence. After a short time, however, an indignant feeling was roused; a voluntary Association formed itself under the name of the Jamaica Committee, to take such deliberation and action as the case might admit of, and adhesions poured in from all parts of the country. I was abroad at the time but I sent in my name to the Committee as soon as I heard of it, and took an active part in its proceedings from the time of my return. There was much more at stake than only justice to the Negroes, imperative as was that consideration. The question was, whether the British dependencies, and eventually perhaps Great Britain itself, were to be under the government of law, or of military license; whether the lives and persons of British subjects are at the mercy of any two or three officers however raw and inexperienced or reckless and brutal, whom a panic-stricken Governor or other functionary may assume the right to constitute into a so-called Court Martial. This question could only be decided by an appeal to the tribunals; and such an appeal the Committee determined to make. Their determination led to a change in the Chairmanship of the Committee, as the Chairman, Mr. Charles Buxton, thought it not unjust indeed, but inexpedient, to prosecute Governor Eyre and his principal subordinates in a criminal court: but a numerously attended General meeting of the Association having decided this point against him, Mr. Buxton withdrew from the Committee, though continuing to work in the cause, and I was, quite unexpectedly on my own part, proposed and elected Chairman. It became, in consequence, my duty to represent the Committee in the House, sometimes by putting questions to the Government, sometimes as the recipient of questions more or less provocative, addressed by individual members to myself; but especially as speaker in the important debate originated in the session of 1866 by Mr. Buxton: and the speech I then delivered is that which I should probably select as the best of my speeches in Parliament.[19] For more than two years we carried on the combat, trying every avenue legally open to us, to the courts of criminal justice. A bench of magistrates in one of the most Tory counties in England dismissed our case: we were more successful before the magistrates at Bow Street; which gave an opportunity to the Lord Chief Justice of the Queen's Bench, Sir Alexander Cockburn, for delivering his celebrated charge, which settled the law of the question in favour of liberty, as far as it is in the power of a judge's charge to settle it.[20] There, however, our success ended, for the Old Bailey Grand Jury by throwing out our bill prevented the case from coming to trial. It was clear that to bring English functionaries to the bar of a criminal court for abuses of power committed against negroes and mulattoes, was not a popular proceeding with the English middle classes. We had however redeemed, so far as lay in us, the character of our country, by shewing that there was at any rate a body of persons determined to use all the means which the law afforded to obtain justice for the injured. We had elicited from the highest criminal judge in the nation an authoritative declaration that the law was what we maintained it to be; and we had given an emphatic warning to those who might be tempted to similar guilt hereafter, that though they might escape the actual sentence of a criminal tribunal, they were not safe against being put to some trouble and expense in order to avoid it. Colonial Governors and other persons in authority will have a considerable motive to stop short of such extremities in future.

As a matter of curiosity I kept some specimens of the abusive letters, almost all of them anonymous, which I received while these proceedings were going on. They are evidence of the sympathy felt with the brutalities in Jamaica by the brutal part of the popula-

[19] Among the most active members of the Committee were Mr. P. A. Taylor, M.P., always faithful and energetic in every assertion of the principles of liberty; Mr. Goldwin Smith, Mr. Frederic Harrison, Mr. Slack, Mr. Chamerovzow, Mr. Shaen, and Mr. Chesson, the Honorary Secretary of the Association (Mill's note).

[20] The charge (on an indictment against two officers for their conduct during the Jamaica rebellion) was six hours long, and covered the entire field of martial law. It was subsequently published (1867) from shorthand notes made in the courtroom.

tion at home. They graduated from coarse jokes, verbal and pictorial, up to threats of assassination.[21]

Among other matters of importance in which I took an active part, but which excited little interest in the public, two deserve particular mention. I joined with several other independent Liberals in defeating an Extradition Bill, introduced at the very end of the session of 1866 and by which, though surrender avowedly for political offences was not authorised, political refugees, if charged by a foreign government with acts which are necessarily incident to all attempts at insurrection, would have been surrendered to be dealt with by the criminal courts of the government against which they had rebelled: thus making the British Government an accomplice in the vengeance of foreign despotisms. The defeat of this proposal led to the appointment of a Select Committee (in which I was included) to examine and report on the whole subject of Extradition Treaties; and the result was that in the Extradition Act, which passed through Parliament after I had ceased to be a member, opportunity is given to any one whose extradition is demanded, of being heard before an English Court of justice to prove that the offence with which he is charged is really political. The cause of European freedom has thus been saved from a serious misfortune, and our own country from a great iniquity. The other subject to be mentioned is the fight kept up by a body of advanced Liberals in the session of 1868, on the Bribery Bill of Mr. Disraeli's Government, in which I took a very active part. I had taken council with several of those who had applied their minds most carefully to the details of the subject — Mr. W. D. Christie, Serjeant Pulling, Mr. Chadwick — as well as bestowed much thought of my own, for the purpose of framing such amendments and additional clauses as might make the Bill really effective against the numerous modes of corruption, direct and indirect, which might otherwise, as there was much reason to fear, be increased instead

[21] Helen Taylor adds: "At one time I reckoned that threats of Assassination where [sic] received at least once a week: and I remarked that threatening letters were always especially numerous by Tuesday morning's post. I inferred that they were meditated during the Sunday's leisure and posted on the Mondays. It might be worth while to collect evidence as to the proportions of Crime Committed on the different days of the week. It may be observed however that in England Sunday is generally used for all kinds of letter-writing, innocent as well as guilty" (note in Columbia MS).

of diminished by the Reform Act. We also aimed at engrafting on the Bill, measures for diminishing the mischievous burthen of what are called the legitimate expenses of elections. Among our many amendments was that of Mr. Fawcett for making the returning officer's expenses a charge on the rates instead of on the candidates; another was the prohibition of paid canvassers, and the limitation of paid agents to one for each candidate; a third was the extension of the precautions and penalties against bribery, to municipal elections, which are well known to be not only a preparatory school for bribery at parliamentary elections, but an habitual cover for it. The Conservative Government, however, when once they had carried the leading provision of their Bill (for which I voted and spoke), the transfer of the jurisdiction in elections from the House of Commons to the Judges, made a determined resistance to all other improvements: and after one of our most important proposals, that of Mr. Fawcett, had actually obtained a majority, they summoned the strength of their party and threw out the clause in a subsequent stage. The Liberal party in the House was greatly dishonoured by the conduct of many of its members in giving no help whatever to this attempt to secure the necessary conditions of an honest representation of the people. With their large majority in the House they could have carried all the amendments, or better ones if they had better to propose. But it was late in the Session; members were eager to set about their preparations for the impending General Election: and while some (such as Sir Robert Anstruther) honourably remained at their post, though rival candidates were already canvassing their constituency, a much greater number placed their electioneering interests before their public duty. Many Liberals also looked with indifference on legislation against bribery, thinking that it merely diverted public interest from the Ballot, which they considered, very mistakenly as I expect it will turn out, to be a sufficient, and the only, remedy. From these causes our fight, though kept up with great vigour for several nights, was wholly unsuccessful, and the practices which we sought to render more difficult, prevailed more widely than ever in the first General Election held under the new electoral law.

In the general debates on Mr. Disraeli's Reform Bill, my participation was limited to the one speech already mentioned; but I made the Bill an occasion for bringing the two greatest improvements which remain to be made in representative government formally before the House and the nation. One of them was Personal, or as it is called with equal propriety, Proportional Representation. I brought this under the consideration of the House, by an expository and argumentative speech on Mr. Hare's plan; and subsequently I was active in support of the very imperfect substitute for that plan, which, in a small number of constituencies, Parliament was induced to adopt. This poor makeshift had scarcely any recommendation, except that it was a partial recognition of the evil which it did so little to remedy: as such however it was attacked by the same fallacies, and required to be defended on the same principles, as a really good measure; and its adoption in a few parliamentary elections, as well as the subsequent introduction of what is called the Cumulative Vote in the elections for the London School Board, have had the good effect of converting the equal claim of all electors to a proportional share in the representation, from a subject of merely speculative discussion, into a question of practical politics, much sooner than would otherwise have been the case.

This assertion of my opinions on Personal Representation cannot be credited with any considerable or visible amount of practical result. It was otherwise with the other motion which I made in the form of an amendment to the Reform Bill, and which was by far the most important, perhaps the only really important public service I performed in the capacity of a Member of Parliament: a motion to strike out the words which were understood to limit the electoral franchise to males, thereby admitting to the suffrage all women who as householders or otherwise possess the qualification required of male electors. For women not to make their claim to the suffrage at the time when the elective franchise was being largely extended, would have been to abjure the claim altogether; and a movement on the subject was begun in 1866, when I presented a petition for the suffrage signed by a considerable number of distinguished women. But it was as yet uncertain whether the proposal would obtain more than a few stray votes in the House: and when, after a debate in which the speakers on the contrary side were conspicuous by their feebleness, the votes recorded in favour of the motion amounted to 73 — made up by pairs and tellers to above 80 — the surprise was general and the encouragement great: the greater too because one of those who voted for the motion was Mr. Bright, a fact which could only be attributed to the impression made on him by the debate, as he had previously made no secret of his non-concurrence in the proposal. The time appeared to my daughter, Miss Helen Taylor, to have come for forming a Society for the extension of the suffrage to women. The existence of the Society is due to my daughter's initiative; its constitution was planned entirely by her, and she was the soul of the movement during its first years, though delicate health and superabundant occupation made her decline to be a member of the Executive Committee. Many distinguished members of parliament, professors, and others, and some of the most eminent women of whom the country can boast, became members of the Society, a large proportion either directly or indirectly through my daughter's influence, she having written the greater number, and all the best, of the letters by which adhesion was obtained, even when those letters bore my signature. In two remarkable instances, those of Miss Nightingale and Miss Mary Carpenter, the reluctance those ladies had at first felt to come forward (for it was not on their part difference of opinion) was overcome by appeals written by my daughter though signed by me. Associations for the same object were formed in various local centres, Manchester, Edinburgh, Birmingham, Bristol, Glasgow, and others which have done much valuable work for the cause. All the Societies take the title of branches of the National Society for Women's Suffrage; but each has its own governing body, and acts in complete independence of the others.

I believe I have mentioned all that is worth remembering of my proceedings in the House. But their enumeration, even if complete, would give but an inadequate idea of my occupations during that period, and especially of the time taken up by correspondence. For many years before my election to Parliament I had been continually receiving letters from strangers, mostly addressed to me as a writer on philosophy, and either propounding difficulties or communicating thoughts on subjects connected with logic or political economy. In common, I suppose, with all who are known as political economists, I was a recipient of all the shallow theories and absurd proposals by which people are perpetually endeavouring to shew the way to universal wealth and happiness by some artful reorganisation of the currency. When there were signs of sufficient intelligence in the writers to make it worth while attempting to put them right, I took the trouble to point out their errors, until the growth of my correspondence made it necessary to dismiss such persons with very brief answers. Many, however, of the communications I received were more worthy of attention than these, and in some, oversights of detail were pointed out in my writings, which I was thus enabled to correct. Correspondence of this sort naturally multiplied with the multiplication of the subjects on which I wrote, especially those of a metaphysical character. But when I became a member of parliament I began to receive letters on private grievances and on every imaginable subject that related to any kind of public affairs, however remote from my knowledge or pursuits. It was not my constituents in Westminster who laid this burthen on me: they kept with remarkable fidelity the understanding on which I had consented to serve. I received indeed now and then an application from some ingenuous youth to procure for him a small government appointment: but these were few, and how simple and ignorant the writers were, was shewn by the fact that the applications came in about equally whichever party was in power. My invariable answer was, that it was contrary to the principles on which I was elected to ask favours of any Government. But on the whole hardly any part of the country gave me less trouble than my own constituents. The general mass of correspondence, however, swelled into an oppressive burthen. At this time, and thenceforth, a great proportion of all my letters (including many which found their way into the newspapers[22]) were not written by me but by my daughter; at first merely from her willingness to help in disposing of a mass of letters greater than I could get through without assistance, but afterwards because I thought the letters she wrote superior to mine, and more so in proportion to the difficulty and importance of the occasion. Even those which I wrote myself were generally much improved by her, as is also the case with all the more recent of my prepared speeches, of which, and of some of my published writings, not a few passages, and those the most successful, were hers.[23]

[22] One which deserves particular mention is a letter respecting the Habitual Criminals Act and the functions of a police generally, written in answer to a private application for my opinion, but which got into the newspapers and excited some notice. This letter which was full of original and valuable thoughts was entirely my daughter's. The fertility and aptness which distinguishes her practical conceptions of the adaptation of means to ends is such as I can never hope to rival (Mill's note).

[23] In the Columbia MS Mill inserted and then deleted the following at this point: "I must add that whatever has been done by us for the diffusion of our opinions and of our principles of action by private intercourse and the

While I remained in Parliament my work as an author was unavoidably limited to the recess. During that time I wrote (besides the pamphlet on Ireland already mentioned) the Essay on Plato published in the Edinburgh Review and reprinted in the third volume of "Dissertations and Discussions"; and the Address which conformably to custom I delivered to the University of St. Andrews, whose students had done me the honour of electing me to the office of Rector. In this Discourse I gave expression to many thoughts and opinions which had been accumulating in me through life respecting the various studies which belong to a liberal education, their uses and influences, and the mode in which they should be pursued to render those influences most beneficial. The position I took up, vindicating the high educational value alike of the old classic and the new scientific studies, on even stronger grounds than are urged by most of their advocates, and insisting that it is only the stupid inefficiency of the usual teaching which makes those studies be regarded as competitors instead of allies, was, I think, calculated, not only to aid and stimulate the improvement which has happily commenced in the national institutions for higher education, but to diffuse juster ideas than we often find even in highly educated men on the conditions of the highest mental cultivation.

During this period also I commenced (and completed soon after I had left Parliament) the performance of a duty to philosophy and to the memory of my father, by preparing and publishing an edition of the "Analysis of the Phenomena of the Human Mind" with notes bringing up the doctrines of that admirable book to the latest improvements in science and in speculation. This was a joint undertaking: the psychological notes being furnished in about equal proportions by Mr. Bain and myself, while Mr. Grote supplied some valuable contributions on points in the history of philosophy incidentally raised, and Dr. Andrew Findlater supplied the deficiencies in the book which had been occasioned by the imperfect philological knowledge of the time when it was written. Having been originally published at a time when the current of metaphysical speculation ran in a quite opposite direction to the psychology of Experience and Association, the "Analysis" had not obtained

---

direct influence of mind over mind, has been almost wholly her work, my own capacities of the kind being almost confined to my writings: and no one but myself knows at how great a sacrifice both of her personal tastes and inclinations and of her health that function was performed by her."

the amount of immediate success which it deserved, though it had made a deep impression on many individual minds, and had largely contributed, through those minds, to create that more favourable atmosphere for the Association Psychology of which we now have the benefit. Admirably adapted for a class-book of the Experience Metaphysics, it only required to be enriched, and in some cases corrected, by the results of more recent labours in the same school of thought, to stand, as it now docs, in company with Mr. Bain's treatises, at the head of the systematic works on Analytic psychology.

In the autumn of 1868 the Parliament which passed the Reform Act was dissolved, and at the new election for Westminster I was thrown out; not to my surprise, nor, I believe, to that of my principal supporters, though in the few days preceding the election they had become more sanguine than before. That I should not have been elected at all would not have required any explanation; what excites curiosity is that I should have been elected the first time, or, having been elected then, should have been defeated afterwards. But the efforts made to defeat me were far greater on the second occasion than on the first. For one thing, the Tory Government was now struggling for existence, and success in any contest was of more importance to them. Then, too, all persons of Tory feelings were far more embittered against me individually than on the previous occasion; many who had at first been either favourable or indifferent, were vehemently opposed to my reelection. As I had shewn in my political writings that I was aware of the weak points in democratic opinions, some Conservatives, it seems, had not been without hopes of finding me an opponent of democracy: as I was able to see the Conservative side of the question, they presumed that, like them, I could not see any other side. Yet if they had really read my writings they would have known that after giving full weight to all that appeared to me well grounded in the arguments against democracy, I unhesitatingly decided in its favour, while recommending that it should be accompanied by such institutions as were consistent with its principle and calculated to ward off its inconveniences: one of the chief of these remedies being Proportional Representation, on which scarcely any of the Conservatives gave me any support. Some Tory expectations appear to have been founded on the approbation I had expressed of plural voting, under certain conditions: and it has been surmised that the suggestion of

this sort made in one of the Resolutions which Mr. Disraeli introduced into the House preparatory to his Reform Bill (a suggestion
which meeting with no favour he did not press) may have been
occasioned by what I had written on the point: but if so, it was
forgotten that I had made it an express condition that the privilege
of a plurality of votes should be annexed to education, not to
property, and even so, had approved of it only on the supposition
of universal suffrage. How utterly inadmissible such plural voting
would be under the suffrage given by the present Reform Act, is
proved, to any who could otherwise doubt it, by the very small
weight which the working classes are found to possess in elections
even under the law which gives no more votes to any one elector
than to any other.

While I thus was far more obnoxious to the Tory interest, and
to many Conservative Liberals than I had formerly been, the course
I pursued in Parliament had by no means been such as to make
Liberals generally at all enthusiastic in my support. It has already
been mentioned, how large a proportion of my prominent appearances had been on questions on which I differed from most of the
Liberal party or about which they cared little, and how few occasions there had been on which the line I took was such as could
lead them to attach any great value to me as an organ of their
opinions. I had moreover done things which had excited, in many
minds, a personal prejudice against me. Many were offended by
what they called the persecution of Mr. Eyre: and still greater
offence was taken at my sending a subscription to the election
expenses of Mr. Bradlaugh. Having refused to be at any expense
for my own election, and having had all its expenses defrayed by
others, I felt under a peculiar obligation to subscribe in my turn
where funds were deficient for candidates whose election was desirable. I accordingly sent subscriptions to nearly all the working
class candidates, and among others to Mr. Bradlaugh. He had the
support of the working classes; having heard him speak I knew him
to be a man of ability, and he had proved that he was the reverse
of a demagogue by placing himself in strong opposition to the prevailing opinion of the democratic party on two such important subjects as Malthusianism and Personal Representation. Men of this
sort, who while sharing the democratic feelings of the working
classes, judged political questions for themselves and had courage
to assert their individual convictions against popular opposition,

were needed, as it seemed to me, in Parliament, and I did not think that Mr. Bradlaugh's anti-religious opinions (even though he had been intemperate in the expression of them) ought to exclude him. In subscribing, however, to his election, I did what would have been highly imprudent if I had been at liberty to consider only the interests of my own reelection; and, as might be expected, the utmost possible use, both fair and unfair, was made of this act of mine, to stir up the electors of Westminster against me. To these various causes, combined with an unscrupulous use of the usual pecuniary and other influences on the side of my Tory competitor while none were used on my side, it is to be ascribed that I failed at my second election after having succeeded at the first. No sooner was the result of the election known than I received three or four invitations to become a candidate for other constituencies, chiefly counties; but even if success could have been expected, and this without expense, I was not disposed to deny myself the relief of returning to private life. I had no cause to feel humiliated at my rejection by the electors; and if I had, the feeling would have been far outweighed by the numerous expressions of regret which I received from all sorts of persons and places, and in a most marked degree from those members of the liberal party in Parliament with whom I had been accustomed to act.

Since that time little has occurred which there is need to commemorate in this place. I returned to my old pursuits and to the enjoyment of a country life in the South of Europe; alternating twice a year with a residence of some weeks or months in the neighbourhood of London. I have written various articles in periodicals (chiefly in my friend Mr. Morley's Fortnightly Review), have made a small number of speeches on public occasions, especially at the meetings of the Women's Suffrage Society, have published the "Subjection of Women," written some years before, with some additions by my daughter and myself, and have commenced the preparation of matter for future books, of which it will be time to speak more particularly if I live to finish them. Here, therefore, for the present, this Memoir may close.

INDEX [1]

Abolitionists, American, 159
Aeschines: speeches, 9
Aesop's Fables, 5
Aldrich, Henry: *Artis logicae compendium* (1691), 85
American Civil War, 158–61
Anacreon, 9
Analysis, habit or discipline of, 67, 83–84, 86, 90
Ancient Universal History. See *Universal History*
Anglada, Joseph (1775–1833), professor of medicine at Montpellier, 37
Annual Register, The (1758 ff.), 7
Anson, George, Baron Anson: *A Voyage Round the World, in the Years 1740–44* (1748), 7
Anstruther, Sir Robert (1834–86), politician, 178
Arabian Nights, 7
Aristocracy, 57, 65, 103
Aristophanes, 9
Aristotle: *Rhetoric*, 9; *Organon*, 12
Association, law of (association psychology), 43, 66, 82–84, 134, 135, 162, 182–83. *See also* Hartley; Psychology
Atheism, 25, 29
Austin, Charles (1799–1874), lawyer, 47–49, 58; influence at Cambridge, 48, 63, 75; contributions to *Westminster Review*, 59; editorship of *Parliamentary History and Review*, 71, 72; in London Debating Society, 76
Austin, John (1790–1859), jurist, 40–41, 45, 58; character, 46–47, 49, 106; argument against primogeniture (*WR*, 1824), 59; contribution to *Parliamentary History and Review* (1826), 72; political and religious opinions, 106–108, 128, 139; *A Plea for the Constitution* (1859), 154–55; *Lectures on Jurisprudence* (1863), 161
Austin, Jonathan, of Creeting Mill, Suffolk, father of John and Charles Austin, 46
Austin, Sarah, née Taylor (1793–1867), translator, wife of John Austin, 108 n.
Ayrton, Acton Smee (1816–86), politician, 169

Bacon, Francis, Viscount St. Albans (1561–1626), 95; *Novum Organum* (1620), 15 n.

Bailey, Samuel: *A Critical Dissertation on the Nature, Measures, and Causes of Value* (1825), 73
Baillie, Joanna: plays including *Constantine Paleologus* (published in *Miscellaneous Plays*, 1804), 11 n.
Bain, Alexander (1818–1903), Scottish logician and psychologist, 147 n., 182; *The Senses and the Intellect* (1855) and *The Emotions and the Will* (1859), 155, 163, 183
Baldwin, Robert (1779?–1858), publisher, 58
Baring, Alexander, first Baron Ashburton (1774–1848), financier and statesman, 61
Bazard, Amand (1791–1832), follower of Saint-Simon, 100
Beales, Edmond (1803–81), president of the Reform League, 171
Beattie, James (1735–1803), 11
Beaver, Philip: *African Memoranda* (1805), 7
Bentham, George (1800–1884), botanist, 36
Bentham, Jeremy (1748–1832): lends books to James Mill, 7; early friendship with the Mills, 35; routine at Ford Abbey, 36 n.; amanuenses, 36 n., 50, 54; practice of "marginal contents," 40; influence on contemporaries, 41, 55, 56, 58, 62; JSM's first reading of, 41–43, 80; ideas on law and legislation, 41–43, 55, 157; founds *Westminster Review*, 56–57; on women's suffrage, 64; attitude toward kings, 65; opinion of poetry, 68; MSS edited by JSM, 69–71; style, 70, 71, 128; theory of government, 94–95; JSM's critiques of, 119, 130–31; compared with James Mill, 122
The Book of Fallacies (ed. Bingham, 1824), 69, 71; *Draught of a New Plan for the Organisation of the Judicial Establishment in France* (1790), 71; *A Fragment on Government* (1776), 71; *Plan of Parliamentary Reform* (1817), 65 n.; *Rationale of Judicial Evidence* (ed. JSM, 1827), 69–71; *The Rationale of Reward* (1825), 68 n.; *Traité des preuves judiciaires* (ed. Dumont, 1823), 69, 70; *Traités de législation civile et pénale* (ed. Dumont, 1802), 41–43, 44

[1] In parenthetical documentation the abbreviations *WR* and *LWR* designate the *Westminster Review* and the *London and Westminster Review*.

187